TOKYO

東京

Steve Wide &
Michelle Mackintosh

plum.

Pan Macmillan Australia

BEFORE YOU GO

THINGS WE LOVE

FOOD & DRINK

INTO THE VORTEX

As soon as we get off the plane in Tokyo, we enter *ukiyo*: the 'floating world' where one lives life in the moment, enjoying nature, food and good company; wafting through crowds and stopping to shop for exquisite handicrafts; or dropping into a bar to relax over beer, sake and whisky of the most amazing quality.

Tokyo is an astounding city. It has a rich history stretching back centuries; its identity reflects and draws on the past, and yet it rewrites its story day by day. Tokyo is cities within cities, towns within towns; it is made of ecosystems that grow in a very organic and intimate way, like flowers pushing through the cracks and fissures of urbanisation. It's the illusion of utter chaos – mad crowds of people rushing about their daily lives – layered over an extraordinarily ordered cluster of urban hubs. This proximity of the staggering metropolis and the habitable village are part of what gives Tokyo its unique character. The paradoxical liveability of a city with such an immense, densely packed population entices increasing numbers of tourists keen to take a peek into the workings of this dynamic, bustling and constantly changing world. The city beckons you to rush headlong into what we call the Tokyo Vortex; once inside, time seems to stand still while everything around you moves so fast it's a blur. You go in one end and come out the other without noticing that hours have passed, and that day has turned to night …

View from the Mori Art Museum on Christmas Day

Tokyo is everything that you imagine it to be: an impossible, sleepless metropolis; a crazy maze of shops and restaurants; a place where the magic of forgotten times still flourishes under the looming majesty of new architecture and cloud-piercing skyscrapers. It's ever-evolving, and yet it stays true to long-held beliefs and traditions.

It is both an urban theme park and a world of ancient wisdom and beauty, where the familiar takes on new dimensions and the unfamiliar blares at you across vast thoroughfares, plays melodies at you in toyshops and train stations, or peeks at you from alleys and side streets. Tokyo is a late riser – that is, if it went to bed at all. An early-morning jog can be a blissfully solitary experience; by contrast, if you're waking up with the city, you're bound to get caught up in rush hour, the sardine-can cram of the morning commute.

Visiting Tokyo for the first time will change your life. It's mesmerising, exciting and resolutely individual, an unrivalled parade of fashion, design, architecture and the best of both high culture and pop culture. It's a city of contrasts; whether you're standing in the middle of the Shibuya scramble, a blur of pedestrians rushing past you while you try to snap that perfect crowd shot, or standing before a small shrine, quiet and contemplative, you will feel the intensity and multi-layered nature of this very special place. All across the towering neon cityscapes, steel-and-glass giants loom over tiny alleys crammed with standing bars and small eateries, where salarymen down hasty beers and bowls of ramen before heading back out into the maelstrom.

Delving into the culture of Japan's largest and most famous city comes with a steep learning curve, but one that you'll happily climb. Whenever we visit, we find it to be an endless toy box of new experiences. Turn any corner and you could be face-to-face with the bizarre, the super-cute, the sensitively creative or the astoundingly beautiful. Back home in Australia, when we hear music on the streets, or smell grilling meat or fresh fish or the pink scent of blossoms, we are immediately thrown back to the memory of Tokyo's giddy spiral.

We find ourselves comparing any city we are in to Tokyo, from the politeness of the people, the efficiency of the customer service, and the scope and precision of the rail system, to the plethora of things you can buy, the convenience of the convenience stores, and the sheer volume of fashion, art, entertainment and experiences on offer.

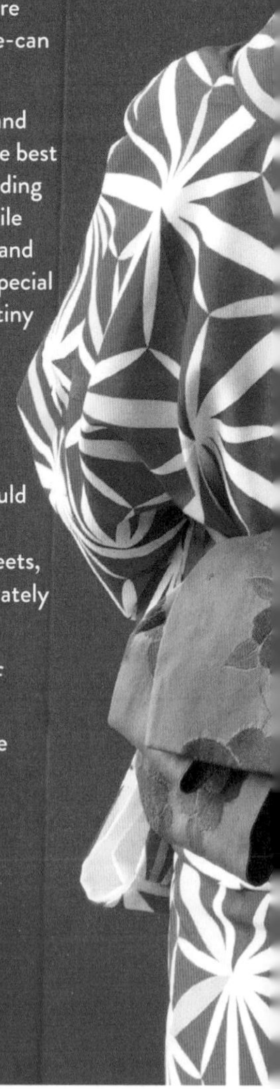

A kimono-clad photo shoot at Sensō-ji

TOKYO

東京

7

INTO THE VORTEX

Chingo-do (Raccoon Dog Temple), Asakusa

We love the seasons in Tokyo: the vibrant pink of the cherry blossoms in April; the steamy air and sudden, heavy rains of the early hot season; the relentless humidity at summer's height, sun baking the streets and glinting menacingly from walls of glass; and the wash of crimson flooding the parks in autumn. The Japanese are understandably obsessed with the seasons – even beer changes flavour and design to mark the time of year – and are constantly coming up with inventive ways to adapt as the weather changes, from high-tech thermals and heated pads in gloves and socks in winter, to cheap yet sturdy umbrellas in the rainy season, and cooling gels, fans and various papers to soak up embarrassing perspiration in summer.

The ever-changing sprawl of micro-cities with their own look and feel – towns within cities, intriguing pockets of social diversity down narrow alleys – can be daunting. Clusters of towering office blocks cast shadows over multistorey retail outlets, which in turn cradle smaller, older, family-owned stores; one street can lead to a sprawling capital, another to a tiny, quiet garden. Your internal compass can be completely knocked out of kilter: you can start your day in one place, end up somewhere else, and realise you've thrown all bearings to the wind and loved every minute of it. At night, after a big day, over a beer or two at a raucous local eatery or some wine at a cool new hangout, you'll wonder if the whole thing actually happened – or was it some elusive, magical dream?

Visually, Tokyo is a city that never fails to impress and delight. One minute you're craning your neck in amazement at a towering contemporary monolith; the next you're smiling goofily at someone kitted out in full costume, luring you into a nearby store. There are cafés that charge you a small fee to drink coffee while playing with the resident cats or hedgehogs. There are food halls crammed with trays of food that make the mouth water and the eyes smile: boxes of treats, unrecognisable edibles and delicacies, all presented in stunning rows and wrapped in such ornate and intricate ways that you almost don't want to open them for fear of damaging the delicate arrangements.

And that's just shopping for food! Retail in Tokyo offers a bewildering (and dangerously habit-forming) array of clothes, toys, stationery, homewares and electronics. The range of products to make your everyday life that much simpler is second to none. There is a kind of natural selection of product and utility in Tokyo that happens at an astounding rate due to the sheer volume of consumers cramming the streets and malls. Even the dull, functional or every day can become something new. Toilets, kitchen utensils, diaries, lunchboxes – everything gets a cute makeover or an inventive spin. We love the way Tokyoites put thought and passion into everything they make and do – the way they juxtapose the old and the new, the crazy and the considered, the beautiful and the chaotic. It is said that what you see on the streets of Tokyo emerges in the West three years later. While this is not true of everything – there are some things you will see in Tokyo that will never emerge in the West – Tokyo is nevertheless a barometer for endless style and invention.

Those visiting Tokyo on a budget can rest easy, too. Despite the widely held belief in the West that Tokyo is a super-expensive city, some of the best things to do in Tokyo are cheap – even free! The lunch sets and *bentō* boxes are not just value for money, they're a culinary treat that can't be missed. Quality toys and gadgets are everywhere – Tokyo is full of kids' things that adults will love – and bargains can be picked up in vintage clothes, new fashion and second-hand music.

Kiyosumi Teien

Amid all of the commerce, the big brands and the world-changing technology, creative Tokyo asserts its independence. With an estimated 13 million people in the capital alone, standing out requires some serious thought. Some turn to the outrageous, the experimental and the shocking. Others take what is already available and push it into new territories – or just make it so beautiful that you have to have it.

Art in Tokyo is mind-blowing: always surprising, constantly changing and often challenging and frustrating in the best of ways. The city's galleries are world-class, and you always feel like you're getting so much more than you paid for. The Mori Art Museum (p. 357) in particular is amazing; pop in at any time, even if you don't know what's on – you're bound to be entertained and inspired. There's even a view thrown in; on the level before you ascend the escalator to the gallery proper is a circular catwalk of glass that gives you a god's-eye view of the staggering scope of this colossal metropolis.

Getting a handle on Tokyo might seem like an insurmountable task. There are several ways of approaching it; you just have to find what works best for you. You could break it down into sections, localities and suburbs – well-known places that you've read about and always wanted to visit. You could zone in on big areas and their various satellites. Or you could just wander, allowing yourself to get lost and discover new experiences, flavours and ideas. For this book we have decided to approach it slightly differently, to slice the Tokyo cake up into three large portions: big areas that are tied together, for the most part, by a central theme, an era (or eras) and a history. Our hope is that anyone overwhelmed by Tokyo's vastness will be able to see how the city came together: how it grew from a bustling fishing port named Edo into one of the world's megacities, and how the many facets of Japan and Japanese culture came to be reflected, celebrated and nurtured in each of the three zones.

This book is a celebration of contemporary Tokyo. It's a tightly edited list of our tried-and-tested favourites. It's for people who want to get an up close and personal look at the real Tokyo: the hidden finds, the architectural marvels, where to go to get into the thick of it and where to go to escape the madness. It's an account of the things that we have discovered and love to do in Tokyo that we hope will serve as inspiration for anyone who wants to live like a local or gain a little more of an understanding of the culture. Tokyo is so diverse that it will be a different experience for different people. You will want to make your own discoveries, hunt out your own inspirations and forge your own paths, but our specific way of approaching the splendours and quirks of the different sections of Tokyo will hopefully give you a kind of blueprint to navigate this monolithic playground.

So let's tackle Tokyo together, experiencing the Japanese talent for bespoke culture, culinary delights and outrageously good shopping that will have you wanting to cross oceans again and again. The order in which you explore the three areas in this book is up to you, and you will probably benefit from using your mood as a gauge. Feel like quiet contemplation? Visit Traditional Tokyo (p. 152) and its shrines or inspiring neighbourhood walks. Want to lose yourself in the lifestyle? Dive headlong into Modern Tokyo (p. 232), with its dizzying central cities of Shinjuku and Shibuya and its tranquil neighbourhood hubs. Feel like shopping, gaming, letting loose, and getting a bit crazy? Hit Central Tokyo (p. 190) ake a seat at a pachinko parlour; go gadget- and manga-mad in Akihabara; grab some toys in Tokyo Station's Character Street; or go high-end shopping in Ginza and splash out on masterful sushi or delectable *wagashi* (traditional sweets; p. 124). Tokyo has all this, and so much more. It's time to take a step into the vortex.

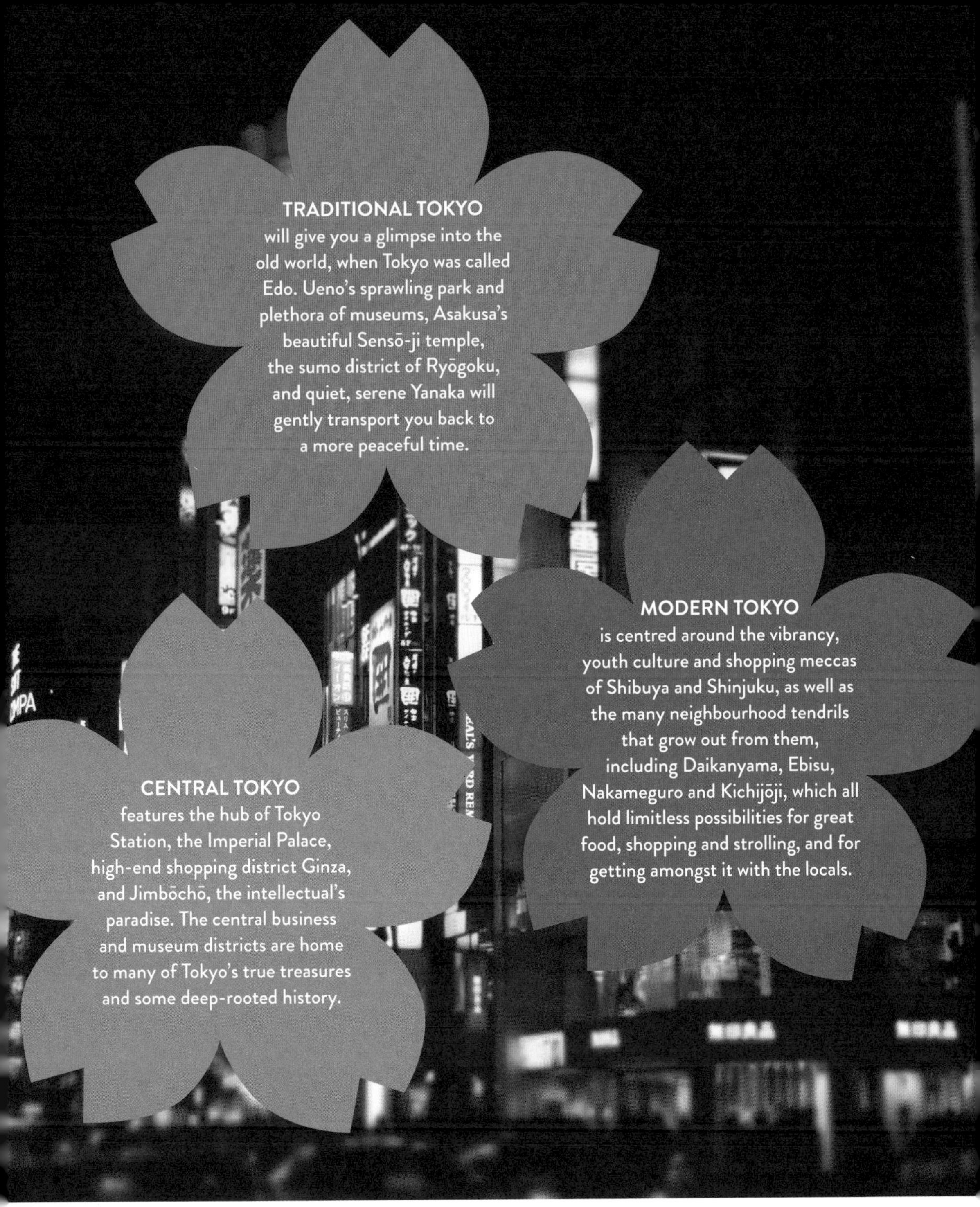

TRADITIONAL TOKYO
will give you a glimpse into the old world, when Tokyo was called Edo. Ueno's sprawling park and plethora of museums, Asakusa's beautiful Sensō-ji temple, the sumo district of Ryōgoku, and quiet, serene Yanaka will gently transport you back to a more peaceful time.

CENTRAL TOKYO
features the hub of Tokyo Station, the Imperial Palace, high-end shopping district Ginza, and Jimbōchō, the intellectual's paradise. The central business and museum districts are home to many of Tokyo's true treasures and some deep-rooted history.

MODERN TOKYO
is centred around the vibrancy, youth culture and shopping meccas of Shibuya and Shinjuku, as well as the many neighbourhood tendrils that grow out from them, including Daikanyama, Ebisu, Nakameguro and Kichijōji, which all hold limitless possibilities for great food, shopping and strolling, and for getting amongst it with the locals.

Shinjuku at night

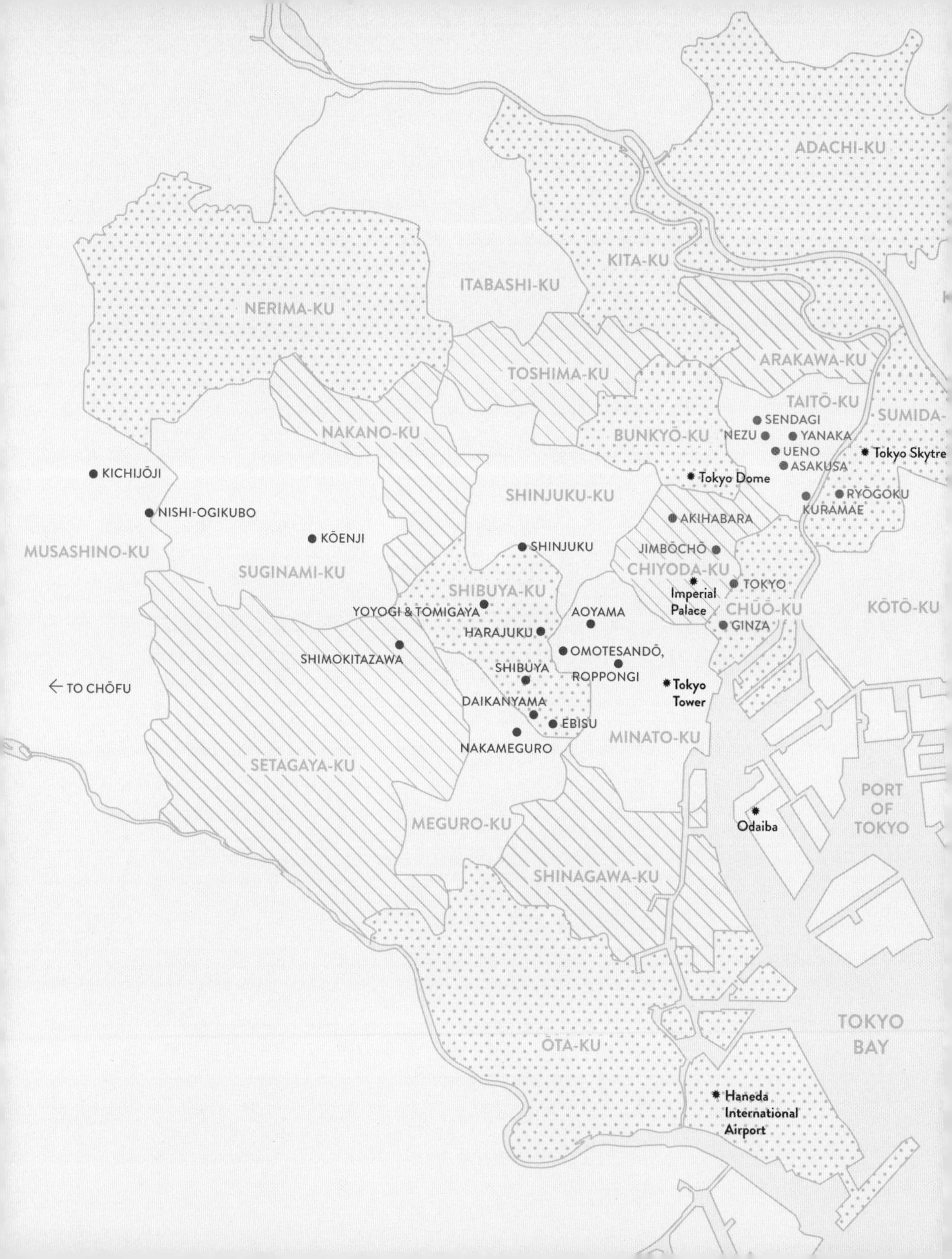

ADACHI-KU
KITA-KU
ITABASHI-KU
NERIMA-KU
ARAKAWA-KU
TOSHIMA-KU
TAITŌ-KU
SUMIDA-
NAKANO-KU
BUNKYŌ-KU
SENDAGI
NEZU
YANAKA
UENO
Tokyo Skytre
ASAKUSA
KICHIJŌJI
Tokyo Dome
SHINJUKU-KU
RYŌGOKU
KURAMAE
NISHI-OGIKUBO
AKIHABARA
KŌENJI
JIMBŌCHŌ
MUSASHINO-KU
SHINJUKU
CHIYODA-KU
SUGINAMI-KU
TOKYO
Imperial Palace
SHIBUYA-KU
CHŪŌ-KU
KŌTŌ-KU
YOYOGI & TOMIGAYA
AOYAMA
HARAJUKU
GINZA
SHIMOKITAZAWA
OMOTESANDŌ,
ROPPONGI
SHIBUYA
← TO CHŌFU
Tokyo Tower
DAIKANYAMA
EBISU
NAKAMEGURO
MINATO-KU
SETAGAYA-KU
PORT OF TOKYO
Odaiba
MEGURO-KU
SHINAGAWA-KU
TOKYO BAY
ŌTA-KU
Haneda International Airport

TOKYO AREA MAP

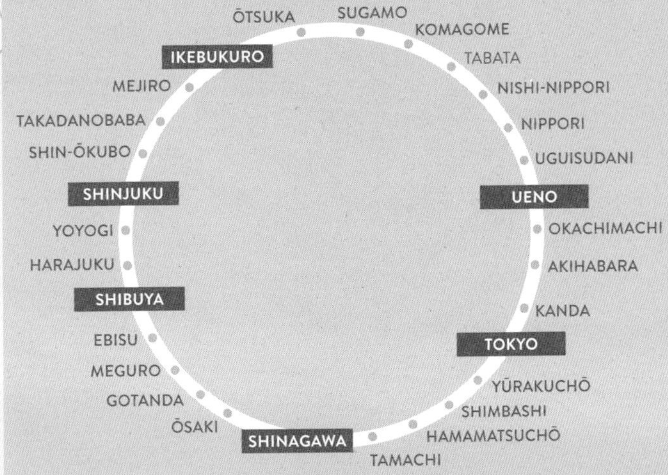

The JR Yamanote Line (above) is a handy jump on and off 'circle' line, perfect for your first day out or to get your bearings. Choose stations close to each other for the perfect day itinerary.

● TRADITIONAL TOKYO ● CENTRAL TOKYO ● MODERN TOKYO ✸ SIGHTS

BEFORE YOU GO

– Tokyo: A potted history
– The eras of Tokyo
– A city for all seasons
– Tokyo customs

Rare books in Jimbōchō

TOKYO: A POTTED HISTORY

At the end of the eighth century, Emperor Kanmu relocated the imperial capital of Japan from Nagaoka-kyō to Heian-kyō, the city now known as Kyoto, where it would remain for more than one thousand years. So how is it that Tokyo came to unseat Kyoto as the capital of modern Japan?

When the powerful political leader and Imperial Regent of Japan, Hideyoshi Toyotomi, died in 1598, he left his five-year-old son Hideyori Toyotomi in the care of five of his trusted regents until the boy was old enough to take Hideyoshi's place as Imperial Regent. However, one of Hideyoshi's five regents, ambitious warlord Ieyasu Tokugawa, had other plans. He took the other regents and their armies to war, defeating them in 1600, a victory that granted him ultimate power. Emperor Go-Yōzei (who was a figurehead only and had very little political clout) appointed Ieyasu shogun, or military leader, in 1603, giving Ieyasu's rule over Japan legitimacy and officially beginning the age of the Tokugawa shogunate (1603–1868), or the Edo period (p. 26).

Ieyasu chose the busy fishing port of Edo as the shogunate's seat of power (Kyoto remained the official capital), setting up house in what is now the Imperial Palace in modern-day Tokyo (p. 340). Social classes became heavily delineated, with the feudal lords and nobility at the top, then the samurai, followed by the farmers and finally the merchants and artisans. By 1635, under the rule of Ieyasu's grandson Iemitsu, Japan had closed its borders in a bid to stem the growing influence of Christianity, which Iemitsu felt was a threat to the strength and peace of Japan. Foreign trade was limited to a small number of Dutch and Chinese merchants at specific ports, and Japan remained cut off from the world for more than 220 years.

During this time of *sakoku*, or 'closed country', the city of Edo flourished – but its social hierarchy became even more divided. Two regions were formed: Yamanote, where the well-to-do lived, and Shitamachi, literally translated as 'downtown', where people lived in shanty towns and relied on handicrafts and manual work to survive. Buffeted by the variety of destructive fires, storms, earthquakes and wars that locals called the *Edo-no-hana*, or 'flowers of Edo', the downtowners developed an extraordinary resilience and a range of useful skills. This, combined with a strong work ethic, turned Edo into one of the world's most creative and inventive hubs, a trait which still sets Tokyo apart today. Areas became known for pottery, wood and paper crafts, or the manufacture of household items. Many of these specialist areas still exist, and are great destinations for anyone with particular interests. These include Yanaka's paper shops (p. 181), Kappabashi's street of kitchenware (p. 157) or Jimbōchō, with its many vintage booksellers (p. 214). High arts like ikebana (flower-arranging), singing and the tea ceremony flourished in early Edo, and were highly regarded throughout Japan. Kabuki, a form of theatre known for its elaborate costumes and makeup, became extremely popular, especially around the areas of Kabukichō and Yoshiwara, which were also the red-light districts of the time. Yamanote high-borns were known to frequently slum it in the downtown area so that they could visit the Yoshiwara courtesans.

The *komon*, a type of kimono characterised by repeating patterns, became popular. Stripes and purple dye were in vogue. Handcrafted everyday objects and ornaments were in high demand, and local craftsmen were considered to be masters of their skills. Artists who specialised in *ukiyo-e* ('pictures of the floating world'), colourful paintings and woodblock prints that captured the hedonistic lifestyle of Edo at the time, generated an extraordinary output, and are now iconic in Japanese culture. It was here that famed woodblock artist Katsushika Hokusai, who was born and based in Edo, created his famous landscape series *Thirty-six Views of Mount Fuji* – of which the instantly recognisable *The Great Wave off Kanagawa* is part.

It was the arrival of Commodore Matthew Perry's fleet of American gunships in the Bay of Edo in 1853 that finally opened Japan up to the world once more. Perry negotiated for the ports of Shimoda and Hakodate to be made available for world trade. This led to an explosion in demand for foreign goods, which in turn led to inflation – and the resulting increase in the cost of living caused discontentment among the people of Japan. During this state of unease, Emperor Meiji wrested power from the Tokugawa regime. In 1868, Meiji (and the imperial seat of power), who still resided in Kyoto, moved to a bustling and lively Edo, and from here the city's fate was sealed. That year, Edo was renamed Tokyo, meaning 'eastern capital'.

In the period that followed the opening of the country – known as the Meiji era or Meiji Restoration, p. 32 – it was as though Japan had a cheat sheet for the industrial revolution and beyond. Japan caught up, drew parallel with and ultimately overtook the rest of the world in many areas. Since the opening of Japan's first railroad in 1782, successive innovations have seen it become the envy of rail systems all over the world.

Japanese art and craft spread to the world, and the influence that *ukiyo-e* and Hokusai had on Impressionism is incalculable. Culture and technology from the West were swiftly

Chitoko Kusakabe in formal kimono, early Shōwa era (top right)

Chitoko Kusakabe and friend, Shōwa era; *Sakura* tea; Incense at Inokashira Benzaiten (clockwise from top left)

adopted: in 1862, Ginza's 'bricktown', a Western-style fireproof housing zone, was established; in 1883, the Rokumeikan, a Western-style building that hosted dances and parties, was built. No longer in vogue, the long-standing male hairstyle of a topknot and bald patch was replaced by the *zangiri* or *jangiri* ('random crop'), a cut with sideburns and a quiff (think Elvis Presley) that, by 1888, had been adopted by 90 per cent of Japanese men. Other Western influences emerged, including the rise of the private detective as a profession, the preference for beer over sake, and even driving on the left side of the road.

The Japanese military also progressed in leaps and bounds. They attacked and occupied parts of China, Korea, Russia, Taiwan and Micronesia, before allying with fascist nations Germany and Italy. Japan entered the Second World War with a surprise attack on American forces in Pearl Harbor in 1941; by the end of the war, they'd conquered much of the Asia-Pacific, and only surrendered when the United States dropped atomic bombs on Hiroshima and Nagasaki in 1945, bombs which caused horrific civilian injuries and fatalities. Tokyo also suffered some 100,000 fatalities and sustained heavy damage that year due to the United States' Operation Meetinghouse. Tokyo could do nothing but regroup and revitalise.

The city excels at bouncing back, and after Japan's surrender in the Second World War, the Emperor and government saw an opportunity to collaborate with the West. During and after the postwar American occupation of Japan, Tokyo experienced unprecedented growth and development. The 'new Tokyo' was unveiled to the world at the 1964 Olympic Games, with new housing, office, hotel and stadium construction; infrastructure and technology improvements; and vending machines on the streets. However, rapid rebuilding turned out to be a double-edged sword, marred by corruption and environmental damage. Fast development led to a rise in commerce and living standards, but the city's new buildings were often unpolished. The cityscape took on a look that has often been described as 'dull and grey', with the phrase 'concrete jungle' being bandied around more than once.

Creativity and craft bubbled under the surface, though, and Japan, while flying under the radar in a world that had started to travel, began to flourish once again. The rise of salaryman culture was rapid. Expansion into the suburbs as people sought housing away from the workplace meant the expansion of the rail network. Shibuya and Shinjuku quickly became areas for commerce and shopping. The aesthetic of this period, known as the Shōwa era (p. 40), is a charming, retro mishmash of prewar German and Austrian 'cuckoo-clock chic', postwar Americana, and elements of modern Japanese culture.

The approaching 2020 Olympic Games have set Tokyo onto a new path of development. The ugly prefabs of postwar Tokyo are being knocked down, and inventive new architecture is taking their place. The ever-changing nature of Tokyo continues. Like its history, the city is multi-layered, its stories both hidden in small, secluded pockets and written on its towering, glossy facade. New construction, phenomenal leaps in technology and a further opening up to Western culture all continue to make Tokyo one of the world's most astounding cities, a truly unique and inspiring destination alive with possibilities.

THE ERAS OF TOKYO

Since the year 645 AD, the history of Japan has been divided into named periods and eras that correspond to the reign of various rulers, significant historical events, or cultural paradigm shifts. The two periods most significant to the history of Tokyo are the Edo period (1603–1867), which is divided into 35 eras, and Modern Japan (1868–2019), which is divided into four eras: Meiji, Taishō, Shōwa and Heisei.

A more modern ride at Hanayashiki, an Edo-period amusement park

江戸時代

EDO PERIOD
(1603–1868)

FINDING THE EDO PERIOD IN MODERN TOKYO

——— The Edo period is named for the city of Edo, or as we know it today, Tokyo. The Edo period transformed the former fishing village into the default capital, as the seat of power for the Tokugawa shogunate, and saw the rise of a middle class that was keen to leave the drudgery of long hours of work behind and instead seek out entertainment, leading to the popularisation of arts and culture. Although Japan was cut off from the rest of the world (with the exception of specific ports that traded with the Netherlands, China and Korea), the closed society flourished under its own rules.

The heart of Edo was the Asakusa area. People from all over Japan moved there, and crafts and trade boomed. The city was filled with highly skilled craftspeople, among them indigo dyers, whose fabric had entered the mainstream; many of the beautiful fabric techniques are still used and admired today. People lived in *nagaya*, communal buildings made up of linked, common living spaces that allowed neighbours to share day-to-day tasks like cleaning, preparing food, making clothing and crafting items. Trade led to a variety of goods becoming available, and the concept of the corner store, where people could shop for everyday items, was born.

Although society was organised by a strict hierarchy, certain social lines were blurred: common people went to imperial events, and imperial people went to common events. People had time to enjoy kabuki theatre, sumo wrestling and the arts, and many of these elements of Edo Tokyo are still alive within the capital today.

It was the birth and rapid rise of printing and the subsequent creation of *ukiyo-e* ('floating world') woodblock prints that would have a massive impact on the West when Japan eventually opened its borders. From the Impressionists onward, many of Europe's most treasured artists were influenced by the prints. Japonaiserie was huge in Paris and helped shape the likes of Van Gogh, Monet, Degas and Toulouse-Lautrec, who bought many *ukiyo-e* prints and adopted the screen-printing technique.

Walking the streets of Yanaka, Nezu and Sendagi, an area called Ya-Ne-Sen (p. 180), will give you a feel for life in old Edo. Kuramae (p. 154), Ryōgoku (p. 166) and Asakusa (p. 154) are also great places to visit to be transported back to the time of the floating world.

Ukiyo*: 'the floating world'.*
An escape from the everyday
through art, extravagance,
style and hedonism

Ase o fuku onna (Woman wiping sweat), Kitagawa Utamaro, 1798 (opposite)

ART

- Modern Rinpa, a revival of a style of painting featuring natural subjects and gold leaf
  Key artist: Hōitsu Sakai (1761–1828)
- *Ukiyo-e* ('floating world') woodblock prints
  Key artist: Katsushika Hokusai (1760–1849; p. 20)

CRAFT

- *Aizome*, indigo dyeing
- *Shodō*, the art of calligraphy (p. 378)

CULTURE

- Kabuki theatre (p. 366)
- Sumo wrestling (p. 172)
- *Sentō* (public bathouses)

EXPERIENCES

- Edoyu, Ryōgoku, an Edo-themed bathhouse (p. 168)
- Hanayashiki (1853), Asakusa, an Edo-period amusement park (p. 158)

FOOD

- Castella cake
- Green tea
- *Inari* sushi (fried tofu pockets stuffed with sushi rice)
- Soba noodles
- Sushi
- Tempura
- *Tsukemono* (pickles)
- *Unagi* (eel)

GARDENS

- The East Gardens of the Imperial Palace, Ninomaru section (1593), Chiyoda (p. 340)
- Koishikawa-Kōrakuen (1629), Bunkyō (p. 345)
- Rikugi-en (circa 1700), Bunkyō (p. 345)

LANDMARKS

- Kuromon ('black gate'; late Edo period) at the Tokyo National Museum, Taitō (p. 362)

LITERATURE

- Monzaemon Chikamatsu (1653–1725), a writer of *bunraku* (puppet theatre) and kabuki theatre, considered to be Japan's Shakespeare
- Chiyo-ni Fukuda (1703–1775), widely regarded as one of Japan's greatest haiku poets
- Haiku poetry
  Key text: *Oku no Hosomichi (The Narrow Road to the Deep North*; c. 1694) by Bashō Matsuo (1644–1694)
- *Kusazōshi* (literature illustrated with woodblock prints)
  Key text: *Nise Murasaki Inaka Genji (The False Murasaki and the Rustic Genji*; 1829) by Tanehiko Ryūtei (1783–1842)
- *Ukiyo-zōshi* ('books of the floating world'), writing about daily life in Edo … and its brothels
  Key text: *Kōshoku Ichidai Otoko (Life of an Amorous Man*; 1682) by Saikaku Ihara (1642–1693)

MUSEUMS

- Edo-Tokyo Museum, Sumida (p. 360)
- Edo-Tokyo Open Air Architectural Museum, Koganei (p. 360)
- Sumida Hokusai Museum, Sumida (p. 363)
- Tokyo National Museum, Taitō (p. 362)

MUSIC

- Hand-flute soundscapes in melodic minor keys
- *Biwa*, a lute-like instrument
- Koto, a type of plucked string instrument, a member of the zither family
- Shakuhachi, a wooden flute used only by Zen Buddhist monks

TEMPLES & BUILDINGS

- Gokoku-ji (1681), Bunkyō
- Kan'ei-ji (1625), Taitō (p. 334)
- Nishinomiya Inari Shrine (1727) at Sensō-ji, Asakusa (p. 334)

Tea and *wagashi* at Fukiage Tea House in Rikugi-en (opposite)

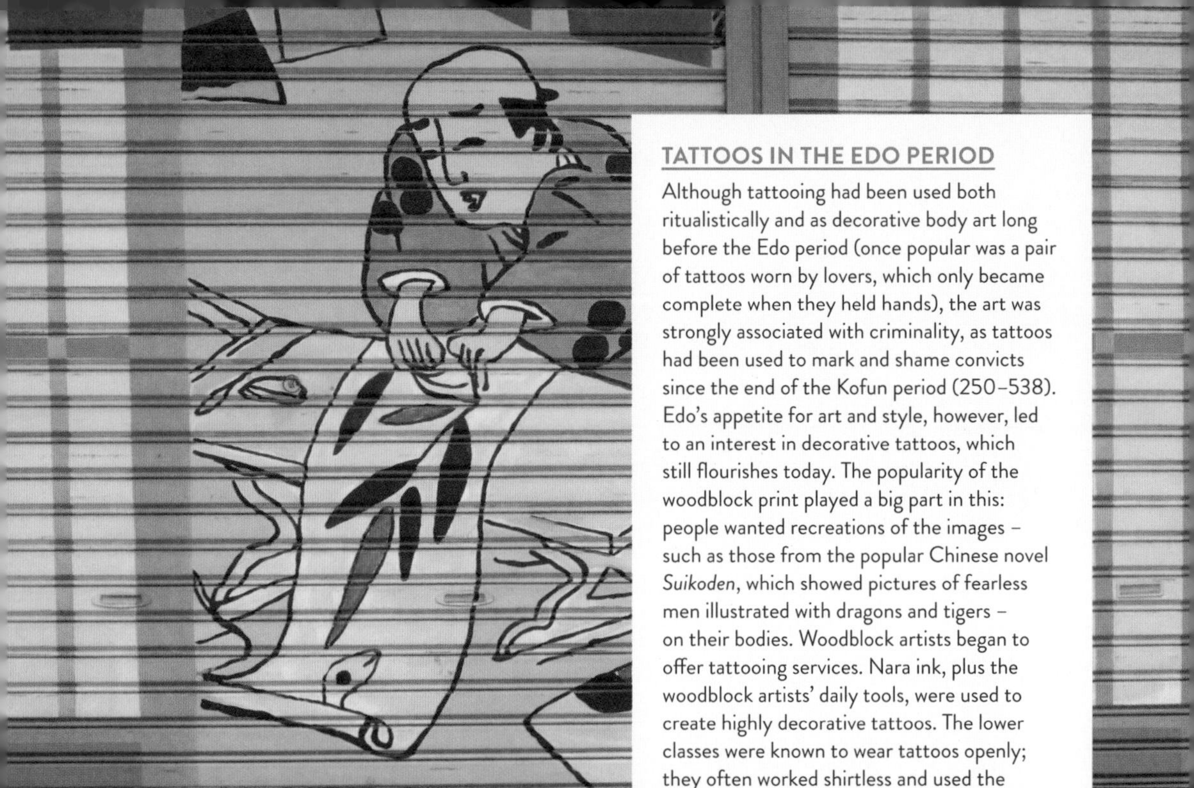

TATTOOS IN THE EDO PERIOD

Although tattooing had been used both ritualistically and as decorative body art long before the Edo period (once popular was a pair of tattoos worn by lovers, which only became complete when they held hands), the art was strongly associated with criminality, as tattoos had been used to mark and shame convicts since the end of the Kofun period (250–538). Edo's appetite for art and style, however, led to an interest in decorative tattoos, which still flourishes today. The popularity of the woodblock print played a big part in this: people wanted recreations of the images – such as those from the popular Chinese novel *Suikoden*, which showed pictures of fearless men illustrated with dragons and tigers – on their bodies. Woodblock artists began to offer tattooing services. Nara ink, plus the woodblock artists' daily tools, were used to create highly decorative tattoos. The lower classes were known to wear tattoos openly; they often worked shirtless and used the illustrations to beautify their upper bodies. It's thought that the rich also had them, secretly hiding under their clothing. Certainly, firemen of the age, who were considered heroic figures (there were a lot of fires), were well known for having tattoos.

Paintings on buildings in Asakusa (opposite); *Roshi Ensei lifting a beam*, Utagawa Kuniyoshi, 1798–1861 (above)

明治時代

MEIJI ERA

(1868–1912)

FINDING THE MEIJI ERA IN MODERN TOKYO

—— The Meiji era, also known as the Meiji Restoration, brought an end to shogun-ruled Japan. The emperor regained control from the shogun due to civil unrest, and for the first time in more than 1000 years, he moved the imperial capital of Japan – to Edo, which was renamed Tokyo ('eastern capital'), and had already been the default capital for years as the centre of power for the shogunate. This was the start of the true modernisation of Tokyo, and the beginning of the Japanese industrial revolution. The Ginza and Tokyo areas became the new centre, moving the power base away from Asakusa and the Sensō-ji Buddhist temple. Banks, commerce, industry and consumerism began to make their mark. With the opening of the Yamanote railway line in 1885, people had more freedom to move, to work or to explore Tokyo. Japan had just opened its borders after a long period of isolation, and it began to adopt the world trends of the late nineteenth and early twentieth centuries at a staggering pace.

The West influenced everything in Tokyo, from architecture to food choices. New buildings looked very European on the outside while maintaining a foundation of traditional Japanese design techniques, a style called *giyōfu* ('pseudo-Western style') architecture. Working people began to wear Western clothes, and the very wealthy started a trend called *yōfuku* ('Western-style clothes'), a fusion of Western and Japanese fashion that was considered the height of modernity. Women still wore kimono, but the silhouettes changed to fall in line with a more Western aesthetic. The fabric patterns became more abstract; brighter colours could be worn by all age groups; and two-piece kimono were popular. Women no longer shaved their eyebrows or blackened their teeth, trends popular in pre-Meiji-era Tokyo. Going out to eat became popular and meat became a staple of meals, while early *yōshoku* ('Western-style food') dishes like pizza and crumbed and deep-fried morsels started a love affair that shows no sign of fading.

So grab a Meiji chocolate bar and catch the Yamanote Line (p. 192) to Tokyo Station (p. 198) to marvel at the architecture and get amongst the general hubbub like a Meiji-era proletarian. Afterwards, head to Ginza (p. 202) and stop in at the Shiseido Parlour (Shiseido Building; p. 365) for afternoon tea, followed by a stroll around Ginza's streets. You'll be living the Meiji dream, feeling the excitement of rebirth and new possibilities.

The end of shogun rule and the start of the Meiji Restoration

The Meiji Emperor, standing, with the imperial family of Japan, Torajirō Kasai, 1900 (opposite)

ART

- Oil painting introduced to Japan
- *Nihonga* ('Japanese-style painting'), an artistic movement combining traditional Japanese painting techniques with those of the Pre-Raphaelite and Romantic movements
  Key artists: Shunsō Hishida (1874–1911), Kiyoshi Kobayakawa (1899–1948), Goyō Hashiguchi (1880–1921)
- *Yōga* ('Western-style painting'), an artistic movement emphasising European conventions and techniques
  Key artists: Seiki Kuroda (1866–1924) and Hōsui Yamamoto (1850–1906)

CULTURE

- Japan's first universities established
- Western sports like baseball, soccer and rugby find popularity

EXPERIENCES

- Ginza Kimuraya, Ginza, a Meiji-era bakery still producing bread and sweets according to recipes from the 1800s (p. 135)

FOOD

- *Bīfu suteiki* (steak)
- Coffee
- Hato Saburē biscuits
- *Karē raisu* (curry rice)
- *Katsu* (deep-fried meat and seafood)
- *Korokke* (crumbed meat, seafood or vegetable croquettes)
- Meiji chocolate
- *Taiyaki* (fish-shaped pastry with a sweet filling)
- Pizza and bread

GARDENS

- Gardens at Hotel Chinzanso Tokyo (1861), Bunkyō
- Kiyosumi Teien (1880), Fukagawa (p. 345)

LITERATURE

- Yukichi Fukuzawa (1835–1901), creator of *Meiroku Zasshi (Meiji Six Journal)*, often described as 'the Japanese Voltaire'
- *Wagahai wa Neko de Aru (I Am a Cat*; 1905) by Natsume Sōseki (1867–1916)

MUSEUMS

- The Koishikawa Annex at the University of Tokyo, Bunkyō
- National Museum of Nature and Science (1871), Taitō (p. 362)

MUSIC

- Japanese musicians and composers experiment with Western classical music, military-style marches and school songs
- Renewed interest in the traditional music of the Edo period

TEMPLES & BUILDINGS

- Kabuki-za theatre (1889), Ginza (p. 368)
- Meiji Shrine (1920), Shibuya; built in the Meiji Emperor's honour after his death (p. 334)
- Mitsukoshi Nihonbashi (1904), Chūō (p. 208)
- Shiseido Parlour (1902), Ginza
- University of Tokyo (1877), Bunkyō
- Yasukuni Jinja (Yasukuni Shrine) (1869), Chiyoda (p. 334)

TRANSPORT

- Tokyo Station (1914), Chiyoda (p. 198)
- Yamanote Line (1885) (p. 192)

Tokyo Station (top); Meiji Shrine (bottom)

大正時代

THE TAISHŌ ERA

(1912–1926)

FINDING THE TAISHŌ ERA IN MODERN TOKYO

The Taishō era might have been almost as short-lived as a cherry-blossom season, but it was a pivotal point in Tokyo's transformation into a fully modern city, not to mention a tremendously chic time. Surviving examples of Taishō-era graphic design, especially postcards and magazine covers, tell a tale of style, sophistication and forward thinking – which is perhaps why the aesthetic of this period is sometimes known as 'Japanese Deco'. Western cultural influence was still strong, with the introduction of jazz music marking the beginning of a long obsession for Tokyoites. Kimono took on a wonderful modernist feel, and Tokyo had its own equivalent of the Roaring Twenties' flapper: *moga*, short for 'modern girls'. There was nothing more stylish than a *moga* in *yukata* (a light cotton kimono), with bobbed hair with a fringe.

A feeling of freedom and unfettered possibility abounded in the brief period before the world drowned in nationalism and dogma; the phrase 'European romanticism' is often used to convey the spirit of the time, also known colloquially as *Taishō roman* ('romantic'). Politically, power was shifting towards the democratic parties, and the era is sometimes referred to as the Taishō democracy. Early leftist movements developed ideas of social welfare and workers' rights, and the age of the salaryman and the working woman was born.

But all was not right with the world: Japan's foreign investment overstretched the country's capital reserves, and everything was overshadowed by Japanese military growth. Then, on 1 September 1923, one of history's greatest natural disasters struck. In a tragedy that still haunts Tokyo today, the Great Kantō Earthquake – and the 40-foot-high tsunami that followed it – killed more than 100,000 people and destroyed more than 570,000 homes. Many examples of architecture from the Taishō era and earlier were lost either in the earthquake, or in bombing raids on Tokyo during the Second World War.

Woman Holding a Black Cat, Yumeji Takehisa, 1919 (opposite)

ART

- Goyō Hashiguchi (1880–1921)
- Shinsui Itō (1898–1972)
- Taikan Yokoyama (1868–1958)
- Yumeji Takehisa (1884–1934), an iconic artist of the Taishō era who blended traditional Japanese art with the techniques of Western painting

BUILDINGS

- Hibiya Public Hall (1926), Chiyoda
- Jiyu Gakuen Myonichikan (1921), Toshima, a Frank Lloyd Wright–designed building housing a girls' school known as the 'House of Tomorrow'
- Mitsui Honkan (1929), Chūō, originally built in 1923, destroyed in the Great Kantō Earthquake (p. 36) and faithfully rebuilt

CRAFT

- Meisen silk, bold patterns and unusual colour schemes were used in kimono for the first time

CULTURE

- The '*bunka* boom': *bunka* ('culture') became more accessible, leading to great advances in film and photography

EXPERIENCES

- Akarimado, Asakusa, a Taishō-inspired European coffee house
- Kayaba Coffee (1916), Yanaka, a Taishō-era European coffee house

FOOD

Western-influenced foods, once a staple of high society (think steak with a demi-glace sauce in a Ginza restaurant) became a staple of eateries in the Taishō era.

- *Karē raisu* (curry rice)
- *Katsu* (deep-fried meat and seafood)
- *Kissaten* (European-style coffee houses; p. 142)
- *Korokke* (crumbed meat, seafood or vegetable croquettes)
- *Omuraisu* (soft omelette filled with fried rice)

LITERATURE

- Naoya Shiga (1883–1971), the 'god of the novel'

MUSEUMS

- Tokyo Metropolitan Teien Art Museum (1933), Minato
- Yumeji Art Museum, Bunkyō

MUSIC

- Jazz was introduced in the Taishō era and remains hugely popular in Tokyo today.

Kissaten signage (left); Shiseido packaging (centre); *Omuraisu* (right)

Hibiya Public Hall (top); Kayaba Coffee (bottom)

昭和時代

THE SHŌWA ERA

(1926–1989)

FINDING THE SHŌWA ERA IN MODERN TOKYO

——— The Shōwa era is exceptional for the stark contrast between its early days and its later years. Early Shōwa saw a city struggling to rebuild after being decimated by the Great Kantō Earthquake and conventional bombing raids on the city during the Second World War.

Against all odds, from postwar darkness there came light, and the late Shōwa era was characterised by colour, exuberance, fun and freedom. Like West Germany, Japan flourished under the demilitarisation policies of its American occupiers. Money that would have been siphoned into defence instead went into the development of technology, making Tokyo one of the world centres for electronics, gadgetry, computers and construction. The Japanese economy grew three times faster than its Western counterparts.

Many people are nostalgic for the late Shōwa era, when life seemed easier and Tokyo experienced huge economic growth. New shopping meccas made Tokyo modern, while just enough of the old world ran in the veins and arteries of the city's streets. Lazy summer days were spent in beachside towns like Atami, or strolling along the closed-off streets of the Ginza boulevard. Pop culture, manga, *otaku* (obsessive fandom) and Tokyo *kawaii* (cute) all began their steady climb to prominence, both in Japan and the West. A burgeoning video-game empire took its first brave footsteps. Western music began to shape Japanese sounds, leading to an explosion of creativity and experimentation that still influences modern music today.

Thanks to the postwar American occupation of Japan and the 1964 Olympic Games in Tokyo, American culture became an obsession for many Japanese people. Embracing the culture of the West was an action heavily endorsed by Emperor Hirohito. This meant that the late Shōwa era's cultural aesthetic was heavily laden with Americana, including Elvis Presley, rock and roll music, whisky, Coke, beer, coffee, hamburgers, denim, cowboys and American cigarettes.

The Shōwa era saw *izakaya*, establishments similar to pubs that sold alcohol and fast food, become a Tokyo staple. Similarly, *yokochō*, the lantern-strewn laneways inhabited by small mom-and-pop eateries, yakitori joints and bars sprung into life, and remain a major draw for Tokyo locals and tourists alike to this day.

People often use the word natsukashii *for the Shōwa era. It means a feeling of nostalgia for days gone by*

Magazine cover by Jun'ichi Nakahara, 1913–1983 (opposite)

ART

- Fluxus, an international experimental art movement
  Key artists: Ay-O (b. 1931), Yoko Ono (b. 1933)
- Metabolism, an architectural movement that combined megastructures with the idea of organic growth (p. 348)
- Mono-ha, an artistic movement exploring the interplay between natural and industrial materials
- Tarō Okamoto (1911–1996)
- Tetsumi Kudo (1935–1990)
- The Gutai group, Japan's first radical postwar artistic movement, which rejected traditional art styles

CULTURE

- Atari, Sega and Nintendo video games
- Gachapon (capsule toys) and vending machines (p. 228)
- Godzilla
- Osamu Tezuka, manga artist
  Key texts: *Kimba the White Lion* (1950), *Astro Boy* (1952)
- Sony Walkman

FASHION

- Japanese Minimalism
  Key Artists: Issey Miyake, Kenzo, Rei Kawakubo (Comme des Garçons), and Yohji Yamamoto

FILM & TELEVISION

- Japanese New Wave, a highly regarded film movement that rejected the conventions of traditional Japanese cinema
- *Monkey* (television series; 1978–1980)
- *Nora Inu* (*Stray Dog*; 1949), dir. Akira Kurosawa (1910–1998)
- *Prince Planet* (television series; 1965–1966)
- *Samurai I: Musashi Miyamoto* (1954), dir. Hiroshi Inagaki (1905–1980)
- *Suna no Onna* (*Woman in the Dunes*; 1964), dir. Hiroshi Teshigahara (1927–2001)
- *The Samurai* (television series; 1962–1965)
- *Tōkyō Monogatari* (*Tokyo Story*; 1953), dir. Yasujirō Ozu (1903–1963)
- *Tōkyō Nagaremono* (*Tokyo Drifter*; 1966), dir. Seijun Suzuki (1923–2017)
- *Tōkyō Orinpikku* (*Tokyo Olympiad*; 1965), dir. Kon Ichikawa (1915–2008)
- *Tampopo*; 1985), dir. Juzo Itami (1933–1997)

GARDENS

- Hama Rikyū Gardens (1946), Chūō (p. 345)
- Gardens at the National Shōwa Memorial Museum, Kudan-Minami (p. 345)

LITERATURE

- *Asakusa Kurenaidan* (*The Scarlet Gang of Asakusa*; 1930) by Yasunari Kawabata (1899–1972)
- *Haru no Yuki* (*Spring Snow*; 1966) by Yukio Mishima (1925–1970)
- Kenzaburō Ōe (b. 1935)
- Manga (comics and graphic novels)
- *Suna no Onna* (*The Woman in the Dunes*; 1960) by Kōbō Abe (1924–1993)
- *Tetsujin 28-go* (*Gigantor*; 1956–1966) manga by Mitsuteru Yokoyama (1934–2004)

MUSEUMS

- National Museum of Western Art (1955), Ueno Park (p. 354)
- National Shōwa Memorial Museum, Kudan-Minami (p. 345)
- Yasukuni Jinja (Yasukuni Shrine, 1869), Kudan-Kita, a controversial shrine to those who died serving the Emperor of Japan in wars from 1867 to 1951, including the Second World War (p. 334)

Monchhichi toys; Flora, Bonnie and Reiko Waycott; Manga and record packaging (opposite, clockwise from top)

和服モンチッチ
ゆかたモンチッチ
¥2,590 税込

ロボットヒーロー大行進
遊星少年

MUSIC

- Cuban music
- *Kayōkyoku* ('pop tune'), the Westernisation of Japanese music and the basis for modern J-pop
  Idol kayō: a style with solo artists singing moody songs
  Mood kayō: a style influenced by jazz and Latin music
- Kyu Sakamoto (1941–1985), singer and actor
  Key tune: '*Ue o Muite Arukō*', also known as '*Sukiyaki*', was the first Japanese-language song to reach number one on the American charts
- Rock and roll
- The birth of Japanese hardcore and metal
- The birth of Japanese electronica and experimentation
  Key artists:
  Yellow Magic Orchestra, Ryuichi Sakamoto (b. 1952)
- Tōru Takemitsu (1930–1996), composer

STREETS

- Golden Gai, Shinjuku (p. 250)
- Harmonica Yokochō, Kichijōji (p. 303)
- Nonbei Yokochō, Shibuya
- Showa-dōri, Ginza
- Yurakūchō, Chiyoda, under the railway tracks (p. 194)

TEMPLES & BUILDINGS

- Bunkamura (1989), Shibuya (p. 360)
- Ginza Wako (1932), Ginza (p. 203)
- Hotel Okura Tokyo (1962), Toranomon, a must-see for any fan of mid-century modern architecture (p. 349). Its beautiful main lobby is set to reopen in 2019.
- International House of Japan (1955), Roppongi
- Isetan Shinjuku (1933), Shinjuku (p. 129)
- Nakagin Capsule Tower (1972), Ginza (p. 349)
- National Diet Building (1936), Chiyoda
- Nippon Budōkan (1964), Chiyoda (p. 354)
- Shizuoka Press and Broadcasting Center (1967), Ginza (p. 354)
- Tsukiji Hongan-ji (1934), Tsukiji
- Warou Flats (1930–37), Azabu
- Yoyogi National Gymnasium (1964), Shibuya (p. 351)

Nippon Budōkan (left); Nonbei Yokochō (right); Hotel Okura Tokyo lobby (opposite top); International House of Japan (opposite bottom)

INSPIRED BY SHŌWA

SHOKO SEKO, ARTIST & MAKER

What do you love to make?

I love making very Japanese things, like *maneki neko* (lucky cats), *okiagari-kobōshi* (roly-poly dolls) and origami.

What is your favourite medium to work in?

My favourite mediums are plush fluffy fabrics, ceramic and clay.

What is your favourite piece you are making right now?

I'm making plush toys and *kingyo* (goldfish).

You love the 1960s. What is the allure of the Shōwa era for you?

The Shōwa era was very eccentric and unique, and many goods for export were made in Japan. To me, it was an era when people were free to just make things.

Who is your favourite maker?

Takara Co. in the early years, San-ei Co., Iwai Co., Shiba Seisakusyo, Kodama, Oike, Tsukuda, Nintendo, Sanrio and Konami.

What do you like to collect?

I like collecting creepy and cute things from all over the world.

WWW.MILBEETOY.COM

平成時代

THE HEISEI ERA
(1989–2019)

FINDING THE HEISEI ERA IN MODERN TOKYO

——— Modern Tokyo has grown and shed many skins over the years. The envisioned near-dystopian *Blade Runner* neon metropolis has actually morphed into a contemporary consumerist megacity with efficient transport, green spaces and an eye for recycling and environmental protection. It is a city of layers: look up, look down, look across, go underground. No matter where your gaze falls, you'll find a dozen things jostling for position. World-class art, world-class universities, robots, tech behemoths and an evolving landscape of futurist architecture; these all coexist (and compete) with tiny-house architecture, the grassroots industries of craft coffee and beer, the low-tech revival, vaping, vintage shopping, and the modernisation of traditional forms of eating and making.

Japan's younger generations just don't want the salaryman lifestyle anymore. The inhabitants of Heisei Tokyo are striving for a world where the ideas and skills of the past are celebrated and used to make the ideas of the future better; a world where the style of the past is recalibrated, and music, books, toys and magazines are 'emotionally recycled' to ensure that past lessons are appreciated, heeded or reinvented, but not forgotten.

Shibuya (p. 234) and Shinjuku (p. 246), as hubs of youth culture, have become the epicentre of Tokyo's creative rebirth, which also sends its tendrils out to young and innovative focal points like Shimokitazawa (p. 317), Daikanyama (p. 295), Kichijōji (p. 303) and Ebisu (p. 287). It's this vibrant, dynamic and forward-thinking atmosphere that feeds – and is fed by – the massive influx of tourism from around the world.

Doraemon exhibition at the Mori Art Museum, 2018 (opposite)

ART

- Hiroshi Sugimoto (b. 1948)
- Kohei Nawa (b. 1975)
- Takashi Murakami (b. 1962), founder of the Superflat movement
- Yayoi Kusama (b. 1929)
- Yoshitomo Nara (b. 1959)

BUILDINGS

- Chloé (2006), Aoyama (p. 352)
- Comme Des Garçons (1999), Aoyama (p. 352)
- Louis Vuitton (2002), Shibuya (p. 365)
- Mode Gakuen Cocoon Tower (2008), Shinjuku (p. 352)
- Prada Epicenter (2003), Aoyama (p. 352)
- St Mary's Cathedral (1964, 2007), Bunkyō (p. 351)
- SunnyHills (2013), Aoyama (p. 352)
- TOBICHI and TOBICHI 2 (2014), Aoyama (pp. 212 & 352)
- Tokyo Skytree (2012), Sumida (p. 161)

CULTURE

- A Bathing Ape (BAPE), clothing company founded in Ura-Harajuku
- Kubrick and Bearbrick toys
- Pokémon
- Sailor Moon
- Washi tape and craft culture

EXPERIENCES

- Tokyo City View Observation Deck at the Mori Art Museum, Roppongi (p. 357)
- Gundam robot sculpture, Odaiba (p. 353)

FASHION

- Japanese streetwear
  Key Brands: A Bathing Ape, Evisu Jeans, Onitsuka Tiger, Undercover
- Global dominators
  Key Brands: Uniqlo, Muji
- Women's fashion
  Key brands: Tsumori Chisato, Cosmic Wonder, Minä Perhonen
- Harajuku, an umbrella term for Japanese street fashion, made famous by Harajuku girls
- Cosplay, a style involving dressing up like characters from anime, manga, movies or video games
- *Decora*, an over-the-top style featuring rainbow outfits (and hair) and dozens (or even hundreds) of accessories
- *Dolly kei*, a style based on European fairy tales
- *Ganguro*, a style featuring tanned skin, bleached hair and brightly coloured outfits
- *Gyaru*, an ultra-feminine style based around glamorous outfits, wigs, false eyelashes and elaborate manicures
- Lolita, a style influenced by the Victorian and Edwardian eras
- *Mori girl*, a soft and natural style utilising layers and floaty fabrics

FILM & TELEVISION

- *Tetsuo: The Iron Man* (1989), dir. Shinya Tsukamoto (b. 1960)
- *Hana-bi* (*Fireworks*; 1997), dir. Takeshi Kitano (b. 1947)
- *Ringu* (*Ring*; 1998), dir. Hideo Nakata (b. 1961)
- *Battle Royale* (2000), dir. Fukusaku Kinji (1930–2003)
- *Dare mo Shiranai* (*Nobody Knows*; 2004), dir. Hirokazu Kore-eda (b. 1962)
- *Death Note* (television series; 2006–2007), dir. Tetsurō Araki (b. 1976)
- Studio Ghibli and Hayao Miyazaki (b. 1941)
  Key films: *Mononoke-hime* (*Princess Mononoke*; 1997), *Sen to Chihiro no Kamikakushi* (*Spirited Away*; 2001), *Hotaru no Haka* (*Grave of the Fireflies*; 1988), *Tonari no Totoro* (*My Neighbor Totoro*; 1988), *Hauru no Ugoku Shiro* (*Howl's Moving Castle*; 2004)
- *Tenten* (*Adrift in Tokyo*; 2007), dir. Satoshi Miki
- *Tokyo Sonata* (2008), dir. Kiyoshi Kurosawa (b. 1955)

LITERATURE

- Banana Yoshimoto (b. 1964)
- Cell phone novels: literary works written on mobile phones, usually sent direct to readers via SMS
- Haruki Murakami (b. 1949)
  Key texts: *Noruwei no mori* (*Norwegian Wood*; 1987), *Nejimaki-dori kuronikuru* (*The Wind-Up Bird Chronicle*; 1997), *1Q84* (2009–2010)

MUSEUMS

- 21_21 Design Sight, Roppongi (p. 362)
- D47 Museum, Shibuya Hikarie building, Shibuya (p. 237)
- National Museum of Modern Art, Chiyoda (p. 354)
- Yayoi Kusama Museum (2014), Shinjuku (p. 363)

MUSIC

- Japanese minimalist pop
  Key artists: Lullatone, Cornelius
- *Kawaii* metal
  Key artist: Babymetal
- Shibuya-kei ('Shibuya style'), a music scene inspired by 1960s culture, French pop and kitsch, among other things
  Key artist: Pizzicato Five
- J-pop and J-rock
  Key artists: AKB48, Kyary Pamyu Pamyu, Perfume
- J-indie
  Key artists: Shonen Knife, The 5.6.7.8's

Treats at Isetan food hall

National Art Center, Roppongi (top); Minä Perhonen exhibition at Spiral Gallery, Aoyama (bottom)

A CITY FOR ALL SEASONS
季節

FUUBUTSUSHI: THE THINGS, FEELINGS, SCENTS AND IMAGES THAT EVOKE MEMORIES OR ANTICIPATION OF A PARTICULAR SEASON

——— The transient beauty of the seasons is key to understanding the Japanese people's deep affinity with nature. While most countries are at the mercy of the seasons to some extent, in Japan it shapes the way people experience life. The food, the festivals, the products in shops, the activities: are all informed by the unique atmosphere that each season brings. Cinematic master Yasujirō Ozu captured this appreciation for the seasons in his famous 'Noriko Trilogy' series of films. They are all odes to the seasons, and all use seasons as a metaphor.

The masterful way in which Tokyo is designed gives each area a chance to shine in at least one of the seasons. Streets are planted en masse with trees that bloom seasonally: cherry blossoms and magnolias in spring, plum blossoms in winter, hydrangeas and lush greenery in summer, and ginkgo and maple trees in autumn. Boating on the lakes in parks is a ritual in spring, summer and autumn. Picnics in summer and ice-skating rinks and *onsen* (hot springs) in winter are anticipated as the seasons slowly reveal themselves.

There is a kind of nostalgia connected to the seasons, a wistfulness that acknowledges the inevitability of change. Seasons are markers of time, and bring to mind the remembrance of things past and the promise of the future. In traditional Japanese aesthetics, there is a concept called *yūgen*, which can be summed up in a quote by aesthetician Zeami Motokiyo as 'a profound, mysterious sense of the beauty of the universe … and the sad beauty of human suffering'. The seasons are the epitome of this: the falling leaves of autumn; rebirth from death in spring; sprouting life in the warmth of summer; and winter's harsh reminder that life brings with it trials and sadness, meaning that we should truly appreciate moments of great beauty.

Sakura soft-serve ice cream at Inokashira Park

SUMMER

夏

Itadaku mono wa natsu de mo kosode: A padded jacket is an acceptable gift, even in summer

NATSU

JUNE–AUGUST · RAINY SEASON, HOT DAYS, RUTHLESSLY HUMID

Summer in Tokyo is hot, but it's not just the heat, it's the humidity. Make no mistake – it is unbelievably humid. Humidity hair is a thing; forget trying to keep wavy hair straight. Those who have previously declared themselves 'non-sweaters' will find themselves soaked through. Add the mid-summer rains, and you have a season to be reckoned with. That's summer in Tokyo, and it doesn't deviate from its malicious schedule.

Escape the heat by visiting a gallery, walking through cool, cavernous train stations, or popping into air-conditioned shops and cafés. Air conditioning is a lifesaver: usually icy cold, especially in department stores, it sets you up for a few more hours outside. The Yamanote Line is a great place to cool down; ride around for a while until you are ready to step out again. Take advantage of Tokyo's beautiful green spaces (p. 336), but dress for *natsubate*, the physical fatigue of summer. Convenience stores and drink machines will have you marvelling at all the options to beat the heat. Try a *kakigōri* (shaved ice) dessert for a true Tokyo experience (p. 126). Keep hydrated and remember that you can duck inside somewhere interesting if the heat and humidity get too much for you. Tokyo has brilliant sunscreens (p. 222), so make sure you're covered. Flannels to mop your brow and hats to protect you from the sun are essential.

Finally, some notes on the rainy season. The Japanese have 50 words for rain, which tells you something. Tokyo has typhoons from May to October, with peak season running from August to September. Expect heavy rains and winds of up to 100 kilometres per hour. During a typhoon, if a place that you expected to be busy seems deserted, chances are everyone else has gotten wind – pun intended – of the fact that a typhoon is on its way. Rain can start in the morning and not let up all day. A patterned umbrella or lightweight raincoat will brighten the cloudiest of days.

Tanabata celebrations in Tokyo (opposite)

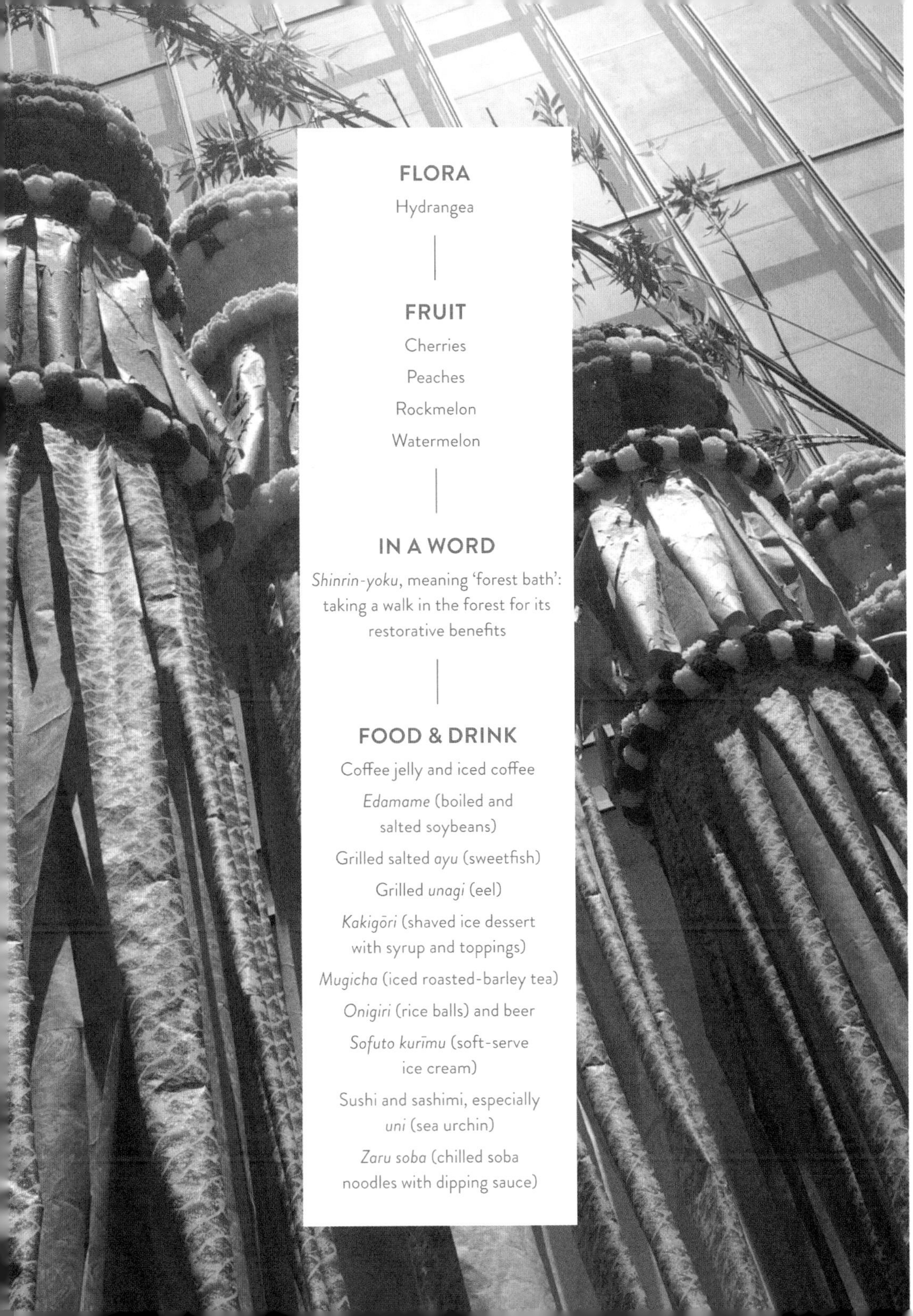

FLORA

Hydrangea

FRUIT

Cherries

Peaches

Rockmelon

Watermelon

IN A WORD

Shinrin-yoku, meaning 'forest bath': taking a walk in the forest for its restorative benefits

FOOD & DRINK

Coffee jelly and iced coffee

Edamame (boiled and salted soybeans)

Grilled salted *ayu* (sweetfish)

Grilled *unagi* (eel)

Kakigōri (shaved ice dessert with syrup and toppings)

Mugicha (iced roasted-barley tea)

Onigiri (rice balls) and beer

Sofuto kurīmu (soft-serve ice cream)

Sushi and sashimi, especially *uni* (sea urchin)

Zaru soba (chilled soba noodles with dipping sauce)

SUMMER FESTIVALS

Japanese festivals are colourful and vibrant, with incredible street food. Tokyo has its own spin on tradition, and puts on some of the biggest and best festivals in Japan. If you time your travels to coincide with a festival, you'll not only experience something completely unique, but you'll also learn about Japanese culture to boot. If you find a festival that interests you, it may be worth planning your next holiday around it. There are many summer festivals, or *natsu matsuri*, in Tokyo; here are five of our favourites.

HARAJUKU–OMOTESANDŌ GENKI MATSURI SUPER YOSAKOI

Harajuku–Omotesandō Traditional Dance Festival

Late August

A bright and colourful festival in and around Omotesandō (p. 252)and Yoyogi Park (p. 342). Expect a riot of colour, costumes, singing, dancing, some very enthusiastic musicians and a general party vibe. Anyone wanting to immerse themselves in traditional Japanese dance will find this festival endlessly fascinating.

HOZUKI-ICHI

Lantern Plant Festival

July 9–10

The lantern plant, with its brightly coloured pods that hang in clusters, is so beautiful that it deserves its own celebration. Various summer fairs – most notably the one at the Sensō-ji temple (p. 334) in Asakusa (p. 154) – honour lantern plants by hanging bunches of them, showing off their vibrant colours and, later, their skeletal, decaying beauty. Florists also stock lantern plants and allow them to slowly wither with age: another potent, short-lived symbol of the transience of life.

SHITAMACHI TANABATA MATSURI

Shitamachi Star Festival

Early July
(five days around 7 July)

In Japan's old quarters, on a long stretch of road between Asakusa (p. 154) and Ueno (p. 174), the *Shitamachi Tanabata Matsuri* is celebrated with street parades, singing and dancing, street food and general frivolity. Tanabata is celebrated across Japan and commemorates the story of celestial lovers Orihime and Hikoboshi, who were forbidden from meeting by the Sky King except on the seventh night of the seventh month, when they can cross a bridge over the Milky Way and unite as long as it's not raining. This festival is our favourite, with its colourful and beautiful decorations that flutter in the wind. With the Skytree (p. 161) and hundred-year-old temples as its backdrop – a hybrid landscape of old and new – the festival really feels like a true Tokyo tradition. There are quite a few Tanabata celebrations held around Tokyo, so if you love the idea of this festival or would prefer to experience a smaller version, ask your hotel front desk or Airbnb host for their favourite in the city.

Tanabata also has its own specific *wagashi* (traditional sweets; p. 124). Shaped like leaves, the sweets represent the old custom of writing a wish on paper mulberry or bamboo leaves. These days, people write wishes on strips of paper called *tanzaku* in the hope that they will be granted.

SUMIDAGAWA HANABI TAIKAI

Sumida River Fireworks Festival

Last Saturday in July

This famous fireworks festival takes place in Sumida, one of Tokyo's traditional areas. It has roots in the Edo period dating back to 1732, but the current incarnation has been a fixture on the Tokyo festival calendar since 1978. Nearly a million people congregate to see the stunning fireworks display on the banks of the Sumida River. It's a family-friendly event, with the fireworks starting at 7 pm and lasting a little over an hour. Wearing a *yukata* (summer kimono) to the festival is popular and a really fun way to get into the spirit of things.

OBON

Festival of the Dead
Mid-August

Obon, the tradition of paying respect to loved ones who have passed away, manifests in highly personal rituals at home and family visits to temples, shrines and graveyards. It's a very popular time of year for travel as family members reunite to honour their ancestors, so plan your movements carefully if you are in Tokyo when Obon is being held.

Obon celebrations can take on an almost riotous joy. Kimono-clad families participate in *rokudō mairi,* attending shrines and temples and calling for deceased family members. Obon is a wonderful time to go for a dusk cemetery walk (Aoyama, p. 267, Yanaka, p. 183, and Yasukuni Jinja, p. 334, are beautiful examples) to see glowing lanterns and the gentle rituals and bonds of family history. At Obon festivals you'll find fun, colourful festival food, costumes and rituals: equal parts celebration and deep spiritual respect. Dusk and night-time events have incredible lighting displays, and often host over-the-top parades and spectacles, too. Dancers in bright costumes perform *Bon odori* ('Obon dance'), a circular dance accompanied by traditional drums and music. Watching bystanders can be called up onto the stage – a stunning sight, as most people also wear *yukata* (summer kimono) for this festival. Many businesses close for Obon holidays, usually for a few days around 15 August.

SUMMER EXPERIENCES

Two of Tokyo's (and the world's) best music festivals take place in summer, offering an huge array of national and international bands, events, food and general abandon. No music-festival obsessive can say they have done it all until they have included these two major events on the global music calendar.

Fuji Rock Festival
Last weekend of July

Summer Sonic Chiba
Early to mid-August
(two-day festival)

SUMMER ESCAPES

Shopping meccas and art enclaves are a perfect escape from the elements, as they're warm in winter and icy cold in summer. Roppongi Hills has the Mori Art Museum (p. 357) and some great ramen in the subway station (Afuri Ramen, p. 109), as well as many other food and drink options you'll want to explore. Shopping complex Tokyo Midtown (p. 275) has the 21_21 Design Sight museum (p. 362) on its grounds, and the Suntory Museum of Art (p. 357) inside, a changing gallery space that is part of Roppongi's art triangle. Fujifilm Square (p. 365), where you can catch some great photography exhibitions, is just outside Tokyo Midtown.

Visiting all of these locations barely requires going outside, and there are various hubs around town that afford the same kind of protection while letting you experience some of Tokyo's best offerings.

AUTUMN

秋

Ichiyō ochite tenka no aki wo shiru:
A falling leaf shows that autumn has come

AKI

SEPTEMBER–NOVEMBER · COOL AIR, SHORTER DAYS, LEAVES CHANGING COLOUR

—— As the weather starts to cool and days become shorter, the hot and humid Japanese summer gradually makes way for autumn. The season's perfect travel weather brings many visitors and a host of seasonal activities to the city, including autumn-leaf viewing, cherry-blossom viewing's lesser-known sibling. Golden light glinting through avenues of trees that are turning from green to deep red or every shade of rich brown is a hauntingly beautiful sight.

A poetic marker of the changing of the seasons, leaves turning shades of crimson, copper and ochre usher in the cooler weather and herald that the end of the year is nigh. The falling leaves and the suggestion of winter's bare, frosty months brings an air of contemplative sadness. Festivals and activities reflect this, with thoughtful strolls being popular. Walking in the crisp air around the city's streets, parks and gardens, rusty leaves swirling around your feet: it's magical and melancholy.

Autumn in Tokyo is more than just a feast for the eyes. The season is host to a very important moment in the Japanese culinary calendar: when the first rice harvest of the year appears in shops. And keep an eye out for autumnal specialties: autumn-leaf-themed food and seasonal warm drinks are as beautiful as they are delicious.

FLORA

Ginkgo leaves

Maple leaves

FRUIT

Apples

Grapes

Nashi pears

Persimmons

Yuzu citrus

IN A WORD

Shūshi, meaning 'autumn melancholy', a feeling of deep sadness associated with the season

FOOD & DRINK

Chestnuts

Eggplant

Ginkgo nuts

Horse mackerel

Mushrooms

New rice

Salmon

Sweet potato

AUTUMN COLOURS

MOMIJIGARI

Autumn-leaf viewing

Mid-November to early/mid-December

If you want to experience the most beautiful autumn landscapes, our pick would be two Edo-period gardens: Rikugi-en (p. 345) and Koishikawa-Kōrakuen (p. 345). These thoughtfully planned gardens are the best of the best when it comes to seasonal Tokyo. Rikugi-en has a beautiful tea house and dusk illuminations, and is the venue used for our kimono day out (p. 64).

Icho Namiki, also called Ginkgo Avenue, is another must-visit. The ginkgo trees lining the large boulevard make for a stunning stroll, and when you reach the end of the road you'll find street-food vendors waiting for you.

Other beautiful spots include Kiyosumi Teien (p. 345), Shinjuku Gyoen (p. 343), Shōwa Kinen Kōen in Tachikawa, Jindai-ji Temple in Chōfu (p. 334) and Mount Takao in Hachiōji.

AUTUMN FESTIVALS

KICHIJŌJI AKI MATSURI

Kichijōji Autumn Festival

September (dates vary)

This colourful two-day festival has been holding its own since the 1970s in one of our favourite areas. Day one starts at 11 am outside JR-East Kichijōji station with a street parade that includes portable shrines, costumes, rituals, boisterous chanting, street food and general frivolity, all in a local setting. The Musashino Hachimangu shrine comes alive on day two, a truly spiritual celebration.

TSUKIMI

Moon-viewing festival

Late September/early October

Enjoying the full moon at the start of October has been a popular pastime since the Edo period. The exact dates are based on the Chinese calendar and change every year. The autumn equinox (*ohigan*) and moon viewing both make for a lovely final outdoor event before the winter chill arrives. Many people congregate for early evening picnics under the moon and stars (with lots of sake, of course). While in the West we talk about the man in the moon, Japanese people see a rabbit, or *usagi*, in the moon. So grab some picnic food and some rugs, or get to one of Tokyo's highest points – we recommend Tokyo Tower or Skytree (both p. 161) – and see if you can make out the famous rabbit. The more sake you have, the easier it will be.

SHICHI-GO-SAN

Seven-five-three festival

November 15

Three- and seven-year-old girls and three- and five-year-old boys are celebrated on this day. It is adorable to see all the children dressed beautifully in formal kimono (often for the first time) as they visit shrines (p. 330).

AUTUMN EXPERIENCES

HALLOWEEN

31 October

Head to Hachikō Square (p. 235) in Shibuya in costume if dressing up for Halloween is your bag. It's a crazy mix of locals and tourists, cheesing up the American tradition with an outrageous array of costumes (if you haven't gathered already, Japanese people are fans of costumes). Pumpkin- and Halloween-themed packaging takes over your favourite foods and brands. Loft (p. 212), Kiddy Land (p. 270) and Tokyu Hands (p. 212) usually go crazy with themed toys and trinkets, and theme restaurants get very spooky.

TOKYO ART BOOK FAIR

Late September to early October

tokyoartbookfair.com/en

JAPAN ROBOT WEEK

Mid-October

biz.nikkan.co.jp/eve/s-robot

KANDA SECOND-HAND BOOK FESTIVAL

Late October to early November

jimbou.info/news/furuhon_fes_index.html

TOKYO INTERNATIONAL FILM FESTIVAL

Late October to early November

2018.tiff-jp.net/en

TOKYO RAMEN SHOW

Late October to early November

ramenshow.com

DESIGN FESTA

Mid-November

designfesta.com/en

Halloween treats and Ginkgo Avenue streetscapes

A KIMONO DAY OUT

MICHELLE AND HIKI, RIKUGI-EN

I love print and textile design, and kimono design has always fascinated me, from the patterns, colours and textures that seem to both clash and match perfectly at the same time, to the range of choices and the history. Whenever I am in Japan, I check to see if there is an exhibition I can visit, and I'll always stop in at Mingeikan, the Japan Folk Crafts Museum (p. 360) to admire the beautiful vintage kimono on display.

I revere all of the Ginza ladies who still wear kimono to shop and lunch, and because of this I had never considered hiring one to wear for the day. Firstly, I would not pass as being Japanese and secondly, I felt like it would be impossible to find the kind of kimono I would like to wear.

On a recent trip to Tokyo to photograph the autumn colours, I was having a conversation with my close friend, Hiki. I mentioned that, one day, I would love to feel what it was like to wear a kimono, drink tea and stroll around an Edo garden. Immediately, she offered to organise one of her family kimono for me and to ask her mother, Akane, to dress us for a kimono day out. Akane, a *Noh* theatre student and performer (interviewed on p. 369), learned how to dress herself and others in kimono from watching her mother wear them almost every day. She kindly agreed and asked for a photo of me so she could match the kimono to my colouring and to the autumn environment. Weeks before the event, I was sent an image of the colour pairing Akane had chosen for me. It was a perfect mix of autumn tones, green and purple.

When I arrived at Hiki's apartment, her mother had nearly finished dressing her. Hiki owns a divine blue kimono covered in butterflies. I was struck by its timeless elegance and beauty. I spied my outfit hanging on the wall and immediately got goosebumps. Hiki's grandmother, Chitoko, had bought the fabric and Akane had had it made into a kimono for Hiki when she got married. To be able to wear something so beautiful and with such family significance is something I will forever treasure.

A kimono mat was laid out for me to stand on when my time came. In the meantime, I put on special stockings and stiff socks, or *tabi*. When I reappeared I was asked to stand on the mat with my arms out wide. Wearing kimono requires special one- or two-piece undergarments known as *juban* – in my case, I put on a white cotton under-kimono and a long skirt. Akane strapped the under-kimono around my torso very tightly. She explained that it needed to be very fitted so it would last throughout the day.

When Akane was happy with the collar position and the tightness of the *juban*, the vintage kimono was taken off the hanger and wrapped around me from right to left. A belt, or *koshi himo*, was added next to smooth out excess material and structurally shape the fabric to the body. This belt's purpose is to create clean lines, and is later hidden under the *obi* sash.

Once Akane was finally satisfied with the drape of the fabric, she was ready to put on the *obi* sash. As this element completes the beauty of the overall outfit, it is almost the most important part.

There are so many different ways to tie an *obi*; some are connected to fashion and style, while others have historical and cultural meaning. A full-length mirror allowed Akane to see how the kimono was looking from the other side, and I watched the tumble of heavy fabric being draped and looped around my body. The precision of this process made me realise just how much artistry goes into being a kimono-dresser. The collar of my white under-kimono was straightened and a beautiful green piece of silk known as *obiage* was wedged beneath the *obi*. In the final step, the thin *obijime* belt was fastened with a brooch-like clip *obidome* around my waist. Hiki loaned me a vintage bag with beautiful embroidery to complete the outfit.

We had a cup of tea and then slipped on special sandals known as *zori* (similar to *geta* sandals, but softer). I felt like I was entering a world I'd never dreamed I'd be able to experience.

We chose the Edo-period garden Rikugi-en (p. 345) for our kimono stroll. The beautiful autumn foliage and gorgeous tea room made it a truly memorable day.

Being dressed in kimono in the traditional way takes time – around one-and-a-half hours, to be precise – but I was enthralled and enjoyed every minute of it. That being said, not everyone has the privilege of knowing someone who owns and can dress others in vintage kimono. The kimono rental listings opposite will have you dressed in less time, and for a reasonable price.

KIMONO TYPES

There are different types, or ranks, of kimono, which determine at which occasion and by whom they can be worn. It's a little complex, but as long as you don't wear a *komon* or *yukata* (summer kimono) to a formal occasion, you'll be fine. The styles below are the most commonly worn; others include *tsukesage*, *tomesode*, *tsumugi* and *iromuji*.

Furisode

Worn by unmarried women, these have a big pattern and long sleeves.

Hōmongi

The equivalent of *furisode* for married women (though it can also be worn by unmarried women).

Komon

A stylish kimono made from fabric with small patterns all over it, which can be worn in both semi-formal or casual settings. The kimono that Hiki and I wore were *komon*.

KIMONO RENTAL

Kimono Sakaeya
kimono-sakaeya.com/Tokyo

Aki Kimono Rental
kr-aki.co.jp/user_data/english

Iza Kimono Rental
asakusakirara.jp/en

Omotenashi Nihonbashi
nihonbashi-info.jp/omotenashi

A word we heard a lot on our kimono day out was 'suteki'. It means lovely or charming

FUYU

DECEMBER–FEBRUARY · SUNNY, DRY, CRISP, A LITTLE SNOW (IF YOU ARE LUCKY)

—— We have spent winter in Japan nearly every year for the past 20 years. When Christmas and New Year celebrations are over and everyone is in holiday mode, it feels like we have the city to ourselves. We love everything about winter in Tokyo: rugging up; sipping hot soups; pulling on mittens and woolly jackets and walking through stark wintery landscapes; parks full of bare trees. Winter is a trip to a Tokyo *onsen* (hot spring) after a busy work year, a time to wind down and relax. It's warm sake, *kotatsu* (tables with cosy heated blankets), the possibility of snow. Late nights in a bookstore bathed in warm yellow light. Later nights in cosy bars.

Now, was there something else? That's right: the sales. Winter sales in Tokyo are like no other, replete with bargains, massive mark-downs, special gift boxes and a whirl of shoppers and frantic salespeople: the boldest, brightest and loudest celebration of consumerism you will ever take part in.

Christmas Day is also fun for visitors. In Tokyo it is business as usual, with all shops and eateries open. A few days later, the city starts closing for New Year, Japan's biggest holiday. Train stations and airports start to get congested and businesses can shut for a few days to up to a month. The city empties. If you are looking for a party city in which to celebrate New Year's Eve, perhaps make other plans. There are now a few midnight countdowns in Shibuya (p. 234) and other young areas, but the New Year in Tokyo is a time for family and reflection, so many of the places you want to visit may be shut or have very limited hours.

Osechi-ryōri at our friend Coco's house (opposite top); *Kadomatsu* decorations (opposite bottom)

FLORA

Moss

Plum blossom

FRUIT

Mandarins

Yuzu citrus

IN A WORD

Yuki, meaning 'snow'

FOOD & DRINK

Amazake (hot, sweet drink made from fermented rice)

Hot teas

Nabe (a variety of hotpot dishes)

Nikuman (steamed buns filled with meat)

Oden (fish cakes and daikon simmered in a soy broth)

Osechi-ryōri (traditional New Year dishes)

Shiruko and zenzai (sweet red-bean soup)

Soups, including ramen, soba and udon noodle soups

WINTER CELEBRATIONS

OOMISOKA

New Year's Eve

Traditionally, soba noodles are eaten, as long noodles symbolise a long life.

OSHŌGATSU

New Year's celebrations

Preparations start from late December; 1–3 January are public holidays

The first time we got caught up in Tokyo's end-of-year celebrations, we became keenly aware that we were partaking in something new: festivities and cultural activities that went beyond our knowledge of Japanese culture. Ever since, we have been hooked, often skipping Christmas in Australia to spend a month in Japan.

If arriving in Tokyo in mid-December, expect to see a mash-up of Christmas trees and lights (as Steve says, pretty, classic Nordic-style Christmas images, only without baby Jesus) with the traditional trappings of Japanese New Year festivities.

If you're in Tokyo over the Christmas and New Year period, keep in mind that most businesses are closed on New Year's Day. Try big hotels or busy train stations for food options. The Mori Art Museum (p. 357), Roppongi Hills (p. 275), Tokyo Tower (p. 161) and Tokyo Skytree (p. 161) also remain open.

OSECHI-RYŌRI: FOOD FOR THE NEW YEAR

The stacking lacquerware boxes, hiding jewel-like edible delights, known as *osechi-ryōri* have been around for centuries, but only became a New Year tradition for commoners in the Edo period. *Osechi-ryōri* is traditionally served in two to five *bentō*-like boxes known as *jubakō*, and the morsels on offer include black beans, *konbu* (kelp), fishcakes, prawns, cod roe and more, although each prefecture – and each family – in Japan has its own spin on *osechi-ryōri*. Every ingredient has a meaning – for example, the prawn symbolises longevity (its curved shape being reminiscent of a hunched-over back) – and the dishes are eaten in a specific order, usually from top to bottom. The perfect balance of colours, food groups, artistry and symbolism, this tradition will truly amaze and delight you with its beauty and thoughtfulness.

Head to a department store for a glimpse of what's on offer – just a glimpse, mind you. You'll soon realise that this is not a cuisine for the budget traveller. The price tag is high because of the work required to prepare the food and the premium quality of the ingredients. If you are ever invited to New Year's Day at a Japanese friend's house and are offered *osechi-ryōri*, don't pass up this opportunity of a lifetime. Remember to take a gift and convey how honoured you are!

OZONI: NEW YEAR SOUP

Our friends Hiki and Ryo took us out for *ozoni*, another New Year food tradition, a few days after New Year's Day. The *ozoni* we tried was a clear broth of dashi and miso with vegetables and *mochi* (rice cakes). As with *osechi-ryōri*, *ozoni* recipes are different in each prefecture and family.

NEW YEAR'S SAKE

When shops and some cultural spaces reopen after New Year's Day, usually on 2 January, it's a tradition to serve samples of the first sake from the barrel. Huge new barrels almost overflowing with fresh sake are opened and tastings are offered to customers. It's great to get involved, try a few different kinds and then buy your favourite.

NEW YEAR'S DECORATIONS

Kagami-mochi

Consisting of two *mochi* (rice cakes) with a mandarin on top, this is a slightly unusual but prevalent New Year decoration. We always look out for gift versions to take home. We've seen glass variations in swanky department stores, and even a miniature capsule toy one.

Kadomatsu

These vertical structures made of bamboo and pine (and sometimes kale and blossom) are placed at doorways to invite the Shinto spirit Toshigami into the premises. They are quite expensive to buy, and are always sold in pairs. Look for them out the front of big businesses, hotels and public facilities.

Shimekazari

Michelle is a little obsessed with *shimekazari*, a wreath-like decoration that adorns the entryways of houses and buildings during the New Year festivities. They are simply constructed from straw rope, sometimes with paper, leaves and other elements woven in, and are said to ward off evil spirits. In Tokyo, they are generally displayed from mid-December and are discarded soon after the New Year. *Shimekazari* differ greatly from prefecture to prefecture (the Kantō region, where Tokyo resides, favours a looped-rope design), so if you are travelling through Japan during the New Year period, you will have the opportunity to become an expert on the intricacies and artistry of *shimekazari*. As it is with Christmas trees, the natural ones are the most beautiful, but the price and convenience of the plastic ones means that artificial options have become more popular.

Shimekazari (top); *Kagami-mochi* (bottom)

Hatsumōde at the Meiji Shrine

HATSUMŌDE: THE FIRST SHRINE VISIT OF THE YEAR

On New Year's Eve in Japan, people eat *toshikoshi* ('year-crossing') soba and participate in Hatsumōde, the first shrine visit of the year.

Eating soba noodles is considered good luck, as the long noodles symbolise long life, and the ease with which soba noodles are cut while eating represents the letting go of any hardships from the previous year. It is considered bad luck to eat *toshikoshi* soba at midnight, though, so join a queue in town early!

Hatsumōde starts at midnight on New Year's Eve/New Year's Day, when bells ring in the new year, and continues for days afterwards. The first time we participated in Hatsumōde we felt like part of a collective hoping for luck for the New Year ahead. The Meiji Shrine and Sensō-ji (both p. 334) draw the largest crowds, so we love visiting Jindai-ji (p. 334) in Chōfu or another one of Tokyo's smaller shrines for a more intimate experience. Having said that, everyone should visit one of the larger shrines at least once, as the energy and atmosphere is incredible. The crowds are thick but flow perfectly towards their main goal, the shrine itself, where people can say (or write) prayers for the coming year. You'll be amazed by how such a large group of people manages to move through the shrine in such an ordered and respectful manner (you'll certainly reassess group behaviour in your own country).

WINTER EXPERIENCES

KOTATSU

A *kotatsu* is a low table covered in a blanket, underneath which a heater is either built in or placed. 'Warm legs, warm heart'! Michelle's feet are always cold, so for her this is one of the best ways to while away a winter afternoon (especially if you are drinking warm sake and eating *zenzai*, sweet red-bean soup, or ramen). Totoshigure in Shimokitazawa (p. 317) is the poster child for cosy dining, with tables that jut out onto the streets. Seek out your own and make yourself comfortable for the day (and/or night!). If you're taking a long train journey, try finding a *kintetsu* train, where they actually have seats with heaters under blankets.

ONSEN

What's a trip to Japan without a visit to an *onsen* (hot spring)? There are some great *onsen* in Tokyo that have outdoor baths. We highly recommend the invigorating experience of a hot bath on a freezing cold day; it's pretty close to heaven.

AMEYA-YOKOCHŌ MARKET

This shopping street, which follows the train line near Ueno Station, is crazy around New Year, with thousands of people madly buying things for their celebrations.

FUKUBUKURO

As if Japan's January sales weren't already exciting enough, enter *fukubukuro*, or 'lucky bag' shopping. Merchants put together grab bags full of mystery items at a substantial markdown, and while you won't know what you get until it's bought and paid for, it's always worth it. Pick your favourite label or store and get a hold of one of their grab bags. Inside will be items at a fraction of their original cost. There are some true bargains to be had, and *fukubukuro* extends to gadgetry, toiletries, clothes, toys, food (especially sweets) and even convenience store purchases.

OTHER WINTER EXPERIENCES

JANUARY SALES

Mid-January
Tokyo-wide

SUMO GRAND TOURNAMENT

Mid-January
sumo.or.jp/EnTicket/year_schedule

ICE SKATING

Throughout winter
- *Tokyo Midtown (p. 275)*
- *Meiji-jingu Gaien Ice Rink, Harajuku*

WINTER ILLUMINATIONS

Dates vary
- *Omotesandō Hills (p. 262)*
- *Roppongi Hills (p. 275)*
- *Midtown Christmas (p. 275)*
- *Tokyo Dome City*

BONENKAI: 'FORGET THE YEAR' PARTIES

Bonenkai are office parties to end all office parties. Workers attend several *bonenkai* at the end of the year: it's a whole-company affair. They usually book out restaurants across the board, so you might find it hard to get into your favourite spot around this time. Expect to see very drunk people staggering out onto streets, laughing and talking energetically, or being helped along by slightly more sober friends. Women, men, bosses and underlings: no-one is immune from 'overdoing it'.

WINTER FESTIVALS

SETSUBUN

Bean-throwing Festival
2–4 February

Want to get rid of last year's demons? During *Setsubun*, people throw beans out the door or at family members wearing a demon mask to ward off evil spirits. This is a very popular family-friendly tradition and is loads of fun. Masks and beans can be bought in stores across the city. Look out for packages of roasted soybeans with Mr and Mrs Demon on them and ready your throwing arm. Festivities can be found at Zōjō-ji (p. 334), Sensō-ji (p. 334) or the Shimokita Tengu Matsuri (Long Red-nosed Goblins Festival). Don't forget to chant, '*Oni wa soto! Fuku wa uchi!*' ('Demons out, good fortune in!').

Setsubun packs for sale, Sun Road, Kichijōji (opposite)

Many larger stores set up a New Year gift section around this time, so if you want to take a New Year–themed present home, there are plenty of lovely souvenirs. Independent handicraft stalls pop up in big commercial areas. Yanaka Ginza (p. 188) and the tiny alleys around it offer a great day out at this time of year, especially if you're looking to see kagami-mochi and shimekazari stalls.

SPRING

春

Rakka eda ni kaerazu: The fallen blossom returns not to the bough

HARU

MARCH–MAY · WARM SUNSHINE, GENTLE WINDS, FALLING PETALS

——— As the cold weather makes way for the gentle winds of spring, Tokyo is transformed by flower viewing and festivals, new financial and school years and the celebratory Golden Week, a full week of public holidays. Spring delicacies and favourites like young bamboo shoots and fresh strawberries fill markets and stores. The extreme sport of predicting the exact opening of the first cherry blossom at Yasukuni Jinja (Yasukuni Shrine; p. 334) takes over the public consciousness and the anticipation of family time and holidays leading up to Golden Week provides more joy.

Spring in Tokyo – and across Japan – is famed for the fragile, fleeting beauty of *sakura*, or cherry blossoms. Locals and visitors alike gather for *hanami* (flower viewing) in parks and gardens across the city to witness first the opening of the blossoms, followed by the floating and falling of the petals – the *sakura* snow – and finally the carpet of pink that blankets the ground. There is a saying in Japanese: *mono no aware* (literally 'the bitter-sweetness of fading beauty'). It conveys the feeling of the poignancy, beauty and sadness of transient things. Pathways strewn with fallen petals, beauty lost. Some believe the *sakura* snow is the most beautiful part of *hanami*: a celebration of fleeting moments, an acknowledgement that the intensity of such brief encounters makes them mean that much more.

FLORA

Sakura (cherry blossom)

FRUIT

Strawberries

IN A PHRASE

Mono no aware, meaning 'the bitter-sweetness of fading beauty'

FOOD & DRINK

Bonito

Broad beans

Cabbage

New potatoes

New tea

Spanish mackerel

Wasabi

Young bamboo shoots

SPRING SAKURA

HANAMI

Cherry-blossom viewing

The fragility of the cherry blossom; the sacred viewing of flowers. *Hanami*, from the words *hana*, meaning 'flower', and *mi*, meaning 'to see', is a quintessential Japanese custom, and one you absolutely must take part in if you're in Tokyo at the right time of year. The city turns precious shades of pink for a limited moment in time, usually no more than a week. When the blossoms arrive, everything takes on a kind of magical festival atmosphere. It's a time to catch up with friends, participate in activities, eat delicious seasonal food, and drink sake. *Sakura*-themed *bentō* boxes and traditional Japanese sweets are popular. People come together to celebrate with picnics and sake under the trees. Paper lanterns are threaded through the trees to keep the magic going into the evening and beyond, maintaining the beauty of the flowers into the night. This is known as *yozakura*, or 'night *sakura*'. We've been in Tokyo and experienced earthquakes, typhoons and snow, and nothing keeps the public from shopping ... except a day out in blossoms.

SPRING FOODS

Head to a department-store food hall in spring and you'll find *sakura*-themed everything – a major challenge to your self-control, as you'll want to try it all. Convenience stores are a great way to see all the seasonal packaging on offer. Many brands sell out early (*sakura*-themed Kit Kat, Kirin and Yebisu, for example), so if you see something you like, buy it!

HANAMI DANGO

These sweet dumplings, typically eaten at *hanami* picnics, are always served in threes: one pink, to symbolise cherry blossoms; one white, to symbolise snow; and one green, to symbolise grass.

SAKURA MOCHI

This *sakura*-flavoured rice cake, wrapped in pickled cherry-blossom leaves, is delicious. We head to our favourite stores (Higashiya Man, p. 267, and Toraya, p. 129) and line up early so as not to miss out. A pop-up stall inside Kudanshita Station on the way to Kitanomaru Park (p. 340) is also a stand-out; as well as *sakura mochi* it sells *ichigo daifuku* (strawberry *mochi*), a chewy *mochi* rice cake wrapped around sweet red-bean paste and a juicy strawberry. *Oishii!*

SAKURA WAGASHI

If you have never tried *wagashi* (traditional sweets, p. 124) before, this is your moment. The artistry around *sakura*-themed *wagashi* is astounding, it can be difficult to justify biting into one and ruining its beauty. Tea infused or flavoured with *sakura* is also a treasure of the season, so make it your business to have a sit-in tea and sweets afternoon if you are in Tokyo for *hanami*.

SAVOURY FOOD

While the cherry-blossom sweets are particularly beautiful, we also enjoy seeing petals and flowers on our rice dishes. *Hanami bentō* boxes and *onigiri* (rice balls) with tiny pink flowers – everything is a frenzy of pink – are so lovely that you'll want to buy one of everything.

OTHER SPRING FOODS

- Pink sake and pink champagne
- Pink *sakura* soft-serve ice cream
- *Sakura*-themed packaging for chocolate, beer, candy … and everything else!

PARKS AND GARDENS WITH SAKURA

Yanaka Cemetery, Yanaka (p. 183)
- Quiet and gentle atmosphere
- Beautiful at dusk
- A contemplative stroll

Shinjuku Gyoen, Shinjuku (p. 343)
- Entry fee
- Alcohol-free
- Picnic-friendly
- Family-friendly

Nakameguro Canal, Nakameguro (p. 299)
- Great for river strolls
- Young, international crowd
- Pink sake and champagne
- Street-food stalls
- Dogs in prams

Ueno Park, Ueno (p. 342)
- Street food
- Swan boats
- Picnic-friendly
- Family-friendly
- Good for a day of visiting museums

Inokashira Park, Musashino (p. 342)
- Swan boats
- *Sakura*-themed food
- Family-friendly
- Alcohol-friendly
- Picnic-friendly

Kitanomaru Park, Chiyoda (p. 340)
- Picnic-friendly
- Great for long walks
- Boating along the river

Yoyogi Park, Shibuya (p. 342)
- Young, international crowd
- Pink sake and champagne
- Street-food stalls
- Picnic-friendly
- Live music

SPRING FESTIVALS

HINA MATSURI

Doll's Day or Girl's Day
March 3

This festival is centred around girls and praying for their health and happiness. It is celebrated in homes across Japan by displaying a pair of *hina* dolls on red velvet. These ornamental dolls, a woman and a man representing the Emperor and Empress, are taken out a few days before March 3 and put away soon after.

Hina Matsuri is a time for girls' parties, kimono, *amazake* (a hot, sweet drink made from fermented rice) and sweets, including green or three-coloured *mochi* (rice cakes) and *ichigo daifuku* (strawberry *mochi*). It's a great time to be in Tokyo, as you can go and see vintage *hina* doll collections at Hotel Gajoen (1-8-1 Shimomeguro, Meguro hotelgajoen-tokyo.com) and try all the festive food. Check with your hotel or Airbnb host for other doll exhibitions around town. Department stores and public places can have wonderful displays and themed events.

JINDAI-JI YAKUYOKE GANZAN JIE DAISHI SAI

Jindai-ji Temple Daruma Doll Fair
Early March

Michelle collects *kokeshi* dolls (tall, narrow wooden dolls) and Steve collects *daruma*, dolls in the shape of a stocky, red, bearded man that are modelled after the founder of Zen Buddhism, Bodhidharma. The area of Chōfu around the Jindai-ji temple (p. 334) is known for its *daruma* dolls, and each March they hold a fair where you can buy dolls and participate in *daruma* festivities. They are a symbol of good luck, and therefore a perfect gift to bring home for any facial-hair obsessed loved ones (and make sure you buy one to sit on your work desk, too). Come early and pick your favourite from one of hundreds of stalls. There is a whole ritual based around writing wishes on a *daruma*'s blank eye and filling in the other eye a year later if the wishes come true. You can spend a day taking your chosen doll to different places for inscriptions and hoping for good luck.

NEW FINANCIAL & SCHOOL YEAR

April 1

April 1 is the first day of both the financial year and the school year in Japan. It represents new beginnings and is a day of hope and anticipation for the year ahead. It can also coincide with *hanami* (flower viewing) – when it does, it takes on a festive and joyous atmosphere.

GOLDEN WEEK

Late April to early May

Japanese people don't get much annual leave from work, but they do have a lot of public holidays. The phrase 'Golden Week' was coined in the 1950s to mark a week full of public holidays, and it is one of the busiest travel times of year in Japan. The public holidays are Shōwa Day (29 April), Constitution Memory Day (3 May), Greenery Day (4 May) and Children's Day (5 May). Some businesses shut completely during this time, and many workers take time off in between the public holidays to spend time with family. Many Tokyoites leave the city to visit families in other prefectures, so you may find Tokyo to be a little less crowded than usual.

SPRING EXPERIENCES

KOINOBORI AT TOKYO TOWER

Late April to early May

This is Tokyo Tower's (p. 161) take on the tradition of *koinobori* ('carp streamer'), when families would display a windsock shaped like a carp at the entrance of their homes for any young boys living there. It's now part of Kodomo no Hi, or Children's Day (see Golden Week, above).

More than 300 colourful carp streamers float and fly around Tokyo Tower to symbolise the wish for children to grow up healthy and happy. Masses of carp-shaped windsocks swimming in the sky is a sight to behold if you are in Tokyo for Golden Week.

OTHER SPRING EXPERIENCES

ANIME JAPAN
Late March
anime-japan.jp/en

TOKYO RAINBOW PRIDE
28 April–6 May
tokyorainbowpride.com

DESIGN FESTA
Mid-May
designfesta.com/en

SUMO GRAND TOURNAMENT
Mid-May
sumo.or.jp/EnTicket/year_schedule

TOKYO INTERNATIONAL ART FAIR
End of May
tokyoartfair.com

Koinobori at Tokyo Tower (top); *Hanami* picnics (bottom)

Hanami at Chidorigafuchi moat

One of our first experiences of hanami *was at Shinjuku Gyoen (p. 343). It took almost an hour in an orderly queue to get to the bag-search station, and then we queued again to deposit 200 yen into a machine before finally being let loose into the gardens. Shinjuku Gyoen is a sprawling park where trees bloom both early and late. There were couples, families (there is a no-alcohol policy), older people and people on their own, with everyone sharing a quiet respect for nature and more group laughter than we have ever heard. Community spirit, sharing, collective pride and love for this tiny piece of beauty. Everyone was happy and it was infectious.*

At Nakameguro Canal (p. 299), pink lanterns were hanging everywhere, displaying logos of local businesses. The drinking started around at 10.30 am, and it was a fun, young-ish crowd of locals and internationals. Food stalls, pink champagne and pink sake were readily available. We enjoyed amazake *(a hot, sweet drink made from fermented rice),* hanami dango *(sweet dumplings) and a* sakura*-themed* bentō *box.*

We have learned a lot about Japanese culture through its celebration of cherry blossoms. Collective happiness and love of nature's beauty take over the city for a few fleeting days. Something we never expected to see is men of all ages concentrating on taking photographs of the small, pale pink flowers. As essential as they may be, pictures really do not do justice to the feeling and atmosphere, to the deep, dark wood of the trunks and the fragile pink flowers that give the trees an almost mystical feeling, accented by the delicate warm days and cool evenings – and all the laughter floating in the air.

OMIYAGE

The beautiful tradition of *omiyage* involves bringing a gift home to friends, family and even co-workers after a holiday or business trip. *Omiyage* are no mere souvenirs, though. Each city, small town or village has its own specialty products, sweets, food or characters, and they all come in beautiful packaging. Neighbouring cities compete, and rival stores try to outdo each other on quality and value.

As Japan's biggest city, Tokyo has amazing *omiyage*, so stock up on presents for family (and make sure to put yourself into the mix). Limited-edition packaging is a big thing in Japan. Some products for sale in Tokyo may be a Tokyo-only offer, where only a limited quantity has been made. If you see a queue for *omiyage*, you should probably join it.

Posting internationally is relatively inexpensive from Japan. Why not take advantage of the amazing paper, tapes and packaging products (p. 210), wrap a present and send it from Tokyo? Japanese stamps are beautifully designed, and you can choose from an array of seasonal and limited-edition offerings. Friends and family will get the most wonderful snail-mail surprise when the postie delivers your creation!

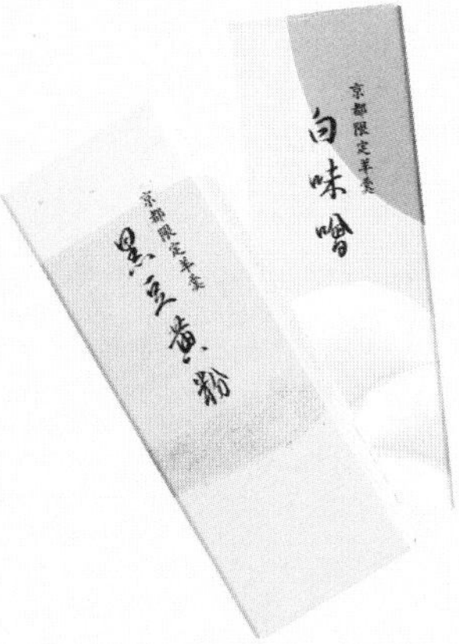

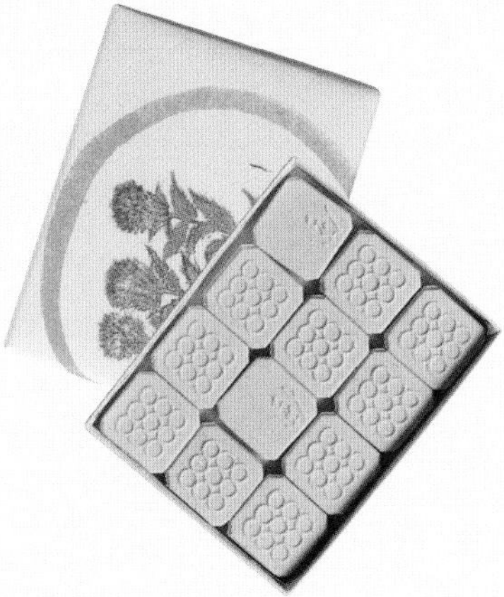

SPECIALTY PRODUCTS

Biscuit tins
Shiseido Parlour's (Shiseido Building; p. 365) biscuit packaging is irresistible.

Hato Saburē
Michelle's favourite dove-shaped biscuits from food halls.

Imo yōkan
Sweet-potato confectionery from Funawa Café, Taito.

Kabuki-themed items
Kabuki masks and goodies abound in the basement gift shops of the Kabuki-za theatre (p. 368).

Kihara Tokyo Icon plates
Small plates made from Arita porcelain decorated with iconic Tokyo designs.

Manga
Many manga specialists in Tokyo stock a small range of English translations.

Paper products
Tokyo is stationery heaven. Isetatsu and Bingoya (both p. 212) sell traditional washi paper designs.

Sampuru
Plastic food models! Kappabashi Dōri (Kitchen Town; p. 157) has whole stores devoted to *sampuru*.

Shrine & temple gifts
Nakamise Dōri (p. 155) is one of the best spots for *omiyage*. Jindai-ji (p. 334) is great for *daruma* dolls, and Gōtoku-ji (p. 334) for *maneki neko* (lucky cats).

Sumo souvenirs
The gift shops in and around the Ryōgoku Kokugikan (p. 173) sumo stadium are a treasure trove of sumo-themed items.

Tokyo Banana
Banana-shaped, cream-filled sponge cakes that can be found at Tokyo Station, airports and department stores.

Train souvenirs
Trainiart is the one-stop shop for the train-obsessed, and stocks Yamanote Line and Japan Rail souvenirs.

Tsumami kanzashi
Edo-period hair ornaments made from strands of silk that have been formed into birds, flowers and more.

OMIYAGE STORES

Kiddy Land
(p. 270)

Mamegui
Tokyo Skytree Solamachi 4F
1-1-2 Oshiage
Sumida 131-0045
mamegui.jp

Tokyo Station
(p. 198)

Tokyu Food Show
B1F 2-24-1 Shibuya
Shibuya 150-0002
tokyu-dept.co.jp/foodshow

Tokyu Hands
(p. 212)

SPECIALTY OMIYAGE

Asakusa Jinja
(p. 334)

Makanai Cosme – skincare
1-1-3 Nishi-Shinjuku
Shinjuku 160-0023

Mori Art Museum
Art souvenirs (p. 357)

Tokyo Skytree gift shop
(p. 161)

Yayoi Kusama Museum
(p. 363)

TOKYO CUSTOMS
東京習慣

Useful phrases: meet & greet

Hello: *Konnichiwa*

Good morning: *Ohayō*

Goodbye: *Mata ne* ('see you'); *sayōnara* ('goodbye')

——— Japan is a country where customs and behaviour mean everything. Japanese society has strict rules, practices and traditions that govern how to behave – it can become embarrassing very quickly for travellers who don't know the etiquette. Luckily, in Tokyo a lot of these manners are more relaxed, as you would expect from a big city, and when it comes down to it, it's all about being mindful of others. If you just remember to be respectful, kind and helpful, you won't go wrong. It can even be a fascinating learning experience, seeing how the inhabitants of a busy city get through the rigours of the day: how they communicate, how people create atmospheres that alleviate stress, how shop attendants greet and treat you, and how restaurant service sets you instantly at ease.

This helpful guide should have you mastering Tokyo customs and rules in no time. Of course, some of these rules might not apply in certain situations. The 109 building in Shibuya (p. 237) would rather trade on noise and pandemonium than quiet politeness. On the street, brightly coloured trucks pump out the latest J-pop, and cars with squealing megaphones blare out someone's political agenda.

MEET & GREET

——— When meeting someone for the first time, it's okay to shake hands rather than bowing. Locals won't expect visitors to know Japanese customs, but you can still give a small bow to show that you are making an effort. If it is a business situation, having your own business card and presenting it – face up, using both hands to hold the edges of the card – to the person you are meeting will always get you props. If it's a significant meeting, don't forget to bring a gift. A gift from your home country goes down *very* well, so choose something that says a lot about where you come from or who you are. It should go without saying: be on time. Tokyo trains are the most punctual in the world; follow their example. And, as always, try a little bit of the language. It will go a long way.

You'll find manners posters, like the one opposite, all over the city – if you need a little reminding!

Useful phrases: manners

Thank you: *Arigatō*

Please: *Onegaishimasu*

Excuse me: *Sumimasen*

ON TRAINS

Tokyo trains are the lifeblood of the city, shuttling a seemingly endless stream of commuters from one place to the next. Delays are very rare and trains are clean and comfortable: cool in summer and warm in winter. It's a human soup at peak times: absurd crowds that often have to be rammed into carriages by force, something that Tokyoites have come to expect but that visitors find endlessly amusing (or confronting). Don't be afraid to launch yourself into it.

When on a crowded train, always take off your backpack. There's nothing more annoying than being hit by a backpack full of ... what the hell are in those things, anyway? Never talk on your mobile phone; switch it to silent. Feel free to play games on it, though, or read some manga. When in the station, try to obey the arrows on the stairs that tell you which direction to go in, and stick to the right side on the pedestrian walkways.

Outside of peak times, especially if you are travelling to quieter areas, you'll find yourself with a lot more space – you might even get a seat! Which you may then have to give up to anyone elderly, injured or pregnant ... manners, remember?

IN SHOPS

Shopping is one of Tokyo's great pastimes. Shop assistants are charming, gentle and kind, and you should return the favour. There are a few things you can do to be polite while shopping. If it's raining, make sure you put your umbrella in the stand provided, or slip it into the plastic covers that bigger stores provide. You can ask if the shop assistant speaks English – '*Eigo ga hanashimasu ka?*' – and while the reply will usually be 'No,' or, 'Only a little bit,' they will often go on to speak pretty good English. You can ask for your purchase to be gift-wrapped – '*Puresento*'.

Useful phrases: eating

I humbly receive (say before you eat): *Itadakimasu*

It was quite a feast (say when you are leaving): *Gochisōsama deshita*

Do you have an English menu?: *Eigo no menyu arimasuka?*

EATING

—— There are a couple of phrases that will help you in Japanese *izakaya* (pubs; p. 41) or restaurants: '*Nama biru onegaishimasu*' ('A draft beer, please') and '*Umeshu sōda onegaishimasu*' ('An umeshu soda, please'). *Umeshu* is a liqueur made from plums and when added to soda it makes a delicious drink, especially in summer. When it comes to sake or beer, always pour your fellow diners' drinks and let them pour yours in return.

In old-school establishments, you may need to take off your shoes. If you do, you might be given slippers to wear; remember to exchange these slippers for bathroom slippers if you need to use the bathroom.

If your Japanese is limited, ask for an English menu. If all else fails, just point at what looks delicious. If you're in a sushi restaurant, remember to dip the fish side and not the rice side of your *nigiri* sushi into the soy (this prevents disastrous sushi disintegration). When eating yakitori, it can be enjoyed directly from the skewers or slid off with chopsticks – either way is fine. On the subject of chopsticks, never stick them vertically into your bowl of rice, as this is a funeral custom, and never use chopsticks to pass food to someone else.

Don't tip! Outsiders might feel a bit stingy, but it confuses your Japanese hosts: it's as if you are saying, 'You need more money!' Get used to not tipping – we're sure it won't take long.

Never eat or drink while walking. You shouldn't really even drink from a coffee cup on the street or on a train, although we may have had to do this from time to time …

FOOD & DRINK

- Nabe
- Noodles
- Ramen
- Sushi & sashimi
- Tempura
- Tofu
- Yōshoku
- Yakitori
- Katsu
- Wagashi
- Yōgashi
- A Tokyo tipple
- Coffee
- Tea
- Sake

Tokyo distils the delicate and unique flavours of Japan, from street eats to high-end dining, and serves them up to a hungry city. Whether you crave delicate sushi or sashimi made by a master with a lifetime of learning, or just want to duck into a stand-up ramen bar or yakitori joint, Tokyo will dish up something that's sure to become one of your lifetime food obsessions – all with impeccable hospitality and a cold glass of the best beer in the world.

From a fairly narrow core of rice, raw fish, grilled meats and various entrails, the Japanese have forged a surprising array of delectable dishes. The nationwide obsession with (and subsequent perfection of) the noodle is legendary; Japan's noodle soups and broths are addictive. Nutritious, versatile and abundant, seaweed is used in various forms in most meals. In our experience, those who adhere to a typical Western diet at home will end up feeling the health benefits of Japan's food culture. For those who still waver at the idea of trying anything new, the Japanese have mastered a range of dishes from other countries. You can get pizza and burgers in Japan that are among the best in the world.

Tokyo bars serve up some of the most incredible drinks, and their spin on the gastropub or tapas bar, the *izakaya* (p. 41), has a well-deserved reputation for delicious food.

And don't get us started on the sweets! *Wagashi* (p. 124), or traditional confectionery, is an art form unto itself. The shapes are surprising – more like tiny sculptures than food – and the flavours are new and intriguing and usually based around seasonal ingredients. Tokyo also offers a whole range of more Western sweet treats, some with a slight twist, which will keep you hopping from store to store in anticipation of new discoveries.

Steve and Coco sharing a *kakigōri* (opposite)

WHAT'S ON THE MENU?

—— Many stalwarts of Japanese cuisine – sushi, ramen and teriyaki, for example – have made their way onto Western plates (and into our hearts), but that doesn't mean that Japan's lesser-known dishes aren't equally delicious. We always recommend pushing your comfort zone a little when in Tokyo, but if you're not ready to jump into the deep end with your eyes closed, we can vouch for the tastiness of the dishes listed here. You will be able to find most of them in all kinds of establishments, from *izakaya* (pubs; p. 41) and restaurants, to convenience stores, street-food stalls and 'holes in the wall' that specialise in one item.

AGEDASHI DŌFU

An *izakaya* and yakitori-joint staple, and one of Michelle's absolute favourites. These blocks of silky-soft tofu are lightly dusted with potato starch or cornflour, deep-fried and served in a light dashi broth. Tasty *and* good for you.

DONBURI

A favourite among visitors, a *donburi* is simply a bowl of rice with a topping of simmered meat, fish or vegetables. Popular *donburi* include *oyakodon*, rice topped with chicken and egg; *katsudon*, rice topped with a crumbed pork cutlet; and *gyūdon*, rice topped with beef and onions.

GYŌZA

One of Steve's all-time favourites, this Japanese version of the Chinese 'potsticker' dumpling is a tender pocket filled with pork, ginger and spring onion (cabbage, leek and shrimp are also popular fillings). When perfectly cooked, *gyōza* will be crisp and golden brown on the bottom, with tender, steamed tops. *Gyōza* joints are rambunctious, knockabout affairs where you order as you go, while downing beer.

KARAAGE

Chicken is dusted with seasoned flour and deep-fried – resulting in the classic 'Japanese fried chicken'. *Karaage* can be bought in food halls and convenience stores, as well as in *izakaya*, ramen or *tonkatsu* (fried pork cutlet) eateries. *Karaage* is distinct from foods fried in breadcrumbs, such as *ebi* (prawn) or *kaki* (oyster), which are often referred to as *furai* (fry).

OKONOMIYAKI

Imagine a pancake throwing a party and inviting lots of friends, and you've got *okonomiyaki*. Both street food and fast restaurant food in Tokyo (and a major dish in Osaka), *okonomiyaki* is a cross between savoury pancake and frittata. While there are plenty of places that make the dish for you, don't pass up the opportunity to visit one of the many establishments where you can cook your own on a hot griddle. The mash-up nature of *okonomiyaki* makes it the ultimate do-it-yourself: using the ingredients provided, throw together an eggy batter, onions, bean shoots, cabbage, squid, shrimp – at some point you just have to improvise – and make like a chef. Finish your masterpiece with a criss-cross of mayonnaise and tangy, Worcestershire-based *okonomiyaki* sauce to round off a delicious, simple meal. Kids love it.

ONIGIRI

Whether you pick one up at a convenience store for a quick lunch, or go to a place that specialises in them, these triangles of rice with a hint of filling and a crispy nori coat are one of Tokyo's best fast foods. *Onigiri*, or rice balls, are said to resemble a feudal lord, crouching and wrapped in a *yukata* (summer kimono). Fillings can range from salmon flakes (our favourite) to tempura prawn, *umeboshi* (pickled plum), tuna, or half an egg (another good one), with extra flavourings of soy or sesame seeds. There are many vegetarian, brown rice or mixed grain options available. The convenience-store chain Natural Lawson has a great range of vegan *onigiri*.

Vegetarian *onigiri* (opposite)

SHOKUDŌ

Tokyoites, like New Yorkers, have often wandered far from their hometowns, moving to the big smoke to try new opportunities. But being away from home can be tough, and there are times when mum's cooking is the only thing that will comfort a troubled soul. Enter shokudō: mom-and-pop, hole-in-the-wall eateries, similar to diners, which serve up the kind of dishes that a homesick Tokyoite might have had back home cooked by mum. Shokudō usually serve simple dishes like *donburi*, sashimi, tempura, curry, rice and miso – not to mention plenty of booze to help drown your sorrows.

TAKOYAKI

The word *yaki* means 'grilled', and you'll see it attached to a few foods in Tokyo. *Yakiniku*, for instance, is grilled meat. *Takoyaki* – from *tako*, or octopus – is a round ball of wheat-flour batter filled with bits of octopus, tempura scraps, pickled ginger and green onion. Grilled in a special pan that has circular depressions like an egg carton, *takoyaki* are golden and crispy on the outside but still a bit gooey inside. Add shaved bonito, mayonnaise and a tangy Worcestershire-based sauce and you have one of Tokyo's most popular street foods.

TAMAGOYAKI

A rolled omelette that can be found on any *izakaya* menu or as a side at a lot of sushi restaurants, *tamagoyaki* is one of our favourite dishes. Unlike any omelette you will be used to, *tamagoyaki* is usually seasoned with soy, dashi and mirin, rolled into a small block while cooking to create many fine layers of egg, and then finished off with another dash of soy. In order to become a *tamagoyaki*-maker, you need some serious training, and quite often it will take the longest to cook out of all of the dishes you have ordered. Perfection takes time, and the results speak for themselves.

TEISHOKU

Teishoku, or set meals, are made up of a collection of different small dishes, and are a great way to try various Tokyo foods in one go. They are perfect for lunch and can range from the simple to the high-end. If you are travelling on a budget and would like to treat yourself, some high-end establishments offer a trimmed-down version of their *teishoku* at lunchtime, much cheaper than the ones on the dinner menu. Dishes will almost always include miso, rice, *tsukemono* (pickles) and some form of fish – perhaps some sashimi or grilled mackerel. Fresh tofu, *umeboshi* (pickled plum) and various condiments complete the picture.

UNAGI

Like *nattō* (p. 97), *unagi* (eel) might belong in the 'acquired taste' category. *Unagi* is usually served *kabayaki*-style, dipped in a sweet soy-based sauce and grilled. It should be firm and fleshy. When served on a bed of fluffy white rice, it's known as *unadon*. A popular dish in the Edo period (p. 26), Tokyoites love to eat *unagi* in summer and will always eat it on the Doyo no Ushi no Hi, or Day of the Ox, which falls between 20 July and 10 August and signifies the start of the last days of summer.

OPTIONAL EXTRAS

——— Small dishes are often served as starters or sides, in *teishoku* ('set meals', p. 96) or as part of an evening of drinking and nibbling in an *izakaya* (pub; p. 41). The accompaniments below are popular and you are bound to run into them when in Tokyo.

CHAWANMUSHI

A savoury egg custard that is often served as a starter. A small surprise awaits in the centre – usually a mushroom and a small prawn, an edamame bean or a square of ham.

EDAMAME

A great starter, edamame are immature soybeans still in their pods, boiled and lightly salted. Squeeze them out of the pod and pop them into your mouth. Their slight sweetness and firm, creamy texture makes them irresistible.

GOHAN (RICE)

In Japan, rice is used as a side dish to almost everything. The most common type of rice in Japan is short-grain. It's plump, absorbs flavour and separates well when cooked to perfection. Trying rice from different regions of Japan is a must for the food connoisseur.

MISO

Miso, fermented soybeans with salt and *kōji* (fermented rice), rice or barley, is a thick paste that has many moods. It can be used to flavour soups, ramen broths and on *nasu dengaku*, roasted eggplant with a miso glaze. A bowl of rice and a miso soup on a cold day is truly one of life's great joys.

NATTŌ

Made from fermented soybeans and served up with mustard or soy, *nattō* is what you might call an acquired taste. Once acquired, though, many people swear by it. It is a great source of vitamins, minerals and fibre for vegans.

SHŌYU

Shōyu – Japanese soy sauce – is like Chinese soy sauce with benefits. Brewed with added wheat, *shōyu* has a slightly sweeter and more delicate flavour, and accompanies many dishes. *Shōyu* is like a fine wine in Japan and has five distinct varieties (*koikuchi*, *usukuchi*, *tamari*, *shiro* and *saishi shikomi*) with subtle yet notable differences. *Shōyu* is an absolutely essential part of the flavour profile of sushi and sashimi.

TSUKEMONO

Japan has turned pickling into an art form. A small dish of *tsukemono* (pickles) will accompany most meals, and pickles and rice are the best of friends. The most common *tsukemono* are daikon, cucumber, eggplant, burdock, cabbage and carrot. Plums are also pickled to make *umeboshi*, which gives their usually sweet flavour a biting sharpness that fills the mouth.

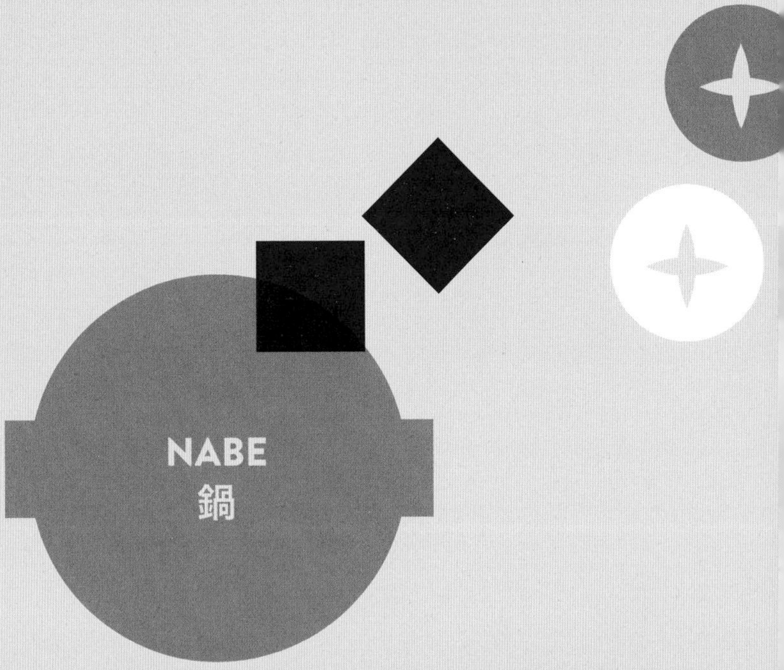

NABE
鍋

——— Popular dish *nabemono* (from *nabe*, meaning 'cooking pot', and *mono*, meaning 'things'), usually shortened to *nabe*, is the Japanese equivalent of a stew: a hotpot of meat and/or vegetables and tofu in simmering broth. *Nabe* includes *oden*, fishcakes and vegetables boiled in delicious stock; *shabu-shabu*, where those feasting use chopsticks to pick up thin slices of meat and swish them in and out of hot broth until they are lightly cooked; and, of course, *chankonabe*, the sumo wrestler's meal of choice.

TYPES OF NABE

CHANKONABE

A hearty hotpot of cabbage, udon noodles, chicken, tofu, fish- and meat-balls and more, *chankonabe* is designed to fortify even the most mountainous wrestler. At one time only sumo were allowed to eat *chankonabe*, but thankfully we can now all dig in. A bubbling broth is accompanied by extras that you pile in, allow to cook for a short while to soak up the flavours of the soup, and then ladle out and enjoy. You would think all of that liquid would mean that *chankonabe* doesn't play well with beer, but you would be wrong. Get everyone together and partake: it's healthy, filling and will start a lifelong craving.

MOTSUNABE

This heavier form of *nabe* was perfected in Fukuoka and features beef or pork offal simmered with cabbage and garlic chives to get its distinct, dark flavour. One for the carnivores whose tastes lean toward the less delicate.

SHABU-SHABU

Most visitors to Tokyo want to try *shabu-shabu* – not just for the taste, but for its truly communal dining experience. A fortifying soup broth with vegetables is accompanied by a plate of thinly sliced raw meat. Pick up the meat with your chopsticks and swish it in and out of the stock until cooked, a process that takes very little time. Spoon the soup into a bowl, add the cooked meat and you're good to go.

ODEN

Oden is probably the most basic version of the *nabe*: boiling broth with vegetables (especially daikon and konjac), fishcakes, meat, eggs and other porous delights. Usually eaten separately, the ingredients can also be consumed together in a delicious soup. This is what you'll see in the bain-marie at most convenience stores. The eggs are particularly good.

YOSENABE

Yosenabe (from *yose*, meaning 'put together') is, as the name might imply, *nabe* that has all of its ingredients cooked together in the same pot. A delicious stew that is the epitome of the one-pot dish, *yosenabe* is the perfect throw-together meal for anyone with limited cooking time and an eye for nutrition.

YUDŌFU

Tofu steeped in delicious *konbu* (kelp) broth. One of Michelle's go-to dishes.

SUKIYAKI

Surprisingly a member of the *nabe* family, *sukiyaki*, a long-time Western favourite, consists of vegetables, tofu and wafer-thin sliced beef stewed in a sweetened *shōyu* (soy sauce) broth eaten with a raw-egg dip.

NABE FIX

Eat like a sumo

You've heard of super-sizing your food, why not sumo-size it?

Vegequarian *chankonabe* at Chanko Tomoegata

FOR CHANKONABE

(p. 171)

FOR ODEN

Azabu Ichigo
2-5-14 Azabu-Jūban
Minato 106-0045
azabu-ichigo.com

Hide
15-5 Maruyamachō
Shibuya 150-0044
ne.jp/asahi/oden/hide

Nakagawa
2-12-3 Kanda-Sudachō
Chiyoda 101-0041

Ogura
6-3-6 Ginza
Chūō 104-0061

Ore no Dashi
7-6-6 Ginza 1F
Chūō 104-0061

Otafuku
1-2-6 Hanakawado
Taitō 111-0033
otafuku.ne.jp

Otakō
3-20-1 Shinjuku
Shinjuku 160-0022
otako.co.jp

Tanaka
3-10-15 Ginza
Chūō 104-0061

FOR SHABU-SHABU

Asakusa Imahan
3-1-12 Nishi-Asakusa
Taitō 111-0035
asakusaimahan.co.jp/english

Ginza Rangetsu
3-5-8 Ginza
Chūō 104-0061
ginza-rangetsu.com/english

Hirata Bokujo
COREDO Nihonbashi 4F
1-4-1 Nihonbashi
Chūō 103-0027
hiraboku.info/shop/tonkatsu/coredo-nihonbashi

Imafuku
1-12-19 Shirokane
Minato 108-0072
kuroge-wagyu.com/if/top_e.html

Kagayaki
2-16-6 Ryusen
Taitō 110-0012

Kyoto Hyoki
Multiple locations
hyoki.jp/en

Matsukiya
6-8 Maruyamachō
Shibuya 150-0044

Seryna
3-12-2 Roppongi
Minato 106-0032
seryna.co.jp/en/seryna/roppongi

Zakuro Muromachi
COREDO Muromachi 4F
2-2-1 Nihonbashi-Muromachi
Chūō 103-0022
r.gnavi.co.jp/gahs601

NOODLES
麺

Noodles in Japan are like pasta in Italy: essential and iconic. They are as ubiquitous as rice and have so many variations that you could eat noodles every day for a year and still find something new. In winter, soba or udon in hot broth with various accompaniments can be close to lifesaving. In summer, a cold soba salad or chilled soba noodles dunked in tasty dipping sauce are perfect dishes for the hot weather. Steve prefers the chewy texture of chunky udon noodles as they soak up the flavours of a sauce or stock, while Michelle prefers the delicate soba noodle, with its ability to be simple or complex.

Noodles are Tokyo's fast food – reliable, delicious, restorative and versatile – and it seems like the city has a noodle eatery on every street. Establishments that specialise in homemade noodles are particularly worth seeking out. Making and cutting soba and udon is a highly regarded skill and watching masters at work through a small window makes your noodle adventure extra special.

CURRY NANBAN

This noodle bowl features soba or udon noodles in a rich curry-flavoured broth.

HIYASHI CHŪKA

This chilled noodle dish is light and perfect for the summer months. It is served in Chinese restaurants and some soba restaurants, and is Michelle's favourite noodle dish.

KITSUNE & TANUKI SOBA

Kitsune (fox) and *tanuki* (raccoon dog) soba are both Tokyo favourites. *Kitsune* soba features deep-fried tofu in broth and *tanuki* has bits of fried tempura batter stirred through the noodles.

NABEYAKI UDON

This one-pot dish includes vegetables, tofu and/or chicken and *shirataki* noodles in a tasty broth.

TEMPURA UDON OR SOBA

Noodles in a delectable broth are accompanied by spring onions and a side dish of tempura prawns and vegetables.

ZARU OR HADAKA SOBA

Cold soba is often eaten with nothing but a simple dipping sauce. Simply mix in some wasabi and spring onion, dip the noodles and enjoy.

TYPES OF NOODLES

HARUSAME

Known in the West as cellophane or glass noodles, *harusame* are usually made from sweet-potato flour, rice flour or mung-bean starch. They are nutritious, delicious and a top pick for gluten-free travellers. Like vermicelli, *harusame* are usually found in dried form and are used to soak up tasty broths, but they are also great in summer salads.

SHIRATAKI

Shirataki, meaning 'white waterfall', are thin, translucent and jelly-like noodles made from a root vegetable called konjac. Gluten-free and very low in calories, they often appear in a dish called *donabe*.

SOBA

One of the most popular noodle choices for Tokyoites. Thin and light brown, soba can be used in soups, as dipping noodles, or in salads. Soba noodles are made from buckwheat flour (soba is also the Japanese word for buckwheat) and have the added benefit of the nutrients thiamine (vitamin B1) and lysine, which aren't found in pasta or udon noodles.

UDON

Thick, white and chewy, udon noodles are made from wheat flour and soak up sauces and soups with aplomb. There are many regional variations: udon can be round or flat, moderately thin or wide and sheet-like (*himokawa*), or even shaped like ears (*mimi* udon). No matter the shape, udon noodles are delicious in a light broth and are often an accompaniment to tempura. Curry udon is also irresistible.

SOMEN

A thinner, lighter form of the udon noodle, *somen* are made from wheat and used most commonly in cold noodle dishes, in soups or in *nagashi somen*, a summer specialty where noodles are floated down bamboo 'waterslides' and scooped up by hungry diners as they go past.

RAMEN

The ramen noodle is a wheat noodle that is thinner than soba or udon, made to sit perfectly in a bowl of rich, savoury soup. It's effectively an ultra-fresh and vastly superior version of the dried two-minute noodle.
For more on ramen, see p. 106.

NOODLING AROUND

A string of possibilities

Seasonal soba noodles in hot broth, with a touch of yuzu citrus and *umeboshi*

Kanda Matsuya
1-13 Kanda
Chiyoda 101-0041
kanda-matsuya.jp

A classic establishment located in a beautiful wooden building with more than 130 years of history. Matsuya in Kanda – an area that seems to have a deep love affair with soba – serves the noodle hot in delicate broths or cold with a side of dipping sauce. Go here for a truly authentic experience served up by masters.

Kanda Yabu Soba
2-10 Kanda-Awajichō
Chiyoda 101-0063
yabusoba.net

The *seiro* noodles at this popular soba joint established in 1880 are made from ten parts buckwheat flour to one part wheat flour, giving them a density unlike that of other soba noodles. The *tensoba*, a noodle soup with crispy shrimp tempura on the side, is a standout.

Nezu Soshian
2-28-8 Nezu
Bunkyō 113-0031

If you want to try a range of dishes in a contemporary setting with great service and a Michelin star to boot, head to Nezu Soshian and feel the soba love.

Sato Yosuke
6-4-17 Ginza
Chūō 104-0061
sato-yoske.co.jp

Come here to try out the smooth and chewy *inaniwa* udon, a flat noodle from northern Japan. It's Ginza, so you'll be getting the high-end udon treatment, but it's worth it. The perfectly made, perfectly rolled and perfectly presented udon noodles come with a range of exquisite side dishes and sauces.

Shin Udon
2-20-16 Yoyogi
Shibuya 151-0053
udonshin.com

Check out the super-cute frontage of this compact udon-noodle house in Yoyogi. Then head inside and see how the masters make these ultra-fresh noodles and pair them with soups, toppings and accompaniments that elevate udon to the next level.

Udon Kurosawa
6-11-16 Roppongi
Minato 106-0032
9638.net/udon

Kurosawa offers a range of super-tasty dishes. The location is fantastic and the interior is a Japanese-style haven of warm woods and cosy booths. It's a tradition here to finish off your meal with an udon bowl. They vary by season but all are exceptional additions to your udon experience. The curry *nanban* is worth visiting Tokyo for – you'll want it every time you're in the neighbourhood.

ALSO TRY MICHELIN-STARRED SOBA

Okina
1-3-10 Ebisu-Nishi
Shibuya 150-0021

Sasuga
2-13-6 Ginza
Chūō 104-0061

Tamawarai
5-23-3 Jingūmae
Shibuya 150-0001

Yamori
3-9-7 Tsukishima
Chūō 104-0052

FOR GOOD MEASURE

Edo Soba Teuchidokoro Asada
2-29-11 Asakusabashi
Taitō 111-0053

Kiyose Soba Kashiwaya
3-35-1 Shimorenjaku
Mitaka 181-0013

Kyotei Daikokuya
4-39-2 Asakusa
Taitō 111-0032

Minogasa
1-3-2 Kanda-Izumichō
Chiyoda 101-0024

Soba & BAR An
The Prudential Plaza 1F
2-13-10 Nagatachō
Chiyoda 100-0014

Buckwheat noodles are gluten friendly, not gluten free

To many foodies, ramen is a religious experience. To Tokyoites, ramen is a necessity. This is the food of the people, the salaryman's go-to, a rowdy affair where the kitchen is always bubbling and sizzling, and the room is alive with cheery banter (although patrons quickly replace conversations with slurps when the ramen arrives).

At its essence, ramen is a thick, tasty broth with noodles, but the dish has subtle variations all over the city. Tokyo broth is usually made from pork and chicken stock, with every shop serving its own variation, to which *chāshū* (marinated pork slices) and noodles are added. The Chinese-style ramen noodle is the norm, though noodle styles can also vary. Garnishes like crisp nori sheets add a hint of the ocean. Bean shoots, shallots and bamboo shoots are standard, but every restaurant will have its own customisations and specialties – even vegetarians will find a place to partake. The boiled eggs braised in soy are our favourite extra.

Ramen dens can be holes in the wall, charming mom-and-pop establishments, standing bars, tiny nooks that seat eight, time-honoured family affairs or respected chains. Each has its own style, its own specialties and its own closely guarded secrets. The typical ramen eatery will have several large pots gurgling away just behind the counter, intensifying stock into an irresistible, unctuous broth before your eyes.

There are anywhere between 6000 and 10,000 ramen shops in Tokyo, and it's possible to plan a whole day around visiting one legendary ramen joint – for good reason. Ramen is fast, filling, delicious and one of Tokyo's true staples.

TYPES OF RAMEN

SHIO RAMEN

Shio (salt) ramen is for anyone with a salty tooth. The chicken-, fish- or pork-broth base is given that extra savoury hit and lingers deliciously on the palate after eating.

SHŌYU RAMEN

For fans of *shōyu* (soy sauce), the broth of this ramen is complex and tangy, and is characterised by a clear broth tinted brown with soy.

MISO RAMEN

Said to have been invented in the 1960s, this ramen uses an *awase* miso broth – a mix of both white and red miso – that gives the ramen stock a big umami kick.

TONKOTSU RAMEN

A specialty of Kyushu, Japan's third-largest island, *tonkotsu* ramen stars a pork-bone broth. Although most ramen varieties are pork-based, *tonkotsu* is distinguished by its creamy white broth, which is made by boiling the pork bones for longer than regular ramen broth.

NIBOSHI RAMEN

This intense, salty ramen has a broth made from small *niboshi*, or young sardines, giving it a unique flavour.

TSUKUMEN RAMEN

Taking its cue from *zaru* soba (p. 102), cold soba noodles meant for dipping, *tsukemen* keeps the noodles and additions separate from the broth and lets you add them at will. The chewier noodle and richer broth – and the option to experiment – make this a popular dish.

WHERE TO START YOUR RAMEN ODYSSEY

Ramen seven days a week

Get inspired by Juzo Itami's classic 1980s film *Tampopo*

Fuunji
2-14-3 Yoyogi
Shibuya 151-0053
fu-unji.com

Tsukemen is the ramen you can artfully arrange to suit your own palate. A chicken soup (*tori paitan*) or a fish broth sits alongside a pile of perfect noodles. Add egg, bamboo shoots, nori, pork belly – whatever you desire. An explosive fish-powder bomb, *gyofun*, is dropped in the centre of the fish broth. It's decadent and delicious.

Matador
2-4-17 Senju-Azuma
Adachi 120-0025
matador.tokyo

A master of *gyūkotsu*, beef-based ramen, Iwatate-san opened Matador in 2011 and has since perfected a recipe for the notoriously difficult ramen. Get the balance wrong and beef ramen can become too strong or too sweet. For anyone who doesn't eat pork or who wants to try a darker, less subtle ramen with slices of beef that almost cover the bowl, Matador is a must-visit.

Seasonal vegetarian ramen from Afuri

Mensho
1-15-9 1F Kasuga
Bunkyō 112-0003
menya-shono.com/tokyo

Mensho is popular for *tsukemen*. They also do a mean *tori paitan*, a luxurious chicken-based broth, and a ramen using lamb instead of pork.

Motenashi Kuroki
2-15 Kanda-Izumichō
Chiyoda 101-0024
ameblo.jp/motenashikuroki

So much goodness just a short walk from all the action in Akihabara. Spy the rusted white sign emblazoned with a steaming noodle bowl and head into this *shio* ramen specialist. The salt ramen is enhanced with dried fish, mackerel and bonito. The pork is slow-roasted; the eggs are perfect; and the extra toppings you can order turn everything up to eleven. Try shrimp dumplings or chicken *chāshū*. Motenashi Kuroki is the kind of place that silences talk of Akihabara's junk-food reputation.

Nagi
Shinjuku Golden Gai
1-1-10 2F Kabukichō
Shinjuku 160-0021
n-nagi.com

Hidden in the old Tokyo barfly maze of Golden Gai (p. 247), Nagi is a cheerful, shoulder-to-shoulder ramen den for the true taste adventurer. The concentrated, deep, salty-sweet broth made from *niboshi* (baby sardines) draws long queues. Order up some chicken skin or pigs' trotters as side dishes. You know you want to.

Take a day trip and visit the noodle museum in Yokohama

Tsuta
1-14-1 Sugamo
Toshima 170-0002
ameblo.jp/yuki-onishi

A soba-noodle shop that garnered a Michelin star for its ramen, and which has a ticketing system that requires a PhD to understand. Yes please! The rules of engagement: 1) get a PhD; 2) queue early to book a ticket and select a time (they open at 11 am); and 3) return at the allotted time and prepare to inhale ramen. The ramen is based around umami flavour: savoury, sharp, tasty. They also do a great *tsukemen*.

ALSO TRY

Afuri
1-1-7 Ebisu
Shibuya 150-0013
afuri.com

Menya Kissou
1-11-3 Tōyō
Kōtō 135-0016

Menya Musashi Bujin
2-18-5 Kanda-Sakumachō
Chiyoda 101-0025
menya634.co.jp/storelist/akihabara

Nakiryu
2-34-4 Minami-Ōtsuka
Toshima 170-0005
www12.plala.or.jp/nakiryu

Shibata
2-25-20 Wakabachō
Chōfu 182-0003

Takano
2-15-10 Nakanobu
Shinagawa 142-0053

Tomita
Takahashi Building 1F
Matsudo 1339
Chiba 271-0092

SUSHI & SASHIMI 寿司と刺身

—— For many years the idea of eating raw fish was the Western diner's nightmare – until we all tried it, of course. Distinct from sushi, which always includes a morsel of vinegared rice, sashimi stands alone. The freshest of fish, sliced thinly and placed on a rice bowl or accompanied by a small salad, is picked up with chopsticks, dipped into soy sauce and then savoured. Fresh sashimi melts in the mouth and is prized for its subtle flavour and texture. It's healthy as well, like much of the Japanese diet. In Tokyo, sashimi can be eaten in sushi restaurants and *izakaya* (pubs; p. 41), or purchased from food halls.

Sushi can be enjoyed in Tokyo with or without causing permanent damage to your credit card – it's entirely up to you. For a memorable experience, you can't go past a high-end sushi restaurant, but for those wanting to keep within a budget, you can still enjoy these thin slices of fish on small pillows of vinegared rice.

The sheer number of options to choose from can be overwhelming if you're not familiar with sushi; some of the most popular include *maguro* (tuna), *sake* (salmon), *aji* (horse mackerel) and *ebi* (cooked prawns), as well as *hotategai* (sliced raw scallop) and *tamago* (delicate segments of omelette). *Inari* sushi is another immensely popular choice: deep-fried tofu pouches simmered in a sweet sauce, then stuffed with vinegared rice. Big money is often shelled out for the more treasured sushi, from creamy orange *uni* (sea urchin) to quality *unagi* (eel) and *toro* (belly tuna). Such variety is perhaps the reason for the phrase *omakase*: 'I'll leave it up to you'. Sushi restaurants offering *omakase* serve diners the chef's selection of the day for a set price.

Conveyor-belt sushi restaurants (p. 269) are becoming increasingly popular in Tokyo, and at 100–400 yen a piece, their sushi is affordable, as well as tasty and healthy. Not to mention ordering food on a screen and having it arrive at your table on a tiny train is fun for small and big kids alike.

TYPES OF SUSHI

NIGIRI SUSHI

Small portions of vinegared rice shaped by hand and topped with sliced fish, seafood or other special ingredients.

MAKIZUSHI

Makizushi is the umbrella term for sushi that is cylindrical and typically wrapped in nori – the kind you might grab on your lunch break.

HOSOMAKI

Hosomaki are the opposite of *futomaki* (*hosoi* means 'thin'): delicate little rolls about two centimetres in diameter, usually containing only one filling, such as cucumber or tuna.

FUTOMAKI

Futomaki – from *futoi*, meaning 'fat', and 'maki', meaning roll – are extra-large sushi rolls, usually five or six centimetres in diameter and often filled with vegetarian fillings like pickled daikon, omelette, cucumber and deep-fried tofu.

CHIRASHIZUSHI

Chirashi means 'scattering', which is how *chirashizushi* is made: by scattering (or arranging) slices of raw fish on top of a bowl of vinegared rice. Filling and fast.

TEMAKI

Temaki are a little like an ice cream – if the cone was made of nori and the ice cream was actually rice and sushi fillings. They are meant to be eaten by hand, hence the name: *te* means 'hand'.

SUSHI & SASHIMI FIX

Ask for the chef's recommendations

JIRO DREAMS OF SUSHI

If you want to prepare your eyes and stomach for Tokyo's sushi ahead of your trip, we recommend watching the documentary *Jiro Dreams of Sushi* (2011; dir. David Gelb). The film profiles the nonagenarian Ono Jiro, sushi master and proprietor of what is probably Japan's most famous sushi restaurant: the ten-seat, Michelin three-star Sukiyabashi Jiro.

If after watching the film you're dreaming of visiting the original Sukiyabashi Jiro in Ginza yourself, you might need to keep dreaming. Reservations are exceptionally difficult to obtain and, in the case of hopeful diners from overseas, must be made through a hotel concierge. You might try your luck at Jiro's son Takashi's branch of Sukiyabashi Jiro in Roppongi Hills, or visit Harutaka (right), which is run by Harutaka Takahashi, a sushi chef who trained under Jiro for thirteen years.

Chefs at work at Katsu Midori

SUSHI DINNERS TO SAVE UP FOR

Harutaka
Omakase for 43,500 yen
8-3-1 Ginza
Chūō 104-0061
ginza-sushi.com/harutaka.html

Sawada
Omakase for 35,000 yen
MC Building 3F
5-9-19 Ginza
Chūō 104-0061

Sushi Iwa
Lunch set for 47,000 yen
8-4-4 Ginza
Chūō 104-0061

Sushi Yoshitake
Omakase for 23,000 yen
3F Suzuryu Building
8-7-19 Ginza
Chūō 104-0061
sushi-yoshitake.com

An *omakase* (chef's choice) lunch is a cheaper option

Don't add too much soy sauce. Dip the fish into the soy sauce – not the rice!

CHEAPER SUSHI OPTIONS

Ganso Zushi
Multiple locations
gansozushi.com

Genki Sushi
24-8 Udagawachō
Shibuya 150-0042
genkisushi.co.jp

Katsu Midori
Seibu Department Store Shibuya 8F
21-1 Udagawachō
Shibuya 150-0042
katumidori.co.jp/shibuya

Sushi Katsura
2-15-4 Tsukiji
Chūō 104-0045

Uogashi Nihon-Ichi
Multiple locations
uogashi-nihonichi.com/english

SASHIMI

RyuGin
Eisu Building, Ground Floor
7-17-24 Roppongi
Minato 106-0032
nihonryori-ryugin.com/en

Takamaru Sengyoten
7-12-3 Nishi-Shinjuku
Shinjuku 160-0023
takamaru-inc.com

Uosho Ginpei Ginza
Asoruti Ginza Hana Tsubaki Dōri Building 5F
7-6-10 Ginza
Chūō 104-0061

TEMPURA
天ぷら

—— These tender morsels of seafood or vegetable fried in light batter and sprinkled with salt can be found in many Japanese eateries, either as part of a meal or as the star of the show. Tempura à la carte, where pieces are made individually, is tempura taken to the next level – an experience not to be missed. Usually prepared in front of you by a master, it's a visual as well as a textural delight.

Tempura can be made using prawns, scallops, whitefish, eggplant, yam, butternut pumpkin, green capsicum, green beans, lotus root, mushroom and *shiso* (perilla) leaf, to name just a few. Special mention goes to *kakiage*, an odd-looking but delicious style of tempura: a fried bundle of mixed seafood and vegetables.

Tempura is usually accompanied by a light dipping sauce or various types of salt. It's perfect served over rice for a light lunch and excellent in a soba-noodle soup. And, of course, tempura goes perfectly with cold beer!

TEMPURA FIX

Funabashiya
3-28-14 Shinjuku
Shinjuku 160-0022

Gachi
Nakajima Building 1F
Shibadaimon 2-6-8
Minato 105-0012

Kondo
5-5-13 Ginza
Chūō 104-0061

Miyagawa
Palace Aoyama 1F
6-1-6 Minami-Aoyama
Minato 107-0062

Tempura Masa
Nishinanabankan Building 1F
7-7-16 Ginza
Chūō 104-0061

Tenmatsu
1-8-2 Nihonbashi-Muromachi
Chūō 103-0022
tenmatsu.com/english.html

Tenya
1-9-1 Asakusa
Taitō 111-0032
tenya.co.jp

TOFU
豆腐

Tofu has come a long way in the West since the seventies, and in many places is now a dietary staple. But the Japanese knew its secrets from the very beginning – particularly how to use it to absorb flavour and make delicious dishes – and it shows. One trip to Tokyo is all it will take to instil a love of tofu in anyone. Whether it's fried tofu in a light savoury sauce, tofu topped with *konbu* (kelp) and dashi stock, or even tofu that forms while you wait at your dinner table, there is at least one dish that will have you – vegetarian, vegan or omnivore – obsessing, just like us.

Tofu comes in a variety of delicious guises: *yudofu* (cooked in a hot broth), *yuba* (a kansai specialty, tofu skin is used in many dishes including soups and Shojin Ryori), *kinu-dofu* (silken tofu), *momen-dofu* (silken tofu with less water, firmer and great for *agedashi dōfu*), *atsuage* (deep-fried tofu) and *aburaage* (deep-fried and used as a pocket for *inari* sushi). The fresh tofu made over a flame while you wait, transforming from soy-milk curd to a silky-soft, jelly-like consistency, is truly sensational with a drizzle of soy sauce. Tofu is also used in many varieties of sweets – the creamy texture lends itself well to tofu ice creams, cheesecakes and more. Clean and packed with everything good, Tokyo's tofu is amazing.

TOFU FIX

Ain Soph Journey
3-8-9 Shinjuku Tokyo
5925-8908
ain-sophjourney.business.site

Chen Mapo Tofu
2F 1-12-32 Ark Mori Building
Akasaka 3505-2228
sasanoyuki.com

Sasanoyuki
2-15-10 Negishi, Taito
3873-1145
sasanoyuki.com

Sorano Shibuya
17-4 Sakuragaokachō
Shibuya 150-0031

Tokyo Shiba Tofuya Ukai
4-4-13 Shibakōen
Minato 105-0011

TIP: *Savoury tofu dishes can come topped with bonito (fish) flakes or cooked in dashi, so make sure to tell waitstaff if you are vegetarian* *(p. 118).*

YŌSHOKU
洋食

——— *Yōshoku* is the Japanese take on Western dishes – familiar to travellers but with a special local spin. Working with flavours and ingredients introduced over centuries by Europeans and Americans, Japan has adapted various Western dishes to suit its diners' palates – and ours! Each dish is delicious in its own right, but recognising a dish and finding it tastes a little bit different is what makes this food such a joyous experience.

After a trip to Tokyo you may start to add a little nori to your pasta

Omuraisu and *hanbāgu* at Isetan

TYPES OF YŌSHOKU

HANBĀGU

Also known as Hamburg steak, and a common item on the menu at *shokudō* restaurants (p. 96), a burger patty is dressed in a delicious sauce and accompanied by a side salad. It may also come with rice, or with curry sauce. You can also get *hanbāga*, the style of burger you're used to, in various fast-food restaurants like Freshness, JS or Mos Burger. We highly recommend Tokyo's delicious (and healthier) take.

KARE

Japanese-style curry, with its complex and subtle flavour profile, is milder in spice, a little darker in colour and slightly sweet – and, like all curry, totally addictive. Unlike many South-East Asian curries, there are no fish products – vegetarians rejoice! You can happily enjoy the many *yasai* (vegetable) curries of Tokyo. Chicken and beef are also popular options, and, as we've mentioned before, a good curry udon (p. 103) is a meal for which you'd cross an ocean.

MENTAIKO PASTA

This Tokyo twist on pasta uses a sauce of preserved spicy cod roe (*mentaiko*), butter and olive oil. It can be topped with nori, mushrooms, shiso leaves and other Japanese ingredients. Michelle loves it, while Steve is not so keen: this is a divisive dish, but Tokyoites are big fans. We have to admit that it has a certain charm. Enjoy with chopsticks!

OMURAISU

As the name might suggest, this is omelette with rice. A thick, fluffy omelette is wrapped around rice that has been bedazzled with peas, ginger and possibly small cubes of meat. Drizzle with mayonnaise and tomato sauce, or even a rich demi-glace sauce, and you have a filling, delicious meal.

POTATO FURAI

Fried potato – or as we know them, fries. A popular dish in yakitori joints and *izakaya* (pubs; p. 41). Great for the Westerner who wants a bit of home to go with their new culinary experiences.

POTATO SARADA

Japanese potato salad is very similar to its Western counterpart – the main difference is that it is made with the slightly spiced and more acidic Japanese mayonnaise, as well as wasabi, giving it a tangier taste with a subtle kick. Sesame oil and vinegar make it uniquely Japanese, but it is still probably the *yōshoku* dish that is closest to the Western version. Ham and pepper are the finishing touches to an irresistible potato salad, found in many *izakaya* and *shokudō* eateries.

Michelle likes to eat her potato *furai* with chopsticks

THINGS WE LOVE

VEGETARIAN & VEGAN TOKYO

You would think that things would be easy for the vegetarian in Tokyo, with its strong Buddhist history. However, most dishes contain seafood in some form, even if it's just shavings of dried bonito or a light dashi stock (which is typically made with bonito). So if you're pescetarian, Tokyo is the perfect place to eat. There is good news for those who don't partake in seafood, though. Vegetarian food options are rapidly on the rise in Tokyo and a little bit of exploration can uncover some amazing vegetarian (and vegan) experiences.

Generally, finding out whether something has meat or not is pretty easy, but if you're worried, write down the Japanese phrase for 'I don't eat meat and seafood' – 'Niku to gyokairui o tabemasen' – and take it with you so you can inform waitstaff. 'Watashi wa bejitarian desu' is 'I am a vegetarian'. Another useful phrase is 'Kono tabemono wa niku aruiwa gyokairui wo harimasuka?', which means 'Does this food contain meat or seafood?' If in doubt, the dishes and listings here are some of the best vegetarian eats in Tokyo.

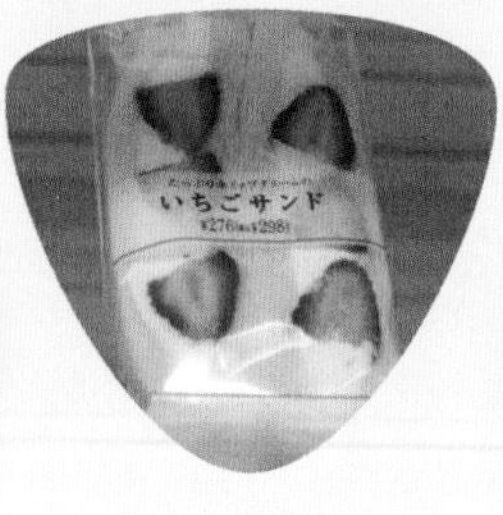

VEGETARIAN-FRIENDLY JAPANESE DISHES

Inari sushi (sushi rice in tofu pouches)

A favourite of vegetarians and non-vegetarians alike, *inari* sushi is a deep-fried tofu pocket that is simmered in a sweet sauce and then stuffed with vinegared rice.

Nattō (fermented soybeans)

This stringy fermented soybean is a staple of Japanese cuisine, not a delicacy, so you can find it everywhere. It's ... unusual to the Western palate (much like the blue-cheese vibe of fermented tofu), but try it out. It's healthy and a lot of people find they quite like its pungency.

Onigiri (rice balls)

Grilled, plain, seaweed, *umeboshi* (pickled plum), adzuki beans ... there are many veggie options when it comes to this ubiquitous Japanese fast food.

Tamagoyaki (rolled omelette)

Recognisable as the pillow of egg that sits atop *tamago* sushi, you can also find *tamagoyaki* on its own, delicately seasoned and incredibly moreish.

Temaki (hand rolls)

These cone-shaped and incredibly convenient sushi rolls come in a number of vegetarian guises, including cucumber, pickles, egg, avocado and *nattō*.

VEGETARIAN OPTIONS IN OMNIVORE SPACES

Convenience stores

- *Anin dōfu* (almond dessert with a tofu consistency)
- Boiled eggs
- *Edamame*, broad beans and corn
- Egg sandwiches
- *Furutsū sando* (fresh fruit sandwiches
- Fruit and jelly (made with agar)
- *Onigiri* (rice balls) with *umeboshi* (pickled plum), seaweed or adzuki beans
- Plain soba noodles with vegetable tempura on the side (note that soba noodles in soup and *zaru soba* dipping sauce generally contain fish)
- Rice crackers
- Salads
- Veggie and yuzu chips

Food halls

Food halls offer a great selection of items. Breads, salads, *onigiri* and plain rice, fruit and vegetables, as well as baked goods from the many bakeries are all good options.

Izakaya

Hiyayakko: chilled tofu (ask for it without bonito flakes – see useful phrases overleaf)

Nama tofu: tofu with ginger and soy (ask for it without bonito flakes)

Nasu dengaku: miso eggplant

Okonomiyaki: savoury pancake – make sure you get it with vegetables only (and note that *okonomiyaki* batter contains egg)

Katsu restaurants

If you're craving a crumbed and deep-fried hit, *tonkatsu* restaurants often serve potato croquettes. Maisen, which you can find in many department-store food halls, even has mini potato *katsu* burgers! Note that the oil used to fry potato croquettes will be the same oil used to fry meat.

Street-food stalls and festivals

Food on skewers is the order of the day when it comes to street and festival food. Happily, vegetarians and vegans can enjoy food on sticks, too.

- Chocolate-coated banana on a skewer
- *Dango*: sweet rice dumplings on skewers
- *Goheimochi*: soy-glazed rice cake on a skewer
- *Kushikatsu*: crumbed and deep-fried food on skewers – try lotus root, mini peppers, mushrooms or egg
- *Taiyaki*: fish-shaped pastry filled with sweet red-bean paste or custard
- *Yaki imo*: baked sweet potato
- *Yaki tomorokoshi*: soy-glazed grilled corn on a skewer
- *Yakiguri*: roasted chestnuts

Yakitori restaurants

Vegetables and other non-meat items will be cooked on the same grill as meat items, but a selection of grilled vegetables (mushrooms, peppers and spring onions) is usually available, as are quail eggs.

VEGETARIAN-FRIENDLY TOKYO EATERIES

8ablish
5-10-17 Minami-Aoyama
Minato 107-0062
eightablish.com

Ain Soph
Four locations
ain-soph.jp

Brown Rice Canteen
5-1-8 Jingūmae
Shibuya 150-0001
www.nealsyard.co.jp/brownrice/welcome

Cityshop
5-4-41 Minami-Aoyama
Minato 107-0062
cityshop.tokyo

Eat More Greens
2-2-5 Azabu-Jūban
Minato 106-0045
eatmoregreens.jp

Mr Farmer
Four locations
eat-walk.com/mf

Muji Café & Meal
Various locations
muji.com

Nōmin Café
2-27-8 Kitazawa
Setagaya 155-0031
hyakushow.com

Tamana Shokudo
3-8-27 Minami-Aoyama
Minato 107-0062
tamana-shokudo.jp

Zen (Shinjuku)
Hanamasa Building 1F
5-10-9 Shinjuku
Shinjuku 160-0022

CHAIN-STORE FAVOURITES

CoCo Ichibanya – vegetarian curry
Multiple locations
ichibanya.co.jp/english

Mos Burger – yasai burger
Multiple locations
mos.jp

RAMEN SHOPS

Afuri Ramen
(p. 109)
Afuri Ramen does a fab seasonal vegetarian ramen. Ask your hotel concierge or Airbnb host to call and check if it is in season.

T's TanTan
Keiyo Dōri
Tokyo Station
1-9-1 Marunouchi
Chiyoda 100-0005
www.nre.co.jp/Portals/0/shop/tantan

Shinjuku Gyoen Ramen Ouka
1-11-7 Shinjuku
Shinjuku 160-0022
www.m-ouka.com

Soranoiro Nippon, Tokyo Station
Ramen Street (p. 199)

CHIC DINNER VENUES

Bon
1-2-11 Ryusen
Taitō 110-0012
fuchabon.co.jp/english/english.html

Tofu Sorano
17-4 Sakuragaokachō
Shibuya 150-0031

Tofu Ukai
4-4-13 Shibakōen
Minato 105-0011
ukai.co.jp/shiba

USEFUL WORDS & PHRASES

Gyokairui: seafood (including fish)

Katsuobushi nashi de onegai shimasu: without bonito (fish) flakes, please

Niku: meat (does not include fish or seafood)

Sakana: fish

Tamago: egg

Yasai: vegetables

GREAT RESOURCES

happycow.net
vegietokyo.com

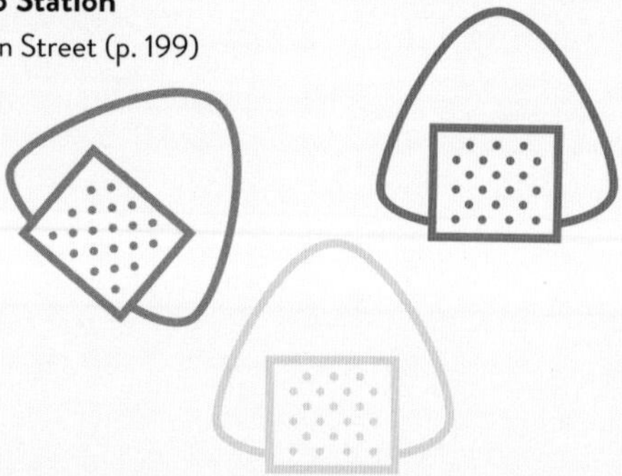

Yaki imo stand near Ginkgo Avenue in autumn (top); *Dango* street stall in Chōfu (bottom)

YAKITORI 焼鳥

A staple at most *izakaya* (pubs; p. 41), yakitori refers to bamboo skewers of meat, typically chicken but sometimes other meat or vegetables (also known as *kushiyaki*), grilled over an open flame. Yakitori is the epitome of fast food: an excellent snack for the office worker on the go. There are many types of yakitori, usually defined by the part of the animal used. Popular options are *momo* (chicken thigh), *tsukune* (chicken meatballs) and *negima* (chicken thigh perfectly paired with spring onion). The more adventurous eater can try *nankotsu* (chicken cartilage), *sunagimo* (chicken gizzard), *shiro* (chicken small intestine) or *hāto* (chicken hearts). There's also something referred to as 'chicken hormone'. Nothing is wasted … unless it's not tasted.

YAKITORI FAVOURITES

Bird Court
3-68 Senju
Adachi 120-0034

Bird Land
4-2-15 Ginza
Chūō 104-0061
ginza-birdland.sakura.ne.jp

Ranjatai
2-12-3 Kanda-Jimbōchō
Chiyoda 101-0051

Toriki
1-8-13 Kinshi
Sumida 130-0013

Torishiki
2-14-12 Kamiōsaki
Shinagawa 141-0021

ALSO TRY

Ginza Torishige
6-9-15 Ginza
Chūō 104-0061

Imai
Rosa Bianca 1F
3-42-11 Jingumae
Shibuya 150-0001
yakitoriimai.jp

Nakameguro Iguchi
1-2-9 Kamimeguro
Meguro 153-0051

Ogawa
Wind Arakichō 1F
9-1 Arakichō
Shinjuku 160-0007

Katsu is a pork cutlet that has been dipped in breadcrumbs and deep-fried. It can then be lathered in rich sauce and eaten with side dishes. *Katsu* has enjoyed great popularity over the years and is a regular dish for locals and visitors alike. Tokyo excels at *katsu* and has a couple of unmissable restaurant experiences.

The king of the *katsu*, *tonkatsu* is pork in breadcrumbs, deep-fried to perfection and enjoyed with a thick fruit-based sauce, shredded cabbage, rice and pickles. Maisen has *ebi* (prawn) *katsu* and potato croquettes too, if you are not a pork eater. *Torikatsu* is *katsu*, but chicken instead of pork. For anyone who doesn't eat pork or red meat, the joys of *katsu* can still be yours.

TONKATSU FAVOURITES

Tonkatsu Maisen
4-8-5 Jingumae
Shibuya 150-0001
mai-sen.com
The *tonkatsu* here is premium and the sauces – a thick plum sauce and a Japanese barbecue-style one – are unctuous and irresistible. There's a take-out window as well, if you feel like eating in a park or on the Shinkansen (bullet train).

Tonkatsu Tonki
1-1-2 Shimomeguro
Meguro 153-0064

Watch the chefs in action as they carve your *hire-katsu* (pork fillet *katsu*) or *rōsu-katsu* (pork loin *katsu*) and serve it up with tasty rice and pickles.

ALSO TRY

Marugo
1-8-14 Soto-Kanda
Chiyoda 101-0021

Muneta
Saneki Building 1F-105
2-37-15 Daizawa
Setagaya 155-0032
tonkatsu-muneta.com

Ponta Honke
3-23-3 Ueno
Taitō 110-0005

Wako
Multiple locations
wako-group.co.jp/en

Yachiyo
Tsukiji-Shijo Building No. 6
5-2-1 Tsukiji
Chūō 104-0045

WAGASHI 和菓子

—— *Wagashi* refers to traditional Japanese confectionery, a beautiful and unique take on sweets. It wasn't until the Muromachi period (1392–1573) that trade with Portugal and Spain brought sugar to Japan, so for many years *wagashi* was a high-end product reserved for the elite. Not so now; anyone can experience these delectable jewels, and for us not a day can go by without nibbling delicately into a precious *wagashi* to discover its subtly flavoured centre.

Japanese confections are highly seasonal, so the time of the year you are visiting will determine what is on offer. The steamy summer months favour *kakigōri* (a bowl of shaved ice with sweet sauce and toppings) and the jelly-like *warabi mochi*. Autumn brings all things chestnut- and sweet potato–flavoured, while spring is a pink *sakura* (cherry blossom) heaven. In winter you can be comforted by *shiruko* (sweet red-bean soup) with *mochi* (rice cakes).

These sweets are artfully created, perfectly reflect the seasons, and appeal to all five senses. Dating back centuries, the techniques, flavours and designs are so carefully executed that you can't help but be moved by the effort and grace that goes into creating one small sweet. If you are like us, it will spark a life-long journey to find the best and most interesting varieties on your Japanese travels.

UNIQUE JAPANESE FLAVOURS

Kinako: roasted soy flour

Yuzu citrus: a delicate, tart flavour similar to lemon

Sakura: cherry blossom – a salty-sour flavour

Matcha: green tea – a popular flavour for ice cream and cheesecake

Sweet potato: popular as an ice-cream flavour, or fried and covered in molasses

An or *anko*: sweet red-bean paste

Tea and seasonal *wagashi* at Wakuden tea house

TYPES OF WAGASHI

ANMITSU

Cubes of agar (a kind of jelly made from algae) and *anko* (sweet red-bean paste), served with a sugar syrup and fruit.

DAIFUKU

A type of *mochi* (rice cake), *daifuku*, meaning 'great luck', is famous in its own right. *Mochi* is wrapped around a delicious, extra-thick *anko* filling. There are many different variations.

DANGO

Rice-flour dumplings filled with red- or white-bean paste, boiled or steamed, and often served on skewers. *Dango* is a common street food for festive occasions.

DORAYAKI

One of Japan's all-time favourite children's characters, Doraemon, snacks on *dorayaki*: two small pancakes sandwiched together with an *anko* filling. You'll find these everywhere, as they are easy to carry and eat on the go.

KAKIGŌRI

Mountains of shaved, flavoured ice, sometimes accompanied by other toppings. *Matcha* (green tea) flavour with sweetened condensed milk is a common combination. Perfect in summer.

KARINTŌ

Small and sweet, with different textures and flavours, these bite-sized candy pieces come in beautiful boxes or brightly coloured packages.

KASHIGATA

Sugary moulded sweets, often given as gifts due to their beauty.

KINTARŌ AME

Small handmade candies similar to rock candy, decorated with the image of folk hero Kintarō, a young boy with superhuman strength.

KONPEITŌ

Introduced by Portuguese traders in the sixteenth century, these handfuls of hard candy are small, sweet and brightly coloured hits of sugar in the shape of small crystals. The name means 'confetti'.

KUZUKIRI

Translucent jelly-like ribbons made from the starch of the kudzu, or Japanese arrowroot, vine. Served chilled with Okinawan black-sugar syrup. The perfect summer treat.

MANJŪ

Heralding the arrival of winter, *manjū* are steamed buns with a Chinese heritage. A dough made of glutinous rice envelops a delicious centre, usually *anko* (sweet red-bean paste) or sometimes *matcha* (green tea). In summer, the translucent, jelly-like *mizu manjū* is popular.

MOCHI

Often rounded and sometimes filled, *mochi* are glutinous rice-flour sweets traditionally eaten around New Year and on Kodomo no Hi (Children's Day, 5 May). *Hishi mochi*, made of pink, green and white layers, is made for *Hina Matsuri* (Girl's Day or Doll's Day, 3 March).

MONAKA

Baked sweets moulded into various shapes, such as *sakura* (cherry blossoms).

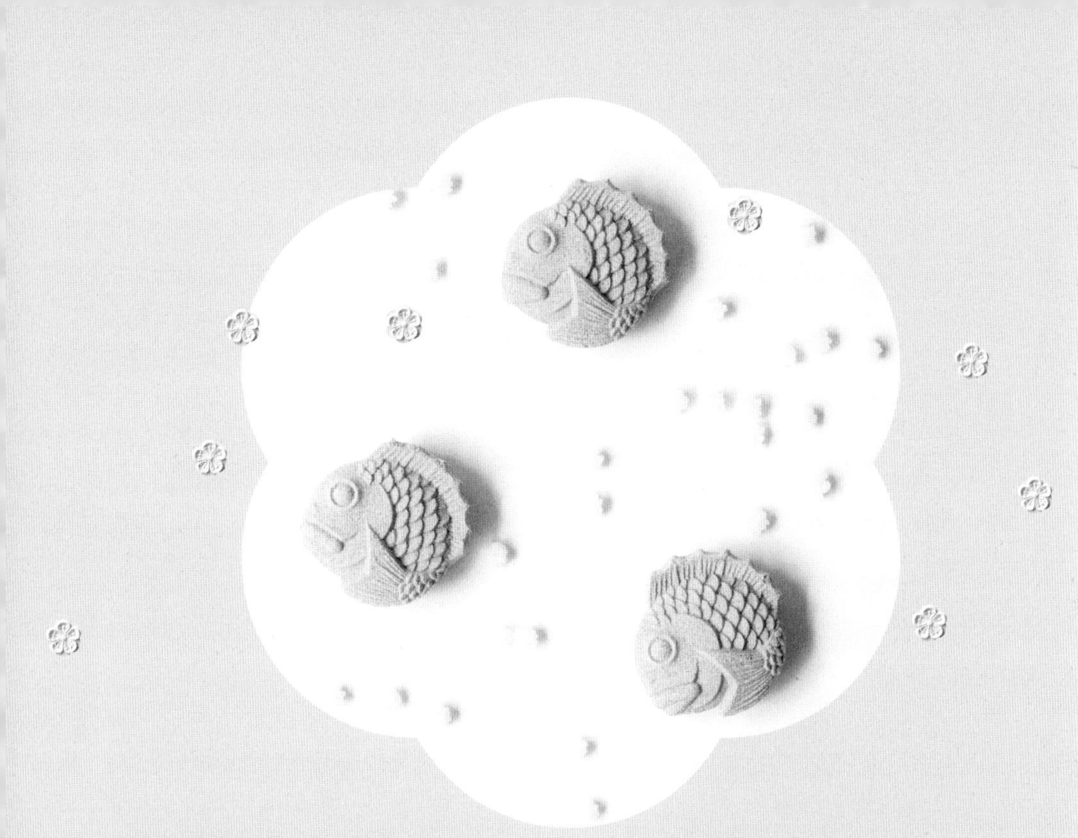

NAMAGASHI

Mostly eaten as an accompaniment to tea ceremonies, this fruit jelly or sweet bean paste is artfully shaped and beautifully presented. Leaf and flower motifs are common, reflecting the seasons.

SENBEI

Sweetened flat rice crackers, usually decorated with a pattern or an emblem. One variation, *edo-gawara senbei*, comes with scenic illustrations that reflect seasonal aspects and landscapes from the Edo period.

TAIYAKI

A waffle-like pastry shaped like a *tai*, or sea bream, wrapped around assorted fillings, including *anko* (sweet red-bean paste), custard and purple sweet potato.

WARABI MOCHI

Although the name suggests that it is a type of *mochi* (rice cake), *warabi mochi* is actually a chewy, jelly-like sweet made of bracken starch and covered with *kinako* (roasted soybean flour).

YŌKAN

A moulded jelly made from agar, red bean and sugar, *yōkan* comes in many varieties. Most often you'll see it in high-end sweet stores, perfectly shaped, delicately wrapped in a seasonal leaf and holding a treasure in its centre: adzuki beans, persimmon, chestnuts, figs or even sweet potato.

ZENZAI

A warm, sweet red-bean soup that is usually served with chewy *mochi*.

Michelle queued for the New Year *konpeitō* and *kashigata* above

Michelle loves chestnut *wagashi* and always queues at Isetan for her favourite variety

Dango and *kakigōri* are so popular that they have their own emojis

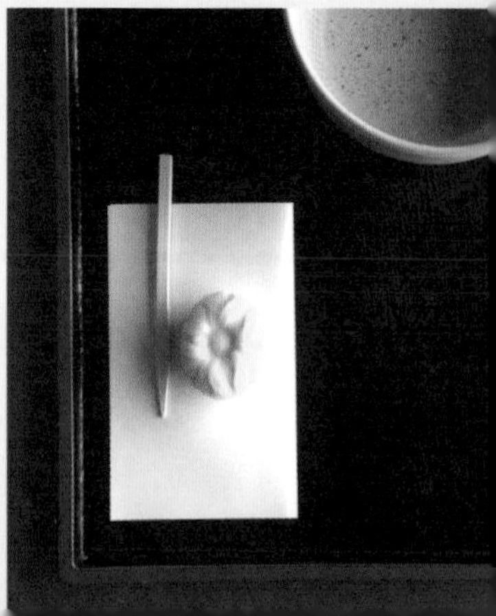

FOR DORAYAKI

Seijuken
1-4-16 Nihonbashi-Horidomechō
Chūō 103-0012
seijuken.com

Usagiya
1-10-10 Ueno
Taitō 110-0005
ueno-usagiya.jp

FOR KAKIGŌRI

Chimoto
1-4-6 Yakumo
Meguro 152-0023
chimoto-yagumomochi.com

FOR SENBEI

Matsuzaki Senbei
5-6-9 Ginza
Chūō 104-0061
matsuzaki-senbei.com

FOR TEA & WAGASHI

Baishinka at Yakumo Saryō
3-4-7 Yakumo
Meguro 152-0023
yakumosaryo.jp/e/baishinka

Higashiya
POLA Ginza Building 2F
1-7-7 Ginza
Chūō 104-0061
higashiya.com

Murasakino Wakuden
3-3-1 Marunouchi
Chiyoda 100-0005
wakuden.jp

Sasama
1-23 Kanda-Jimbōchō
Chiyoda 101-0051
sasama.co.jp

Wagashi Asobi
1-31-1 Kamiikedai
Ōta 145-0064
wagashi-asobi.com

FOR WARABI MOCHI & KUZUKIRI

Kuriya Kashi Kurogi
University of Tokyo
7-3-1 Hongō
Bunkyō 113-0033
wagashi-kurogi.co.jp

FOR YŌKAN

Echigoya Wakasa
1-8-4 Chitose
Sumida 130-0025

Murasakino Wakuden
3-3-1 Marunouchi
Chiyoda 100-0005
wakuden.jp

Toraya
Tokyo Midtown Galleria B1F
9-7-4 Akasaka
Minato 107-0052
www.toraya-group.co.jp/toraya/shops

Wagashi Asobi
1-31-1 Kamiikedai
Ōta 145-0064
wagashi-asobi.com

FOR EVERYTHING

Isetan Department Store Food Hall
3-14-1 Shinjuku
Shinjuku 160-0022
isetan.mistore.jp/store/shinjuku

Various types of seasonal *wagashi* (opposite)

YŌGASHI 洋菓子

—— *Yōgashi* is the name given to Western sweets with a Japanese twist. Stalwarts like sponge cake, cheesecake and éclairs naturally get a makeover in Tokyo, but an eclectic selection of little-known Western cakes have also garnered a new fan base.

Girlfriends and couples gather on weekends for coffee-and-cake dates, a regular Tokyo ritual. As with everything to do with Tokyo, fads and fashions come and go: one minute, chocolate gateaux with *matcha* (green tea) or sesame cookies are competing for the top spot, the next tofu donuts and *matcha* tiramisu are in. Big-name department-store food halls showcase creative mini-cakes shaped like cute animals, seasonal characters, nature and fruits, among other things.

When we're in Tokyo, we always aim to try something new each day. Why not? After all the walking you do, you'll find it quite easy to justify your cake intake – you need a lot of energy to get through the day's activities. Right? To satisfy your sweet tooth, department-store food halls are a wonderful starting point. Our favourites are Isetan in Shinjuku (p. 129), Nihonbashi Mitsukoshi in Ginza (p. 194) and Tokyu Food Show in Shibuya (p. 85).

Just a heads-up: cream won't necessarily taste like cream as you know it, but it is light and sweet. Butter won't necessarily taste like butter, either, but it is … something else.

Sweet potato soft-serve ice cream, department-store cakes, *matcha* cheesecake and *furūtsu sando* (opposite)

Many packaged cakes and sweets are made to last at least a few weeks. Have a good look around for your favourite packaging (Michelle collects tins from sweet stores, for example) and buy some beautiful edible presents to take home. The famous Tokyo Banana and Michelle's favourite Hato Saburē *dove biscuits make great presents, as do crazy Kit Kat flavours. Many of these are available from the airport, but if you see something you like, buy it – there is no guarantee you will be able to find it anywhere else.*

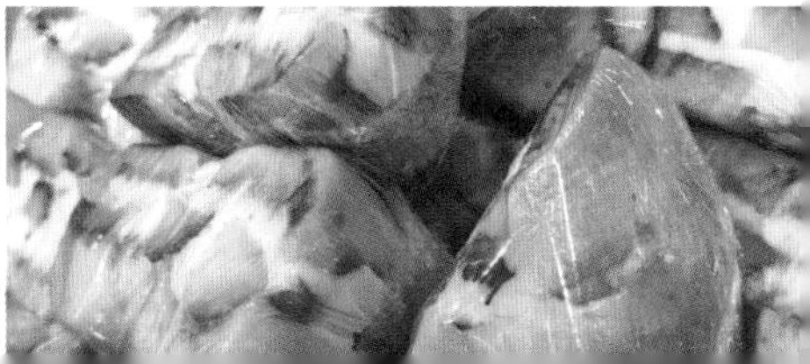

FRENCH-INSPIRED SWEETS

The Japanese have long had an affinity for French culture and cuisine. In Tokyo you can find France's sweet superstars Ladurée, La Maison du Chocolat, Joël Robuchon and Pierre Hermes, which are all ridiculously popular.

CREPES

Crepes can be found at a lot of street-food stalls and dessert houses frequented by the younger set. Fillings can vary, but unlike in Paris, they are almost always sweet: strawberries, kiwifruit, banana, chocolate, Nutella and cream – or all of the above. There are various takes on the crepe, of course. Just join the queue at Harajuku's Gram (p. 258) on any given day of the week to discover them.

MILLE-FEUILLE

The classic French 'thousand leaves' pastry is popular in Japan and can be found either in its original delicate and refined form, or as a 'crepe cake': a layered stack of sweetened crepes from which a slice is carved for you to enjoy with an afternoon coffee.

MONT BLANC

Mont Blanc is one of the most popular desserts in Japan, perhaps because of its subtle chestnut flavour. A sponge cake base is layered with cream and chestnuts, into which a whole chestnut is often pressed for added texture and flavour. The pièce de résistance is the generous amount of chestnut purée piped over the top in long strings.

PARFAIT

You don't have to be on a date to have a parfait, but it helps! The Japanese version of the popular French dessert is a deep well of deliciousness – a mystery trifle that keeps on giving. Expect *matcha* (green tea) sponge, *dango* (rice-flour dumplings), cream, *yōkan* (red-bean jelly), ice cream and more, piled high in a sundae glass. Great to share, but you can take one on by yourself if you've got a sweet tooth.

PURIN

The classic crème caramel is elevated to a delicious, sweet and ever-so-slightly bitter egg-custard pot that you can find in most department-store food halls and convenience stores. *Purin*, or 'pudding', is readily available across Tokyo and often listed first on store menus. When this is the case, you can actually point to it and say, 'Number one.' Steve advises that you do, as *purin* is one of his Tokyo staples.

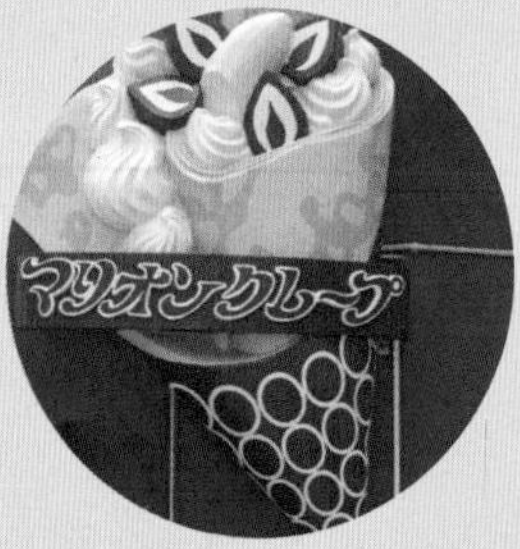

OTHER WESTERN-INSPIRED SWEETS

CASTELLA

This popular sponge cake, often boxed up and given as a gift, was inspired by the Portuguese *pão de Castela*, or 'bread from Castille'. A sugary, thick sponge made using starch syrup, it should appease the most fussy sponge-cake fan.

CHEESECAKE

Matcha (green tea) cheesecake is hands-down Michelle's favourite dessert. Light, puffy and fluffy, airy and creamy, the Tokyo cheesecake is a popular afternoon treat in some of the more hip cafés, and goes well with both coffee and tea.

CHIFFON CAKE

A favourite of the *kissaten* (European-style coffee houses; p. 142), the chiffon cake is a textured sponge lathered in cream. Tokyoites have worked out that it is the perfect accompaniment to the complex flavour of pour-over coffee.

DONUTS

Tokyoites are spoilt for choice with donuts, and the Japanese make an excellent lighter version of the decadent Western pastry. Soybean-pulp donuts and other assorted healthy varieties are delicious, topped with a thin layer of flavoured icing: a true treat without the overload of calories. The more traditional donut options are air-filled, lightly dusted clouds of bliss that will rank among the best donuts you have ever tried.

FURŪTSU SANDO

The fruit sandwich is a phenomenon. Strawberries and cream in bread can be bought at any food hall or convenience store, and in fruit stores. Other variations include kiwifruit, mango, berries, peach and banana.

HONEY TOAST

Made in Shibuya with love, honey toast is the ultimate dessert for groups of teenagers hopped up on an afternoon of game parlours, shopping and gossip, looking for a sugar fix. These chunky, crazy blocks of bread – like a hollowed-out loaf filled with whipped cream and fruit – are great if you want to celebrate a birthday or just have a fun day out. Head to Shibuya (p. 234) and Akihabara (p. 224) in search of honey-toast heaven.

KITTO KATTO

Kitto Katto, or Kit Kats, are hugely popular in Tokyo. They are considered to be good luck due to the similarity between the name Kitto Katto and the Japanese phrase *kitto katsu* ('you're sure to triumph').

Kit Kat flavours run the gamut from cheesecake, sake, pumpkin, wasabi, Mont Blanc, roasted corn, soy sauce, edamame, and melon, to cheese, chilli, banana, baked custard, adzuki bean and blueberry. There have been more than 300 varieties to date. In 2010, the soy sauce Kit Kat was the top-selling candy bar. It's almost a sport for Westerners to grab boxes of the most outrageous flavours for sharing at home. Seasonal varieties are immensely popular, too; in cherry-blossom season, the *sakura* Kit Kat sells out in minutes.

MERONPAN

Sweet melon-flavoured bread shaped like a slice of melon.

ROLL CAKE

Rolled sponge cakes like Swiss rolls, fruit rolls and *matcha* (green tea) rolls are all readily available. They also make a great accompaniment to coffee, or, when packaged, are a great gift if you are travelling to meet friends.

DESSERT DESTINATIONS

Easter-inspired convenience store cakes (top); Harajuku crepes (bottom)

FOR CHIFFON CAKE

Otaco
3-5-1 Asakusa
Taitō 111-0032
otaco-sweets.com

FOR CUTE CAKES FOR KIDS BIG AND SMALL

Café de Miki with Hello Kitty
DiverCity Tokyo Plaza 2F
1-1-10 Aomi
Kōtō 135-0064
sanrio.co.jp/english/store/sh6204120/

Pompompurin Café
Cute Cube Harajuku 3F
1-7-1 Jingūmae
Shibuya 150-0001
pompom.createrestaurants.com/jp/info_harajuku.html

Shiro-Hige's Cream Puff Factory
5-3-1 Daita
Setagaya 155-0033
shiro-hige.com

FOR DONUTS

Floresta Nature Donuts
3-34-14 Kōenji-Kita
Suginami 166-0002
nature-doughnuts.jp/shop/018_koenji

Hara Donuts
1-3-13 Jyūgaoka
Meguro 152-0035
haradonuts.jp

FOR FRUIT DESSERTS

PARLA
2-10-1 Jingūmae
Shibuya 150-0001
par.la

Sembikiya Sohonten Fruits Parlor
2-1-2 Nihonbashi-Muromachi
Chūō 103-0022

FOR HONEY TOAST

Hanito Café Akihabara
1-1-10 Soto-Kanda
Chiyoda 101-0021

Toshi Yoroizuka
Tokyo Midtown East 1F
9-7-2 Akasaka
Minato 107-0052
grand-patissier.info/ToshiYoroizuka

FOR KIT KATS

Kit Kat Chocolatory Ginza
3-7-2 Ginza
Chūō 104-0061
nestle.jp/brand/kit/inbound/en/chocolatory

FOR MERONPAN

Kimuraya
4-5-7 Ginza
Chūō 104-0061
www.kimuraya-sohonten.co.jp

Naniwaya Honten
1-24-2 Kamezawa
Sumida 130-0014

FOR PATISSERIE

Cacao Store
1-6-8 Tomigaya
Shibuya 151-0063

Dominique Ansel Bakery
5-7-14 Jingūmae
Shibuya 150-0001
dominiqueanseljapan.com

Henri Charpentier
2-8-20 Ginza
Chūō 104-0061
www.henri-charpentier.com/eng/shop/ginza-maison

Hidemi Sugino
3-6-17 Kyōbashi
Chūō 104-0031

Il Pleut Sur La Seine
Daikanyama Forum 2F
17-16 Sarugakuchō
Shibuya 150-0033
ilpleut.co.jp

Toshi Yoroizuka
Tokyo Midtown East 1F
9-7-2 Akasaka
Minato 107-0052
grand-patissier.info/ToshiYoroizuka

A TOKYO TIPPLE
東京で一杯

Drinks in Japan – alcoholic and non-alcoholic – can be familiar or startlingly unfamiliar, and sometimes both at the same time.

Sake, the classic Japanese spirit distilled from rice, is also the Japanese word for alcohol in general. Akin to wine in the West, there is an abundance of varieties, regional specialties, quality rankings, tastes and flavours. Tasting and making sake reaches a near-religious fervour in Japan around New Year, when barrels of the first sake of the year are opened. Many shops and food halls in Tokyo will be filled with large lantern-like barrels, ready for customers to taste the fresh sake. Lined up together, the barrels are a spectacular sight.

Beer is as popular in Japan as it is anywhere, and in Tokyo you'll find both a quality and a range of beers that is among the best in the world. Wine is becoming increasingly popular. Tea is an art form, literally, with a ceremony that is deeply rooted in tradition. Coffee has been around in Tokyo since the Meiji era (p. 32), with charming *kissaten* (European-style coffee houses; 142) serving a delectable pour-over utilising high-quality freshly roasted and ground beans. New coffee shops and hole-in-the-wall coffee joints spring up almost daily, serving the finest brews. If you're on the move, vending machines and convenience stores sell a vast range of drinks both hot and cold, soft and hard.

Drinking in Japan can be casual, sophisticated, easygoing or spiritual, depending on what you're looking for.

BEER

Japanese beer is fantastic. There is just something about the varieties on offer, the attention to detail and, yes, the fact that you can buy it at a convenience store. You can even get it in vending machines. Beer is cheap and very, very cheerful. Seasonal varieties abound. Packaging can change from snowflakes and deer in winter, to leaves in autumn and cherry blossoms in *sakura* season. Flavours can change, too. We've tried lemon beer and tomato beer, among others. Only for the brave.

Tokyo in particular is home to one of the greatest beers of all time. Yebisu beer (nowadays made by beverage giant Sapporo) is closely linked with the cool enclave that is Ebisu (p. 287), and you will see Yebisu's logo and namesake Ebisu, the Japanese god of fishermen and luck, everywhere at Ebisu Station. The usual suspects fight for supremacy in the Japanese beer market: Kirin, Asahi and Sapporo make a range of beers that can be grabbed from convenience stores for under 300 yen. Craft beers like Coedo, Suiyōbi no Neko ('Wednesday cat' – the one with the cute cat on it!), Hitachino Nest and Yona Yona can be found in most food halls and convenience stores. If you want to sample a wide range, try places like Craftsman in Gotanda, Tap X Tap in Kanda and Craft Beer Market, which has stores all over Tokyo.

Sake labels, drink machines and seasonal beer

NON-ALCOHOLIC DRINKS

Fruit- and vegetable-flavoured drinks are popular beverages in Japan, and have a lot less sugar than their Western counterparts. Popular flavours include cherry, mandarin, pineapple, apple and orange. Electrolyte and sports drinks like Pocari Sweat will keep you fresh as you pound the pavement. Yoghurt-enhanced drinks and sodas such as Calpis are a favourite of ours (you can even get a can of Calpis and whisky – yoghurt and whisky is actually a tasty combination!) and small boxed soy drinks with unusual or seasonal flavours are another delicious beverage. And while all these drinks are popular, green tea (hot and cold, bottled and canned) dominates the non-alcoholic arena.

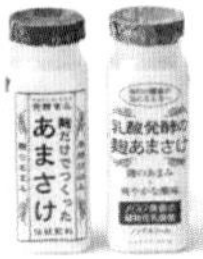

SAKE

The national drink of Japan, found just about everywhere. See p. 148 for more detail.

UMESHU

This plum liqueur is a great drink for the summer months. It's also good if you feel like something a bit more fruity than sake or beer in restaurants. Ask for it with soda and ice.

TEA

Tea, or *ocha*, holds great cultural significance in Japan. See p. 144 for more detail.

WHISKY

Japanese whisky is among the best in the world, and it has a cult-like following in Tokyo. The whisky highball – similar to a scotch and soda – is a fixture at most *izakaya* (pubs; p. 41), and a drink called the freezing black highball is a favourite cooling summer beverage. The popular canned drink *chūhai* is basically a highball made with *shōchū*: the best of both worlds.

SHŌCHŪ

A drink native to the Kyushu region, *shōchū* is a spirit distilled from sweet potato, rice, barley, buckwheat and brown sugar. It's similar to vodka, although weaker in alcohol content. You can drink *shōchū* on the rocks or try it with water, soda or cold green tea (a favourite of ours). It's often said in Japan that *shōchū* gets you 'drunk from the ankles up'. You can be enjoying a *shōchū* or two and when you get up to leave, it hits you …

COFFEE
コーヒー

——— Tokyoites love coffee. Arriving in the Meiji era (p. 32), the coffee obsession took over in the middle of the twentieth century with European-style cafés known as *kissaten* (p. 142); since then, the drink has been loved, changed, reinvented and perfected.

Tokyo's baristas (who have similar facial hair but a different attitude to their Western counterparts) are treated with the same respect afforded to sushi chefs, and are constantly exploring new ways to extract flavour from the bean. One such method is the Kyoto-style coffee-drip tower, which takes more than 50 minutes to create an iced coffee. (Perhaps have a coffee while you're waiting.)

As you might expect, some of the latte art you find in Tokyo is good enough to hang on a gallery wall. From exquisite leaves, flowers and love hearts, to ultra-cute characters and animals, latte art in Tokyo adds a whole new dimension to coffee.

From the retro charm of the *kissaten* and its classic pour-over brews, to the scientific dedication of the contemporary syphon coffee outlet, dig deep into Tokyo coffee culture and you'll find a city that grinds beans with the best of them.

CAFFEINE HITS

POUR-OVER COFFEE

While star baristas and coffee masters *pore over* their coffee style, perfecting the brew-and-flow method, Tokyoites have been elevating the art of the pour-over to high-end status in *kissaten* and cafés since the fifties. Perfectly ground beans, cotton filters and exceptional temperature control make the Tokyo pour-over coffee one of the best ways to enjoy the naughty bean.

AMERICAN DRIP COFFEE

Anyone who has experienced a 'stewed' coffee nightmare at a New York diner will want to try the Japanese take on American-style drip coffee, with its hefty, bittersweet charms. Introduced during the postwar American occupation, drip coffee has become something of a retro fine art in Tokyo.

COFFEE JELLY

One of the seven wonders of the world, the Tokyo coffee jelly is a dessert crossed with a coffee crossed with instant obsession. Whether artfully presented in a high-end *kissaten* (where it can often contain booze) or served as jelly cubes in a tall glass of milk coffee in a chain coffee house, coffee jelly is the perfect way to get your coffee and confectionery hit all in one go. Added to ice cream it becomes a solid affogato. Why should liquid coffee have all the glory? Sometimes solid coffee is the only way to go.

COFFEE IN A CAN

Coffee can be found in various shapes, styles and sizes in Tokyo. Vending machines sell all kinds of drinks, and the varieties and strengths of coffee are vast. Coffee with milk, without milk, extra-strong, hot or cold: they can all be nabbed from a machine for 200–300 yen. If you're feeling a bit rough in the morning or you need an afternoon pick-me-up, a coffee shot will certainly do the trick. Even those who have built up a resistance to strong coffee over the years might find the heady brew in the cans giving them the jitters – a lot of that has to do with the sweetness, so watch out if you like your coffee without sugar.

ICED COFFEE

In summer, an iced coffee is the perfect way to stay cool while getting your morning (or afternoon) pick-me-up. A café iced coffee will traditionally be a tall glass filled with espresso and cold water. You'll have a doll-sized jug of milk and some sugar syrup to lighten it up. It's not your usual iced coffee, but it's delicious and after one or two you'll be flying out the door. In dessert houses you'll find that iced coffee is more like an affogato in a glass, with a shot of coffee complemented by milk and ice cream – just add sugar. Iced coffee can be readily found in drink machines on the street, and after a visit to an *onsen* (hot spring), an iced coffee is a perfect way to rehydrate.

SYPHON COFFEE

Danger: mad scientists at work! Tokyo's syphon-coffee culture is a fascinating spectacle. Pipes, test tubes, beakers and Bunsen burners boil and bubble water and coffee beans to create something special.

KISSATEN

Enjoy coffee
like it's 1965

Old-school coffee houses that came into existence early last century, *kissaten* are both a charming relic of old Tokyo and an exciting new discovery for the coffee-loving traveller. *Kissaten* are family-owned coffee shops and most have endured for decades. They're spaced out across the city and don't spruik themselves, and you won't see much in the way of English. So what does one look for? First, the smell: high-quality coffee beans being roasted lovingly on site. Then, the sound: jazz, almost always jazz, wafting through the air. Finally, the sight: usually a dark wooden exterior, like a cuckoo clock but with a revolving door of customers instead of a cooing bird; and a small and cluttered interior with early twentieth-century Austrian decor, fading white net curtains and the ubiquitous drip-coffee sign.

What you'll notice first is the owners, who have been making cotton-filter and syphon coffee since they were young. They know how to treat customers and how to turn beans and water into tiny china cups full of coffee that delights. There is always a sweet accompaniment and many places are known for their roll cakes, *baumkuchen* (tree cakes) or chiffon cakes. They have odd-sounding specialties like coffee jelly (p. 141), which you really have to try, and their liqueur coffees are not to be missed. Charm, old-world atmosphere and a lifetime of perfecting a brew are all sound-tracked by the owners' favourite jazz or classical music, played right off original vinyl.

Kissaten coffee jelly

KISSATEN

Café de l'Ambre
8-10-15 Ginza
Chūō 104-0061
cafedelambre.com

Café Deux Oiseaux
4-6-28 Asagaya-Kita
Suginami 166-0001

Kayaba Coffee
29-1-6 Yanaka
Taitō 110-0001
kayaba-coffee.com

Kugutsusō
1-7-7 Kichijōji-Honchō
Musashino 180-0004
kugutsusou.info

Monozuki
3-12-10 Nishi-Ogikita
Suginami 167-0042

Nelken
3-56-7 Kōenji-Minami
Suginami 166-0003

Tsuta
5-11-20 Minami-Aoyama
Minato 107-0062

COFFEE JOINTS

About Life Coffee
1-19-8 Dōgenzaka
Shibuya 150-0043
about-life.coffee

Blue Bottle
3-13-14 Minami-Aoyama
Minato 107-0062
bluebottlecoffee.com/cafes/aoyama

Cafe Obscura
1-19-16 Sangenjaya
Sangenjaya 154-0024
obscura-coffee.com

Koffee Mameya
4-15-3 Jingūmae
Shibuya 150-0001
koffee-mameya.com

Light Up Coffee
4-13-15 Kichijōji-Honchō
Musashino 180-0004
lightupcoffee.com

Onibus
2-14-1 Nakameguro
Meguro 153-0051
onibuscoffee.com

Switch Coffee
1-17-23 Meguro
Meguro 153-0063
switchcoffeetokyo.com

Toranomon Koffee
Toranomon Hills Mori Tower
1-1-23 Toranomon
Minato 105-0001
ooo-koffee.com

ALSO TRY

Alpha Beta Coffee Club
2-10-4 Jyūgaoka
Meguro 152-0035
abccoffee.co/cafe

Bear Pond Espresso
2-36-12 Kitazawa
Setagaya 155-0031
bear-pond.com

Nozy
2-29-7 Shimouma
Setagaya 154-0002
nozycoffee.jp

Streamer
Multiple locations
streamer.coffee

Tea in Tokyo is a ritual, a custom, a daily spiritual cleanse, an afternoon out with *wagashi* (traditional sweets; p. 124) or cake, and, of course, an art form accompanied by some of the most beautiful and studied craft in the world. Tea is enduringly popular in India and the United Kingdom, but tea in Japan is something else – almost a religion. Tea varieties are distinct, developed over time and intricately nuanced. Tea houses in Japan are legendary devotional places where the true art of tea is a performance as much as a refreshment.

Tokyo has many opportunities for you to immerse yourself in this sublime tradition, and many gardens host tea houses both old and beautiful or contemporary and architectural. Regardless of design, each one does justice to the long-held tradition of tea-making and drinking, and adds its own particular flourish.

Tea stores feature all manner of extra-special and beautiful tea packaging. Michelle has queued for amazing New Year packaging, as well as the first of the year's tea leaves. We guarantee that if you dip your toe in (figuratively, not literally), it will soon become an obsession.

TYPES OF TEA

HŌJICHA

The main difference between *hōjicha* and other teas is that it is roasted after picking, whereas most tea leaves are steamed. The toasty element gives it a uniquely mild flavour, great for drinking after an evening meal.

Try a hōjicha or matcha latte at one of Tokyo's twenty-first century cafes.

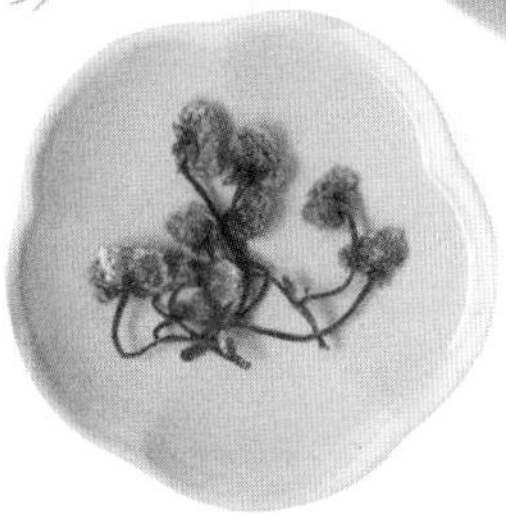

Tea can take on seasonal flavours. Cherry blossom (above) is a favourite in spring time.

CONVENIENCE STORE & MACHINE TEAS

Royal Milk Tea, hot green tea in bottles, cold green tea in bottles (a lifesaver in summer), chai milk tea, olive tea, tea bags with added fruit, powdered *matcha* sachets: there are so many tea options to be found in convenience stores and vending machines, and they are all good.

MATCHA

Many people will be familiar with *matcha*, a finely ground green powder used in most tea ceremonies. The tea is made from plants grown in the shade, the leaves of which have the veins and stems removed after picking and before air-drying. The prepared leaves are then ground with a mortar and pestle to create *matcha*. In the traditional tea ceremony, steeping times and serving temperatures are paramount, as is the presentation. *Matcha* can also be enjoyed at home in a less rarefied atmosphere, simply by whisking hot water into the powder. Versatile and diverse, *matcha* is emblematic of Japan.

SENCHA

Another form of Japanese green tea, *sencha* is made by infusing whole tea leaves in water, unlike the powdered *matcha*. *Sencha* comes in bags and as loose-leaf tea, but will always result in a perfect, restorative, light green-yellow cup of tea.

GENMAICHA

Originally made for the underclass who couldn't afford pure *matcha* or *sencha*, *genmaicha* is made from roasted brown rice mixed with green tea, and has become popular with all parts of society in recent years. Often purported to be good for a poorly stomach, *genmaicha* has a deep and nutty flavour.

JAPANESE GARDENS WITH TEA HOUSES

Kiyosumi Teien – tea house
3-3-9 Kiyosumi Koto
135 - 0024 Tokyo

Koishikawa-Kōrakuen – Kantoku-tei
1-6-6 Kōraku
Bunkyō 112-0004

Nezu Museum Garden – multiple tea houses
6-5-1 Minami-Aoyama
Minato 107-0062
nezu-muse.or.jp/en

Rikugi-en – Fukiage Tea House
6-16-3 Honkomagome
Bunkyō 113-0021

Shinjuku Gyoen – multiple tea houses
11 Naitomachi
Shinjuku 160-0014

TEA HOUSES & STORES

Ishizaki-en
1-10-10 Tomioka
Koto 135-0016

Nakamura Tea Life
4-20-4 Kuramae,
Taito 111-0051
www.tea-nakamura.com

Rakuzan Kagurazaka
4-3 Kagurazaka,
Shinjuku, 162-0825
www.rakuzan.co.jp

Sabo Tea House Yakumo Saryo, Baishinka
3-4 Yakumo,
Meguro 153-0063
yakumosaryo.jp/e/baishinka

Susumu Cha-ten
1-25-5 Jiyugaoka
Meguro 153-0063
susumuya.com

Uogashi-Meicha
4-10-1 Tsujiki
Chuo 104-0061
www.uogashi-meicha.co.jp/en

Tea and *wagashi* at Fukiage Tea House in Rikugi-en; The tea house at Kiyosumi Teien (opposite)

——— Sake, or *nihonshu*, is made by fermenting rice that has been polished to remove the bran husk. The more polished the grain, the less husk there is – and thus the quality of the resulting spirit is higher.

Sake has its own varieties, rankings and regional specialties, as well as a legal designation – *seishu* – on every label. This is a regulation that protects the Japanese sake industry (much like the way certain cheeses are regulated in Italy). As the national drink, sake can be found everywhere: in *izakaya* (pubs; p. 41), food halls, restaurants and bars. What's more, even reasonably priced sake in Tokyo will usually be good quality.

Sake can be served cold, at room temperature, warm or hot. Like tea, it is often served in special ceremonies, warmed in a *tokkuri* (ceramic carafe) and poured into small, saucer-like cups called *sakazuki*. In *izakaya*, sake is served in small bottles with mini cups in porcelain, wood or ceramic. Sometimes sake will be poured into a glass in a lacquerware box, the glass then overflowing and filling the box.

Sake in Japan is crisp and fresh, deep and multi-layered, complex and always surprising. Our primer on sake types is just the tip of the *rice*-berg when it comes to sake, so get out there and experiment. You can even get sparkling sake, with an added sparkle and sweetness that tastes like a (very) dry prosecco. Find the right food pairings and the right level of polishing that suits your palate.

TYPES OF SAKE

TEISEIHAKU-SHU

Teiseihaku-shu is interesting in that it is highly polished, so much so that the sake is said to develop the taste of 'rice itself', and as such it is an acquired taste.

NIGORI

Nigori is unfiltered sake: sweet, pink and cloudy, it has to be served chilled and goes well with spicy food or desserts.

GINJŌ-SHU

The rice used to make *ginjō-shu* has been polished to remove at least 40 per cent of the husk, meaning more impurities have been taken out. An intricate fermentation process leads to a fruity and floral flavour, with more depth than *junmai-shu* and *honjōzō-shu*.

JIZAKE

Fans of craft beer (or craft anything, really) will want to try *jizake*, the sake equivalent. It varies in flavour depending on the brewer, of course; its defining characteristic is that it hasn't been made in an established distillery, but by the hand of a passionate creator.

HONJŌZŌ-SHU

Honjōzō-shu is similar to *junmai-shu*, but it has had distilled alcohol added – not much, but enough to give it a lighter, drier taste.

JUNMAI-SHU

Junmai-shu, or 'pure sake', is sake made from rice, water and a magical ingredient called *kōji*, a kind of mystical mould (*Aspergillus oryzae*, if you want to get scientific) grown on rice. In *junmai-shu*, the rice has been polished to remove at least 30 per cent of the rice husk. With a name like pure sake, one might assume that *junmai-shu* is the pinnacle of quality, but that's not how it works. Each style of sake and its unique distillation process offers a different flavour profile – you have to find the one that appeals to your taste. *Junmai-shu* is fuller, more robust and slightly more acidic than other sakes.

NAMAZAKE

Unlike other sake, *namazake* is not pasteurised, and has to be kept cold; it doesn't last as long as other sake varieties. It is especially refreshing.

AMAZAKE

If you don't drink alcohol but are curious about sake, try *amazake*, a sweet drink made from fermented rice. While low-alcohol *amazake* is more common, there are plenty that are alcohol-free, or as close as can be.

TOKYO BY AREA

- Traditional Tokyo
- Central Tokyo
- Modern Tokyo

TRADITIONAL TOKYO

If you are looking for Tokyo's past, these are the spots to find it. Centuries-old dessert houses; Tokyo's oldest shrine, Sensō-ji; the hallowed halls of sumo at Ryōgoku Kokugikan; and the amazing Edo-Tokyo Open Air Architectural Museum all bring back a little of what it must have felt like to live and breathe in the old city's heyday.

ASAKUSA & KURAMAE; RYŌGOKU; UENO; YANAKA, NEZU & SENDAGI

THE EDO PERIOD (1603–1868), P. 26

—— A playground for entertainers, artists, cultural misfits and vagrants, the city of Edo, as Tokyo was once called, forged the beginnings of the great metropolis we know today. Along with Kyoto and Osaka, Edo was known as *ukiyo*, the 'floating world', and its eponymous period was a time when arts and culture flourished.

Ukiyo-e, an artistic movement of the common people, took hold of the city during the Edo period, influencing not only painting and printmaking techniques, but fashion and lifestyle. Edo's favourite son was artist and printmaker Katsushika Hokusai – most people would recognise his iconic print *The Great Wave off Kanagawa* – and in today's Edo, the Sumida Hokusai Museum (p. 363), a modernist shrine of a building, houses his history and many artworks.

Wander the streets of Yanaka, with its small shrines and village atmosphere; find some craft treasures in Kuramae; try out an old-school *sentō* (public bathhouse); and eat at a 100-year-old soba (p. 103) or *chankonabe* (p. 171) restaurant. You are sure to find some of that old Edo charm you've been seeking.

In true Tokyo style, the traditional Tokyo area also has an eye to the future. It's home to Tokyo Skytree (p. 161), the Asahi Beer Hall (p. 155) and Kappabashi Dōri (Kitchen Town; p. 157), as well as a host of museums in Ueno Park (p. 175). While the wards and districts of traditional Tokyo are among the most popular tourist areas in the city, there are so many tiny streets off the beaten track that it's still possible to feel like you have a slice of old Tokyo to yourself.

ASAKUSA & KURAMAE

——— You get the best of both worlds in Asakusa. In the midst of Tokyo's towering neon futurism, technology overload and consumer culture, you can still visit the Japan of days gone by. Shrines are hidden in verdant gardens; precious buildings stand between towering skyscrapers; and family businesses, run for centuries, still flourish in laneways and backstreets.

Asakusa is home to the spectacular Sensō-ji (p. 334), a seventh-century Buddhist temple where daytrippers can soak up the old-world atmosphere, weaving through the crowds to find their own corner of Zen calm. Leading you towards the temple is Nakamise Dōri (1-36-3 Asakusa, asakusa-nakamise.jp), a colourful promenade dotted with souvenir stands and stalls selling all manner of street food. The festive atmosphere really takes you out of the bustle of the city, and entering the hallowed grounds of Sensō-ji enhances the experience. As one of Tokyo's oldest and most important temples (and reputedly the world's most-visited spiritual site), it attracts a lot of visitors eager to photograph its five-storey pagoda, large main shrine, angular gabled rooftops and the massive red lantern at its entrance. It's all a faithful reconstruction of the original; the buildings and even Nakamise Dōri were bombed in the Second World War. That won't stop you from feeling like you're strolling through a piece of Tokyo's history, however.

From the Asakusa side of Sumida River you can get a panoramic vista of modern Tokyo. One of the most snapped Tokyo scenes, this aspect features Philippe Starck's Asahi Beer Hall (1-23-1 Azumabashi), with its infamous beer-foam swish (dubbed the 'golden poo' by locals), a tapered, gilded blob perched atop. On the skyline it sits side-by-side with the soaring Tokyo Skytree (p. 161); together, they form a distinctive urban vista across the river. The Skytree was named in a public competition and stands proud at 634 metres, the second-tallest structure in the world when it was finished in 2010. It is truly one of the world's premiere tourist destinations, an imposing spire that gives visitors a cloud's-eye view of Tokyo's mind-boggling sprawl.

Sensō-ji and Tokyo Skytree (opposite)

A square slice of neighbourhood between Asakusa's sights and the grungier enclave of Asakusabashi, Kuramae flourishes: small old-world Tokyo handicraft shops and utterly charming contemporary cafés and eateries speckle the narrow streets hidden from the main thoroughfares. In the Edo period, rice granaries lined these same streets, bringing in money – and some wealthy citizens. The rich history and relatively low rents has seen Kuramae become a creative hub, where the young flock to stores selling 'Tokyo-made' in the form of fashion, stationery, leather goods and new products made using old techniques. Of course, cafés, bars and hostels have followed suit. As an added bonus, classic *sentō* (public bathhouses) have been given a revamp, and long-standing mom-and-pop eateries, lulled into a false sense of security by years of familiar faces wafting in and out, are stunned by the sudden influx of new, young and hip customers.

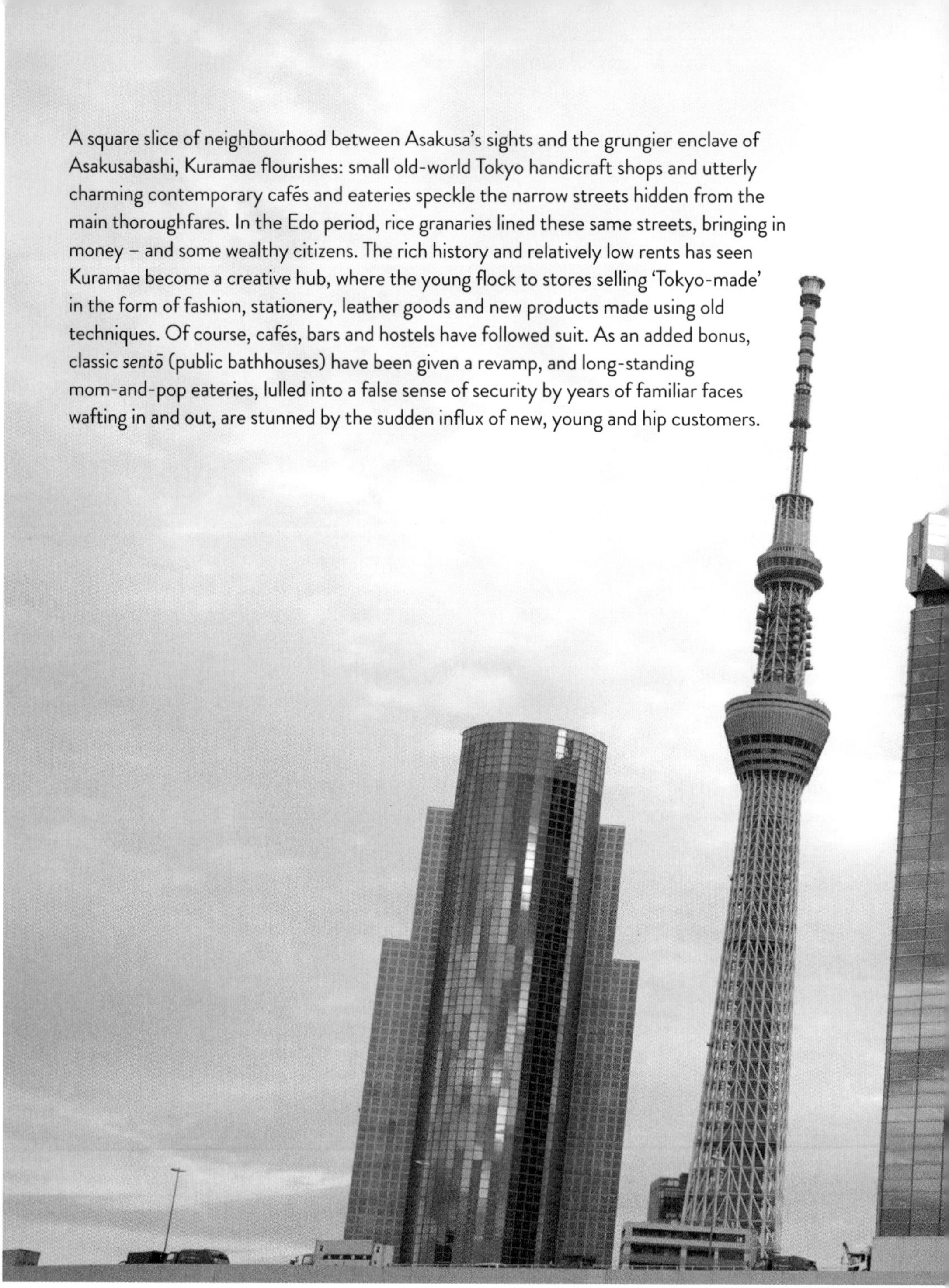

Nearby Kappabashi Dōri (3-18-2 Matsugaya, kappabashi.or.jp/en), or Kitchen Town, will turn your kitchen from amateur to professional with its endless array of cookware, lacquerware, ceramics and, of course, the famous *sampuru*, or plastic display food. Chefs and foodies swear by this street. Given the number of restaurants in Tokyo, you can imagine how well stocked a street devoted entirely to supplying them must be. If you are into the culinary arts at any level, you can get everything you need here at various price points. Take some time to shop the range, from high-end pots and pans, knives, *noren* curtains and elaborate dyed aprons, to cute cookie cutters, wax kitchen paper, children's school lunchboxes, *onigiri* (rice ball) shapers, *sampuru* (plastic food model) keyrings and a range of tiny, ultra-cute implements. Even the non-foodie will find something useful to take home.

Asakusa skyline, with the Tokyo Skytree to the left and the Asahi Beer Hall to the right

Hanayashiki (2-28-1 Asakusa, hanayashiki.net/en) is another spot worth checking out in Asakusa. An amusement park that has operated since 1853 (it claims to be the oldest in Japan and one of the oldest in the world), Hanayashiki is a retro-lover's dream ride of low-tech rollercoasters, ultra-cute character tree houses, psychedelic twirl rides and a host of experiences that used to thrill people before the advent of loop-the-loop rollercoasters and cliff's edge waterslides. The entryway signage, the colours and shapes, and the loudspeakers' jingling music, sound effects and announcements are to-die-for cute. Think the teacup ride at Disneyland, times ten. No doubt terrifying in their day, the low-thrill rides are now a paradise for the faint-hearted.

Hanayashiki pirate ride (above) and ghost train (opposite top right)

Kappabashi Dōri sights

TOKYO VIEWS

A sweeping view of Tokyo is a truly unforgettable sight. The city sprawl as it reaches out to the suburbs, punctuated by clusters of skyscrapers or patches of green, with a backdrop of distant mountains. The endless sky slate grey or bright blue with pillows of fluffy clouds. There are several vantage points where you can get a panoramic view of this extensive metropolis, which is one of the world's largest cities. View enthusiasts might want to try as many different vantage points as possible to really get a sense of the ludicrous scope of Tokyo.

With the Skytree, you get pomp and circumstance. The lower levels are packed with souvenir tourist traps, which in Tokyo tradition means that you can grab some amazing stuff on a budget that will delight everyone back home. Riding the elevator up to the dizzying heights is the future you were promised: a super-fast, vertigo-inducing thrill ride that will have you mistaking a contemporary marvel for an amusement park attraction. The Mori Art Museum's Sky Deck is another impressive spectacle, and Toyko Tower has long been a popular spot.

Most spectacular views don't come for free, but there are a few truly astounding ones that do. For instance, the free view from the Metropolitan Government Building has been a poorly kept secret for some time now. Yebisu Garden Place also has a free view from the thirty-eighth floor: here the Tokyo sprawl is watched over by an uxorious Fuji-san (Mt Fuji) – if you're lucky, that is. Visible Fuji days are scant and completely at the mercy of the elements. Mist, fog and clouds can render Fuji-san, invisible, or at best a pale outline on the distant horizon. Regardless, it's time to take control of your fear of heights and prepare yourself for some truly staggering, truly panoramic vistas of Tokyo.

TOKYO'S BEST VANTAGE POINTS (IN NO PARTICULAR ORDER)

Carrot Tower Observation Deck (free)

4-1-1 Taishidō
Setagaya 154-0004

Cerulean Tower Bar

Cerulean Tower Tokyu Hotel 40F
6-1 Sakuragaokachō
Shibuya 150-8512
tokyuhotelsjapan.com/global/cerulean-h/

Metropolitan Government Building Observation Deck (free)

2-8-1 Nishi-Shinjuku
Shinjuku 163-8001
metro.tokyo.jp

Mori Art Museum

(p. 357)

Odaiba

This man-made island in Tokyo Bay has some great views of Tokyo, and is also home to a few interesting places to visit, including the Fuji TV Building (p. 351), the National Museum of Emerging Science and Innovation (p. 271) and the DiverCity shopping centre, with its massive Gundam robot sculpture (p. 270).

Tokyo Skytree

1-1-2 Oshiage
Sumida 131-0045
tokyo-skytree.jp

Tokyo Tower

4-2-8 Shibakōen
Minato 105-0011
tokyotower.co.jp

Yebisu Garden Place (free)

4-20-1 Ebisu 38F, 39F
Shibuya 150-8522
gardenplace.jp

View from the thirty-eighth floor, Yebisu Garden Place

ASAKUSA & KAPPABASHI WALK

First things first: pop out at Asakusa Station to admire the view of Tokyo Skytree (p. 161) and the Asahi Beer Hall (1-23-1 Azumabashi) across the Azuma Bridge. From Exit 1, take the covered walkway to the Kaminarimon ('thunder gate') and Nakamise Dōri (p. 155), a colourful, festive walkway girded by stores selling everything from tourist trinkets and Japanalia to *wagashi* (traditional sweets; p. 124) and even the occasional high-quality, expensive impulse-buy. There are eateries, shops selling souvenirs, fabric or sweet-potato treats, old *kissaten* (European-style coffee houses; p. 142) and family-run businesses, all side-by-side along a tourist strip that sees hordes of visitors in a day. It is one of the most popular tourist spots in the world, but still manages to retain so much charm. Nakamise Dōri runs all the way up to the Hōzōmon ('treasure house') gate and Sensō-ji (p. 334), so allow yourself to get carried along by the crowd and its melting pot of cultures, creeds, languages and smiling, eager faces, all with the glorious temple in their sights.

Sensō-ji is Tokyo's oldest temple, and the old-world streets and establishments surrounding it make Asakusa a prime spot for a taste of Tokyo's deep past. The temple boasts a huge lantern at the Hōzōmon gate, as well as frightening statues, a towering pagoda and even some small Shinto shrines (which, considering that it's a Buddhist temple, shows a true spirit of peace). Explore the area; there are small shrines (Chingo-do, the Raccoon Dog Temple, is a delight) and many shops and food stalls worth your patronage, as well as vistas to show off your photography skills.

Kokeshi rice crackers on Nakamise Dōri (left); Hōzōmon ('treasure house') gate (right); Chingo-do and Sensō-ji (opposite)

Behind the temple you'll find Hanayashiki (p. 158), an amusement park from 1853 that has a definite fifties-to-eighties feel about it now, a worthwhile stop for anyone into faded retro glamour and Tokyo super-cute. Dotted about the streets are plenty of fabric and *yukata* (summer kimono) shops, *ukiyo-e* woodblock prints and opportunities to get a ride on a rickshaw pulled by an energetic youth. From here, head west, back towards Asakusa Station, to Kappabashi Dōri, or Kitchen Town, the street dedicated to all things cooking and food. Once you cross Kokusai Dōri, slip down Shinso Dōri; you'll be able to tell you're going in the right direction by the statues and signs featuring *kappa*, a salamander-like creature from Japanese folklore. You'll know Kappabashi when you hit it. If you come via the start of the street, the giant chef's-head statue gives it away.

If you approach it from elsewhere, there are still plenty of stores with kettles, pots and pans, ceramics and cookware spilling out onto the street to signal that you have arrived in kitchenware heaven. If you need themed wax paper, plastic samples of food to put in your window, expensive knives and cutlery, *noren* curtains for your entryway, gigantic pots for making ramen broth, Japanese-themed cookie cutters, bamboo steamers, chef uniforms ... well, you get the idea. There's nowhere in the world that will make you want to open your own restaurant like this street. It's a pilgrimage for chefs and cooks the world over, and a joy for amateurs, too.

If you have any energy left after this trek, head to nearby Kuramae (p. 165) for a taste of how modern makers and crafters are reviving an old-school suburb. ⊗

Hakujitsu, Sugita and Kabuki (top left to right); Hakujitsu, SyuRo and Kabuki (middle left to right); Kakimori and Eikyudo (bottom left and right)

KURAMAE WALK

Asakusa, Kappabashi Dōri and Kuramae form a triangle of sorts, so any one can be reached easily from another. Kuramae is a good afternoon stroll: an older part of Tokyo that is having its own revival as younger makers and small cafés pop up among the quiet suburban streets. Get off at Kuramae Station and head to Yorimiti (1-21-2 Honjo, www.yorimiti.co) or Sugita (3-8-3 Kotobuki) for lunch. Yorimiti serves home-style lunches on beautiful ceramics that you can buy from the store. Sugita elevates *tonkatsu* (fried pork cutlet) to new heights. Vegequarians rejoice, as they also have *ebi* (prawn) *tonkatsu* on the menu.

From here, head south to Camera (4-21-8 Kuramae, camera1010.tokyo) for coffee and a fine selection of handicrafts and homewares. The stunning Nakamura Tea Life store (4-20-4 Kuramae, tea-nakamura.com) is just a short stroll down the road. Heading east towards the river, Kokusai Dōri features Proto (Seika Building 2F, 4-20-12 Kuramae, proto-art.stores.jp), for artful homewares, and Maito (4-14-12 Kuramae, maitokomuro.com), who specialise in hand-dyed textiles. Don't miss the old-school Eikyudo *wagashi* (traditional sweets; p. 124) store, established in 1887 and still selling delectable *dorayaki* (red-bean pancakes), *yōkan* (red-bean jelly) and *daifuku* (rice cakes filled with red-bean paste) today.

A right turn into Kuramaebashi Dōri will take you towards the heart of Kuramae. Drop into Yohaku (2-2-7 Torigoe, cnq-yohaku.com) for casual clothing made from quality fabrics. Anyone into stationery can't miss nearby Kakimori (p. 212). Choose your favourite paper and they'll bind it into a book for you onsite, and the range of pens here will make you want to go back to writing by hand. SyuRo (1-16-5 Torigoe, syuro.info) is a must-visit: a design store housed in a beautiful old warehouse space. Pop around the corner and seek out the secret treasure that is Kabuki (1-15-7 Torigoe, kabukiyusuke.com). Here they pair coffee with small, rich slabs of chocolate – the best of both worlds. Not far to the west is Okazu Yokochō ('side-dish alley'; 1-9 Torigoe), a street which still retains the spirit of the fifties and sixties, when it was established. Small pop-up food stalls line this charming little strip.

The Misuji-yu bathhouse (2-13-2 Misuji) is the perfect place for a quick soak. This should give you enough energy to head back east towards the river and pop up the stairs to the magical gallery and shop Hakujitsu (1-7-7 Yanagibashi) to peruse their range of sourced and repurposed Japanese vintage. ⊗

RYŌGOKU
ワイド特集 春場所 五つの見どころ
三横綱それぞれの「決戦前夜」
旭富士・小錦「綱取り」の秘策
5時半から「嵐を呼ぶ男」逆鉾
ほか
ホット対談
二子山勝治
VS
児島襄
大相撲懸賞クイズ
相撲
あっぱれ金剛
大鵬（V32）を追って初場所V23を飾る
力士座談会／クラフ特集・新弟子

——— You don't have to be into sumo wrestling to visit Ryōgoku, but it helps. Home to the famous Ryōgoku Kokugikan sumo hall (p. 173), an 11,000-capacity stadium built in 1985, this is the place to see sumo in training roaming the streets and cramming their voluminous bodies into *chankonabe* (p. 171) restaurants – slightly more spacious than the usual Tokyo eatery.

The original Kokugikan was built in 1909 but was, like many Tokyo landmarks, severely damaged in bombing raids during the Second World War. Because of this, sumo tournaments were held on the grounds of the Meiji Shrine (p. 334) as late as 1954, when another stadium opened in Taitō. This sumo hall operated until 1984, closing to make way for the new Kokugikan. The main tournaments are held in January, May and September, and anyone wanting to see a bout or two should plan carefully, as the times are very specific. However, the stadium features a museum and gift shop that are open whether there are events on or not, so definitely go in for a browse even if you aren't taking in a match.

There is plenty of sumo culture to enjoy outside of the stadium, too. Just strolling the forecourt is a great experience; shrines are laid out along the front and if you're lucky, you might see a sumo or two leaving the stadium, sports bags in hand. Next to Ryōgoku Station is a food hall, a souvenir market with a stage for sumo guest spots, and a small sumo ring in which kids (or embarrassing grown-ups) can practise their moves.

The backstreets are a must for anyone seeking out the sumo food of choice, *chankonabe*, a tasty hotpot crowded with protein and vegetables designed to keep up the sumos' (and your) strength. Expect pieces of chicken, chicken and beef meatballs, seafood and fish in various guises (scallops, clams, salmon and tuna are all popular), yuba (rings of sliced tofu skin), tofu, cabbage and root vegetables (especially daikon), all served in a side dish next to a cauldron of broth that bubbles excitedly in anticipation. You can protein-load by having one *chankonabe* to yourself, but we opt to share one serving, as they are seriously massive. The hardworking sumo wrestler, however, would happily down two servings on his own – and several shots of liquid encouragement along with it. *Chankonabe* is a meal to be reckoned with: warming, restorative and life-affirming sustenance; a challenge and a revelation. Just one thing – you're going to need to walk it off.

Ryōgoku boasts several sightseeing claims to fame that actually have very little to do with sumo wrestlers, so you can walk to these and get some of that *chankonabe* moving through your system. The Edo-Tokyo Museum (p. 360) is a must-see for anyone wanting to explore the Tokyo of days gone by. The museum, built in 1993, has a life-size replica of the Nihonbashi ('Japan Bridge'), a wooden bridge that connected the road from Kyoto to Tokyo during the Edo period, as well as historical artefacts and scale models of Edo buildings. (Its sister museum in Koganei, the Edo-Tokyo Open Air Architectural Museum, p. 360, features reconstructed historic buildings from the Edo period and Meiji era.)

Vintage sumo magazines (opposite)

Fans of the iconic Japanese print *The Great Wave off Kanagawa* will want to check out the Sumida Hokusai Museum (p. 363). One of the shiny new additions to the area, it presents the best of the old world and the new. Edo-period artist Katsushika Hokusai was born and lived most of his life in the area, and in 2016 architect Sejima Kazuyo designed this structural homage to the master printmaker so he could be celebrated in his hometown. The building rises from the ground like a squat sheet-metal insect about to take flight – a glinting steel block that could be the letters H and M fused together, or perhaps an abstract rendition of the Great Wave itself. Either way, it's a striking addition to the landscape.

Fans of tobacco and salt should check out the nearby Tobacco and Salt Museum (p. 365). This 100-yen museum has some great information on both Japanese and foreign salt, a 1.4-ton piece of rock salt and a replica of the Polish St. Kinga statue, carved in rock salt. So much salt, so little time! There is also a surprisingly premium selection of posters and photos relating to tobacco, smoking and the history of smoking in Japan. There are some true treasures, including stunning *ukiyo-e* woodblock prints featuring people smoking, selling or making tobacco and some vintage handicrafts like tobacco pouches, pipes, smoking paraphernalia and cigarette packets. You'll have to go outside if you want to smoke, though.

Just around the corner from the Sumida Hokusai Museum you'll find Edoyu (8-5-1 Kamezawa, edoyu.com). This upmarket *onsen* (hot spring) is the perfect place to relax and unwind if you've downed a few bowls of *chankonabe* or tired out your legs strolling through museums and exhibitions. Edoyu is a stylish *onsen* set over five floors. There are nine baths, all with radium water, including a hinoki cypress bath. One of the standout features is a rock sauna, where you lie on hot rocks in a steaming room. Just remember that this is a no-nude zone. The relaxation rooms are super cosy; you can bundle yourself up in an ultra-soft blanket and lie back, watch television or catch forty winks.

Ryōgoku is also known for its sweet tooth. A stroll around the area gives you plenty of opportunities to try some of Tokyo's best traditional and Western-style cakes, confectionery, parfaits and ice creams. Sample the delightful and the intriguing, from the towering shaved-ice mountains of *kakigōri*, to delectable multi-layered parfait creations. Discover your own favourite treat, whether it's *dorayaki* (red-bean pancakes), *dango* (rice-flour dumplings), *mochi* (rice cakes) or one of the many other Japanese-style sweet experiences on offer. Echigoya Wakasa (p. 129) is a famous *wagashi* (traditional sweets; p. 124) shop operating since the 1700s and is renowned for its *yōkan*, a red-bean jelly often imprinted with leaves and other seasonal emblems.

From Ryōgoku we reconnect with Asakusa (p. 154), where Philippe Stark's Asahi Beer Hall (1-23-1 Azumabashi) sits on the outskirts of the two areas. The top of the Asahi building is home to the Flamme d'Or, or Asahi Flame – one of those classic architecture-meets-design inventions that has divided the community and gained enough notoriety to become a national icon.

Sumida Hokusai Museum (opposite top); Ryōgoku Kokugikan (opposite bottom right)

The golden structure, which resembles a squeezed-out blob of toothpaste, attempts to evoke the image of foam on top of a beer. Resulting 'poo' and 'sperm' comparisons suggest that it wasn't 100 per cent successful. It's certainly an arresting visual, and appears to stand proudly next to the towering Tokyo Skytree (in reality, the Skytree is around 600 metres away). Snap-happy travellers can't get enough of it. Anyone wishing to capture this skyline-meets-surrealist-art moment should note that, although the buildings are on the Ryōgoku side of the river, the best shots can be taken from just over the bridge in Asakusa (p. 154).

If you do cross the bridge for a better view, Tokyo Skytree (p. 161) can be reached easily from here – just grab the Tobu Line from Asakusa Station and go one short stop to Tokyo Skytree Station. The Skytree shuttle also runs from Haneda Airport, Odaiba, Tokyo Disneyland and from Ueno, Wakōshi and Tokyo stations. It's also an easy walk from Oshiage Station.

FIVE OF THE CHUNKIEST CHANKONABE

Chanko Shibamatsu
3-12-19 Nakameguro
Meguro 153-0061
shibamatsu.co.jp
This hearty *chanko* can be ordered with a miso broth, making it lighter than a regular *chanko* and giving it a delicious flavour spin. Chunks of cabbage, mushroom, tofu, *yuba* (rings of sliced tofu skin) and fish- and chicken-balls complete these bowls of hearty goodness.

Chanko Tomoegata
2-17-6 Ryōgoku
Sumida 130-0026
tomoegata.com
Tomoegata is a rambunctious, friendly place and provides the perfect atmosphere to experience the robust nature of *chankonabe*. Look for the picturesque stacks of sake barrels outside and head in to find a small shrine to all things sumo – almost a tiny sumo museum –which gives the entrance a very authentic feel.

Kawasaki Chanko
2-13-1 Ryōgoku
Sumida 130-0026
Kawasaki Chanko was opened in 1937 and still serves up delicious bowls of hefty *chankonabe* to locals – and to the sumo wrestlers who inhabit the nearby 'stables'. Former sumo wrestler Yokoteyama opened this restaurant in order to put a smile on everyone's face. The straightforward *chanko* here is a must for purists and the beaming sign out the front will instantly put you in a good mood.

Kotoguame
Sagara Building 1F
3-4-4 Kinshi
Sumida 130-0013
www13.plala.or.jp/kotogaume
Kotoguame Tsuyoshi is another former sumo wrestler who decided to stay in the business by opening this more sophisticated *chankonabe* must-visit. The popular dish here is the *suisho nabe*, or crystal hotpot, a thinner soup with a salty bite that is stuffed with the usual suspects, which Kotoguame says goes well with a sake or two.

Tokitsunada
Kanda Goro Building 1F
1-21 Kanda-Nishikichō
Chiyoda 101-0054
tokitsunada.net
Former top-division sumo wrestler Tokitsunada Hironori moved from fighting to food when he came out from 'inside the curtain'. Tokitsunada stayed in the business by perfecting a hearty stew. Head in and savour the bubbling bowl of joy. You will be rubbing enormous shoulders with hungry post-match or post-training sumos, aspiring sumo wrestlers, and, if you're lucky, Tokitsunada himself.

For more detail on *chankonabe*, see p. 99.

Chanko Tomoegata (above); Edo-Tokyo Museum (opposite)

SUMO WRESTLING

Steeped in tradition, with its formation reaching far back into history, sumo has become one of Japan's emblematic cultural experiences. Three out of the six yearly tournaments are held in Tokyo, and it is a sport like few others: a trial-by-combat test of strength and tactics, with ritualistic elements that are every bit as important as the wrestling itself. These include the Shinto-inspired salt-purification ceremony, the tassled Shinto-shrine roof that hangs suspended over the ring, and sumo wrestlers' highly regimented diet and lifestyle.

On the surface, the rules are simple: force your opponent out of a small ring, or get him off his feet and onto the ground. It's the nuances that make sumo so intriguing. The ceremony, the tense lead-up, the cat-and-mouse game of launching into the clinch, the slight differences in tactics: it all adds to the overall intensity of the sport.

The match itself might last seconds – few go over a minute or two. The *kimarite*, or winning move, is assessed by the referee and announced to the audience, who will applaud with appreciation. By the way, it's an automatic disqualification if your belt comes undone, so sumo also have to make sure they are trussed up to perfection.

Once a sumo has worked his way up the ranks by beating opponents, he attains the rank of *yokozuna*, or grand champion. It's a hard road to get there, though; most aspects of a sumo wrestler's life are controlled. They live in *heya*, or sumo 'stables', and have disciplined diets and strict training regimes. The sumo meal of choice is a hefty form of *nabe* (p. 98) known as *chankonabe* (p. 167), and it is delicious, so make sure that you get in on the act and order a bowl (p. 171).

Unlike most sports, you can take in your own snacks and sake. Audiences tend to mill around, getting intensely involved in one match and then wandering off to buy some snacks (sold at a premium, of course) or peruse walls of previous *yokozuna*.

TOURNAMENTS

There are three Grand Sumo Tournaments held at the Ryōgoku Kokugikan in Sumida: Hatsu Basho in January, Natsu Basho in May, and Aki Basho in September. Ticket prices vary, but can get very expensive for good seats. Try to find last-minute deals for the best prices and take your own food and booze. Otherwise, you can watch sumo on television; matches are covered in detail and we gained real insights into the sport by watching televised matches and news reports. Pick your own sumo champion and follow his progress!

If you're not in Japan during the Grand Tournaments, you can catch non-tournament or exhibition matches, which you can learn about from the Japan Sumo Association website (sumo.or.jp). It's also possible to visit one of the many stables in Ryōgoku to see young sumo training.

SUMO MUSEUM

Located in the Ryōgoku Kokugikan sumo stadium, the museum is free, but during the three Grand Sumo Tournaments in January, May and September it can only be accessed by visitors with tickets to a tournament event. Historical sumo artefacts and pictures of previous fighters and past tournaments adorn the walls of the museum. If you can't get in, the visitors' centre attached to Ryōgoku Station has some great sumo-related pieces and sumo-themed gifts.

Sumo souvenirs

- Bath salts
- Figurines
- Rice crackers
- Shot glasses
- Stationery
- Textiles with sumo prints
- Washi tape

WHERE TO SEE SUMO WRESTLING

Ryōgoku Kokugikan

1-3-28 Yokoami
Sumida 130-0015
sumo.or.jp/kokugikan

SUMO SHRINES

Ekō-in

2-8-10 Ryōgoku
Sumida 130-0026
Tournaments were held in the grounds of the Ekō-in Buddhist temple before 1909. A short stroll from Ryōgoku Station, fans can visit the temple's monument that serves as a memorial to previous wrestlers.

Tomioka Hachimangū

1-20-3 Tomioka
Kōtō 135-0047
Not far from Ryōgoku you'll find Tomioka, the site where sumo tournaments were held in the Edo period. There are many monuments on the grounds and a small 'treasure house' that features old woodblock prints of sumo wrestlers in action.

UENO

——— Historically, Ueno was part of the Shitamachi ('under city') area of Tokyo, where the working class worked and lived. It still retains much of this feeling today: Ameya-Yokochō's (6-11 Ueno, ameyoko.net) winding streets have a seedy charm, along with cheap eats and cheaper merchandise. Unsavoury-looking bars, clubs and pachinko parlours sit side by side with affordable eateries popular among locals. It's this rough-and-ready charm – and potential to nab a bargain – that makes this area something of a tourist attraction, and you'll find a melting pot of international visitors here, as well as a sizeable chunk of Tokyo's immigrant population. At night, Ameya-Yokochō is a riot of colour and sound: paper menus plastered to walls, the ping-ping of slot machines, and hawkers beckoning you to food stalls, clothes shops or more sinister, mysterious venues up gaudily lit stairs.

In contrast, Ueno Park (Reno Park exit, JR Ueno Station 110-0005) is a peaceful patch of green that holds some of Tokyo's most memorable cultural experiences. Ensconced within Ueno Park you'll find the National Museum of Western Art (p. 354), a Brutalist–modernist hybrid designed by Le Corbusier that is considered his only work in East Asia. Also of note are the National Museum of Nature and Science (p. 362) and Ueno Zoo (9-83 Uenokōen, www.tokyo-zoo.net/english/ueno), distinguished by its huddle of super-cute pandas and its five-storey pagoda, one of three surviving remnants of the park's original temple buildings from 1625. Ueno Park is a prime spot for *hanami* (flower viewing; p. 76) and couples flock there during *sakura* (cherry blossom) season to eat pink soft-serve ice creams and paddle around Shinobazu Pond in swan boats. In autumn, the *Ginkgo biloba* trees shed their canopies of fan-shaped leaves.

Swan boats on Shinobazu Pond, Ueno Park (opposite)

Kiyomizu Kannon-dō temple (top); Ueno Park *sakura* festivities (bottom)

Ameya-Yokochō (top left); Ueno Park *sakura* street stalls and festivities (middle left, top right); National Museum of Western Art (bottom)

TOP KOMBINI BUYS

Forget everything you know about convenience stores. *Kombini* in Japan are convenience stores in the true sense of the word, because they are actually convenient. You can get almost any basic you need. They say you can't have fast, cheap and good, but the things you can buy in a *kombini* really do fit that brief.

It's actually fun to visit a convenience store in Tokyo. Visit enough of them and you'll be able to pick your favourite chain: whether it be 7-Eleven, with its excellent homebrand range and international ATMs; Lawson and its health-conscious sister store Natural Lawson, which boasts a great range of vegetarian food; or the always-friendly Family Mart, with its premium hot-food selection. Cute retro *kombini* like Circle K, Sunkus, Daily Yamazaki or Mini Stop all have their own edge, too. In fact, you could make a day of touring Tokyo's *kombini* and discover something about Tokyo along the way: what people want is considered important – and meeting their needs is good for business. So let's talk about some of the best *kombini* buys.

1. BOOZE (& OTHER DRINKS)

The range of alcoholic drinks in a *kombini* is staggering, and all at a price point for the people. Stocking up before a Shinkansen (bullet train) adventure or just loading up on supplies before bunkering in after a hard day? A *kombini* has you covered. If you don't feel like sinking a few, there is an equally large range of non-alcoholic drinks as well.

2. HEALTH SHOTS

If you've raided the booze section the night before, chances are the next day you'll need a pick-me-up – and the *kombini* is on to it (although for serious hangover cures, hit the pharmacy, as they have a great range – see p. 222). Vitamin C drinks, collagen shots, acidophilus shots, and even the 'fibre mini' for when you're feeling less than regular.

3. CHOCOLATE

Japanese chocolate is less sweet, rich and milky than what you might be used to. There are plenty of seasonal varieties and flavours to try, and once you get into it you might even notice that your favourite chocolate bar at home tastes that little bit too sweet. Dars is creamy and Crunky Balls are addictive. Kit Kats come in many strange flavours (p. 133) and Meiji do a thin, very light slice of heaven.

4. ONIGIRI

The perfect on-the-go snack or lunchtime health hit, *onigiri* are rice balls, usually covered in a crispy wrap of seaweed and filled with salmon, tuna, sweet plum or egg, although there are plenty of variations to choose from. They are handheld delights that satisfy every time.

5. HOT COFFEE

If you find yourself in need of a shot of caffeine, *kombini* usually sell a pretty decent cup to get you by until you find that perfect Tokyo brewhouse. If you just need a drink of something strong and sweet, try the canned coffee. There are so many varieties available, and most of them can also be nabbed in vending machines around town.

6. SNACKS

Convenience stores are snack central, and Japanese snacks tend to be more nutritious, more varied and definitely more interesting than any other. Steamed buns with delicious centres, fried chicken (heated for you and served with a bed of fluffy rice) and a large variety of delectable salads will fill any void. Assorted rice crackers, potato chips, veggie chips, wasabi peas, an absurd range of cup noodles ... the list goes on. Stock up for the day.

7. BENTŌ & PRE-MADE MEALS

If you can't gather the energy to go out (or cook) after a full day of sightseeing, shopping and eating, the selection of *bentō* and pre-made meals are a great dinner option. They might be microwaveable or they might be a fresh salad. For the price, if you need a meal on the go, they'll do the trick.

8. ODEN

This is the assortment of goodies that you will see stewing in the *kombini* bain-marie. Many a visitor has seen it and thought, 'I'm not touching that,' but it's actually just cooked vegetables, meat, fish and eggs all bubbling away happily in broth, like you might have at home. It's kept super-fresh – it hasn't been left there to steep all day. The eggs are particularly good.

9. CLOTHING & ACCESSORIES

Put a fresh spin on it! You can get a change of clothes and some accessories, plus personal grooming products like deodorant, hair gel, lip gloss, body spray, pomade ... you get the gist. If you've pulled an all-nighter, stock up in a convenience store and then head to the pharmacy for a liver tonic and some much-needed eye drops.

10. ICE CREAM

Westerners who don't want to step out of their comfort zone will find a recognisable ice cream or two among the Tokyo tasties, but we think a *matcha* (green tea) ice cream or some Pino minis will hit the spot.

BONUS BUYS

Locals grab the latest manga or something from the great range of magazines to read while travelling to and from work. To add to the convenience, you can also buy tickets for shows, concerts, Tokyo Disneyland, the Ghibli Museum (p. 362) and more. It's fast and easy and, well ... convenient!

YANAKA, NEZU & SENDAGI

You won't find skyscrapers, tower blocks, department stores or masses of shoppers and workers cramming Yanaka's peaceful streets. It's a place where locals stroll or bike around, popping into shrines. The area has many small family-owned eateries (there are lots of privately owned stores in Yanaka, and old-style vendors line the streets), street food, traditional paper stores and new kids with an eye for good food and coffee and a keen understanding of history, tradition and atmosphere. Small pockets of old Tokyo live on here, and if you are staying in the area (new hostels and boutique hotels continue to pop up) it's close to Asakusa (p. 154), Ueno (p. 174) and more tranquil, time-honoured areas, so hire a bike and explore – and get ready to uncover the true spirit of old Edo.

Yanaka street scenes (above); Nezu Shrine (opposite)

With Nezu Jinja (Nezu Shrine, p. 184) as its centrepiece, Yanaka is a tranquil pocket of Tokyo, a place for a gentle saunter through history and home to old-world confectionery and paper stores and newer side-street fashion and vintage outlets. Yanaka is part of Tokyo's historical Shitamachi ('under city') area, which was, as the name suggests, Tokyo's original downtown. Having survived the bombing raids of the Second World War, Yanaka is unique in that it remained intact as an entire town, not just a building here and there, giving its visitors an opportunity to discover some genuine relics of prewar Tokyo.

There are hundreds of small temples and sacred pockets hiding in quiet corners, between shops and buildings or in gardens and groves. Yanaka Cemetery (7-5-24 Yanaka) and the Nezu Shrine are authentic Edo-period Tokyo, while the backstreets offer many examples of where and how the citizens of old Tokyo used to live, eat and shop. Yūyake Dandan (3-13 Nishi-Nippori), or the Sunset Steps, allows visitors a chance to be bathed in the golden glow of the setting sun. Cat-lovers note: Yanaka is also known as 'cat town', and you'll see *kawaii neko* ('cute cats') curled up asleep or prowling the streets and lanes, as well as in various guises as souvenirs in shops along Yanaka Ginza (3-13-1 Yanaka).

Yanaka Cemetery (left); Yanaka street details (right); Nezu Shrine (opposite)

YA-NE-SEN WALK

Ya-Ne-Sen is short for Yanaka, Nezu and Sendagi, three little pockets of Tokyo that offer a treasure trove of Edo-period shrines, craft shops, tiny eateries, gardens, galleries and one of the most beautiful cemeteries you are likely to see.

Catch the Hanzamon Line to Tokyo Metro Nezu Station to visit the Nezu Shrine (1-28-9 Nezu, Bunkyō). On the walk from the station to the shrine you'll pass traditional houses, potted gardens, coffee and craft stores. A wander through the shrine in any season is a totally relaxing and spiritual experience. This is one of Tokyo's most beautiful cultural places, and is a favourite of ours for its timeless beauty, red *torii* gates, fox statues and the beautiful white and blue outfits of the priests (if you are lucky enough to see any wandering the grounds).

If all of the cultural beauty has left you peckish, exit the shrine and walk northeast towards Sendagi Station and pop into Bakery Muira (2-2-15 Sendagi) for morning tea and a pastry. Alternatively, you can double back to Nezu Station, stopping in at Taiyaki of Nezu (1-23-9 Nezu) for the ultimate take on the classic fish-shaped sweet pastry before catching the train one stop to Sendagi.

From Sendagi Station, cross the road to the main street, where you will find some wonderful indie stores. Isetatsu (2-18-9 Yanaka, isetatsu.com) has a beautiful array of Edo-period paper. The striking ruins of Tennō-ji Pagoda (7-9-6 Yanaka) and the small but beautiful temple Daienji (3-1-2 Yanaka) are just some of the many sacred spiritual sites that dot this neighbourhood. Hire a bike from Tokyobike (4-2-39 Yanaka, tokyobikerentals.com) and explore the area. Stop for a pick-me-up at Yanaka Coffee (2-31-3 Yanaka, yanaka-coffeeten.com) and grab lunch at popular newcomer Cibi (3-37-11 Sendagi, cibi.jp), then peruse their perfectly curated selection of homewares.

This area is known for wandering stray cats, and has many stores and cafés with a *neko*, or cat, theme. Try Neko-e-mon (5-4-2 Yanaka, yanakado.com/c_nekoemon.html), where everything is cat-themed, including super-cute cat signage.

Wander south down to Scai the Bathhouse (p. 365) for an art fix, then keep walking until you get to the Shitamachi Museum Annex at the Yoshidaya Liquor Shop (2-10-6 Uenosakuragi) and admire the historical relics of centuries of drinking culture. Then pop into the impressively retro *kissaten* (European-style coffee house; p. 142) Kayaba Coffee (p. 143) for an afternoon bean fix.

Follow your tracks back up the hill until you get to Yanaka Cemetery (7-5-24 Yanaka). If you are in Tokyo for cherry-blossom season, wait until the petals start to fall and visit the cemetery when '*sakura* snow' floats down and covers the walkways and gardens. The soft pink petals resting on the graves is a sight to behold. Novelist Ichiyo Higuchi and Yoshinobu Tokugawa, Japan's last shogun, are two of the many prominent people buried here.

After a contemplative stroll and a meditation on the fleeting nature of life, walk north towards Nippori Station, visiting the Asakura Museum of Sculpture (p. 363) and its beautiful garden, and stopping to browse at tiny stores that have been run by the same families for decades along the way. You could also make a quick detour and visit the Kannon-ji mud wall (5-8-28 Yanaka) for a serious look at Edo-period history.

End your walk at Nippori Station, or take a walk down Yanaka Ginza (3-13-1 Yanaka). If you are a fabric-lover, you'll want to spend a bit of time in and around Nippori, as this is *the* fabric centre of Tokyo. Grab a Nippori map and visit the amazing stores devoted to textiles and material. You may just need two days to do all of this! ⊗

Asakura Museum of Sculpture (right); Yanaka street scenes

CATS, CATS, CATS

As an enduring symbol of luck (and cuteness), the cat, or *neko* in Japanese, is wildly popular in Tokyo. Most Tokyoites lack the room and the time a pet requires, so the cat-obsessed will usually go to one of Tokyo's many cat cafés to get their much-needed fluffy fix. These cafés aren't just cat-themed: they actually have resident cats living there, pampered bundles of fluff that you can pat and talk to (but not pick up). The cat café is a popular destination for locals as well as visitors, who can usually be sorted into one of two groups: those who are missing their own beast back home, and those wanting to get in on that Tokyo cute overload.

Feline characters, items, shops and even bars are fairly common, especially ones featuring the lucky cat, or *maneki neko* – the cat sitting with its left (or, less often, right) paw raised. Stroll down Cat Street (p. 241) from Shibuya to Omotesandō, visit Kiddy Land for cat-themed toys, or find some cat-pattern socks on Takeshita Dōri. Something you'll often see on cars and boxes in Tokyo is the Yamato Transport logo: a cat holding a kitten in its mouth. So *kawaii*.

Maneki neko at Gōtoku-ji

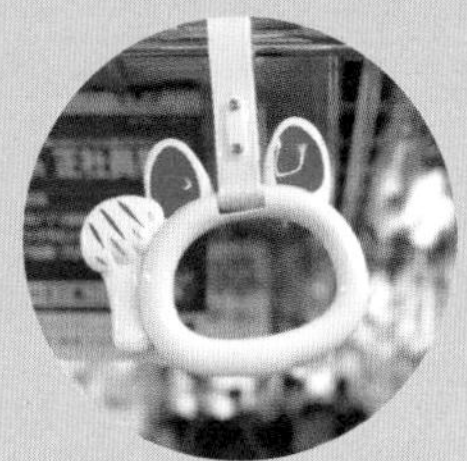

CATS IN JAPANESE POP CULTURE

Cat characters, such as Hello Kitty and Pokémon's Meowth are perennial favourites in both Japan and the West; others are sensations in Japan but haven't quite made the jump across the oceans. Doraemon, for instance, is one of Japan's most treasured anime heroes. This blue robot kitty is highly popular among Japanese children, and often remains fondly in their hearts and minds throughout their lives.

CAT-THEMED ANIME

- *Bananya* (2016), dir. Kyō Yatate (b. 1982)
- *Doraemon* (1973, 1979, 2005–present)
- *Kanojo to Kanojo no Neko: Everything Flows* (2016), dir. Kazuya Sakamoto
- *Natsume Yūjinchō* (*Natsume's Book of Friends*; 2008–2017), dir Takahiro Omori (b. 1965) and Kotomi Deai
- *Neko no Onegaeshi* (*The Cat Returns*; 2002), dir. Hiroyuki Morita (b. 1964)
- *Tokyo Mew Mew* (2002–2003), dir. Noriyuki Abe (b. 1961)

THINGS WE LOVE

CAT BARS

Bar Neko
Ueno-Hirokōji Building 3F
2-8-7 Ueno
Taitō 110-0005
facebook.com/ueno.bar.neko

A cosy bar with a feline host.

Samurai
Mori Building 5F
3-35-5 Shinjuku
Shinjuku 160-0022
jazzbar.business.site

A jazz bar with 1000-plus vintage *maneki neko* (lucky cats).

CAT CAFÉS

Cat Café Cateriam
Mont Blanc Building 2F
2-26-6 Kitazawa
Setagaya 155-0031
cateriam.com

Enjoy one of their adorable cat-themed lattes.

Cat Café MoCHA
Assorti Shibuya 8F
32-12 Udagawachō
Shibuya 150-0042
Cross Avenue Harajuku 4F
1-14-25 Jingūmae
Shibuya 150-0001
catmocha.jp

Cat Café Nyanny
4-8-3 Soto-Kanda
Chiyoda 101-0021
catcafe-akiba.com

Temarino-Oshiro
Kichijoji Petit Mura
2-33-2 Kichijōji-Honchō
Musashino 180-0004
temarinooshiro.com

A village designed to look as though it was built by cats, including a café, stores and petting facilities.

Temarino-Ouchi
Musashi Forum III 3F
2-13-14 Kichijōji-Honchō
Musashino 180-0004
temarinoouchi.com

CAT-THEMED FOOD

Café de Kuroneko-sha
6-30-1 Arakawa
Arakawa 116-0002
cafedekns.blog.fc2.com
Not a café with cats, but a café with cat-themed food.

Floresta Nature Donuts
3-34-14 Kōenji-Kita
Suginami 166-0002
nature-doughnuts.jp/shop/018_koenji
Super-cute cat-themed donuts.

Oshiage Nyanko
3-10-9 Oshiage
Sumida 131-0045
oshiagebunko.com
More cat-themed latte art!

CAT HAVENS

Keio Plaza Hotel
2-2-1 Nishi-Shinjuku
Shinjuku 160-8330
keioplaza.com/rooms/kitty.html
The Keio Plaza Hotel has a selection of Hello Kitty rooms.

Sanrio Puroland
1-31 Ochiai
Tama 206-8588
en.puroland.jp
This theme park is also a must for lovers of iconic cat character Hello Kitty.

Yanaka cats
Yanaka (p. 180) is a beautiful neighbourhood known for its street cats. Yanaka Cemetery (p. 183) and Yanaka Ginza (3-13-1 Yanaka) are famous cat-watching spots.

CAT SHRINES

Gōtoku-ji
(p. 334)

Gōtoku-ji is said to be the birthplace of the *maneki neko*. Legend tells of the feudal lord Naotaka Ii, who was sheltering under a tree in a storm when he saw a white cat waving to him from the tiny temple. The lord entered the temple, and seconds later the tree was struck by lightning. He realised that the cat had saved his life and had the temple rebuilt in spectacular fashion. This shrine to cats will bring you great luck, and has the best *maneki neko* to purchase and take home with you. Add a paw print–covered floor and cat handles to hold onto as you walk, and you're in heaven. We caught the cat train to Gōtoku-ji; we're hoping its popularity will make it a permanent fixture.

Imado Jinja
(p. 334)

Asakusa Jinja (Shinto shrine)
2-26-1 Asakusa
Taitō 111-0032
www.asakusajinja.jp/english

CAT SHOPPING

Tokyu Hands, Kiddy Land and Loft stores stock cat-themed stationery. Cat socks can be found in and around Center Gai in Shibuya (23 Udagawachō) or Sunshine City in Ikebukuro (3-1-1 Higashi-Ikebukuro); Tabio Socks (multiple locations) also occasionally theme it up.

Lucky You!
2-17-6 Kichijōji-Honchō
Musashino 180-0004

If you're a feline fan, there are many ways to combine your love for cats with your trip to Tokyo

Read the famous Meiji-era novel Wagahai wa Neko de Aru (I Am a Cat; 1905) by Sōseki Natsume (1867–1916)

Read Haruki Murakami's The Wind-up Bird Chronicle (1995), which features a cat named Noboru Wataya

Visit the maneki neko (lucky cat) street sculpture out the front of Muji in Shibuya (B1F, 21-1 Udagawachō)

Drink a cat beer or two – look out for Suiyōbi no Neko ('Wednesday cat'), the beer with a cat on its label

If you're visiting the Ghibli Museum (p. 362), catch the Nekobasu (cat bus) from Mitaka Station

Watch Studio Ghibli's Neko no Onegaeshi (The Cat Returns; 2002), dir. Hiroyuki Morita (b. 1964)

Temarino-Oshiro cat café; Michelle and a Floresta donut; Temarino-Oshiro entrance (clockwise from top left)

CENTRAL TOKYO

Tokyo Station and the circle of suburbs radiating out from it mark a centre of sorts in a city without an exact centre. The area encompasses the cultural delights of the Imperial Palace and its garden (p. 340), the Kabuki-za theatre (p. 368) and Tokyo Station, which is almost a city in itself. Ginza and Marunouchi's high-end shopping, Akihabara's electronic wonderland, and the books district of Jimbōchō also come under its expansive sphere.

TOKYO; GINZA; JIMBŌCHŌ; AKIHABARA

THE MEIJI ERA (1868–1912), P. 32; THE TAISHŌ ERA (1912–1926), P.36;
EARLY SHŌWA ERA (1926–1989), P. 40

Central Tokyo is where twentieth-century Tokyo came into its own. It flourished during a time when the Japanese looked to the West for inspiration, while maintaining their own unique take on the world. You'll find some great examples of European-influenced and modernist architecture here: the Tokyo Station building (p. 198); the Wako (p. 203), Takashimaya (p. 251) and Mitsukoshi (p. 194) department stores; the Nakagin Capsule Tower (p. 349); and the Shiseido Building (p. 365), to name just a few. Open ports and the industry and trade that came from them brought a wealth of new ideas to the growing metropolis. Banks, boulevards, and retail were the area's defining features. Certain wards became known as destinations to buy specialist items – books, pickles, kimono, fish, electronics – and the crowds started flocking. All this, along with a travel hub – Tokyo Station – that connected the capital with the rest of the country, made central Tokyo one of the city's most important spaces. It was a nexus for new ideas, and after the devastation of the Second World War, it rose from the ashes to form the core for new beginnings.

TOKYO

The Yamanote Line opened in 1885 and made central Tokyo easily accessible. It's still the most popular train line in the city, and you can make like a mid-century Tokyoite and jump on and off at the stations of Yūrakuchō, Tokyo and Akihabara for a taste of what old and new central Tokyo has to offer.

——— Tokyo the city – not to be confused with Tokyo the capital – is a vast area that sprawls out from Tokyo Station's mad hive of activity. If you really need to get your bearings in Tokyo (and let's face it: in a place this size, who doesn't?) a good starting point is Tokyo Station and the two special wards that flank it, Chiyoda and Chūō.

In Chūō, to the east of Tokyo Station, the neighbourhood of Kyōbashi is a powerhouse of commerce, a grid of wide streets with office blocks and imposing skyscrapers that cast shadows over cool enclaves, cosy eateries and secret places in narrow lanes. People don't really live here; they commute to work in the firms that fill the area's many mirror-armoured buildings. Salarymen and other office-workers crowd the streets, and the alleys and lanes are full of small bars and eateries of all shapes, sizes, tastes and historical origins. Kyōbashi was a central hub for twentieth-century Tokyo; Tokyo's first banks, the Bank of Japan and the Bank of Tokyo, are perched on its fringes and have seen many a transaction – domestic and international – over the years. Along with Chiyoda and its Imperial Palace, Kyōbashi, as the country's seat of financial power, ruled Tokyo and controlled the capital, flourishing in the Taishō era (1912–1926). The architecture here often reflects that, although ongoing organic growth, regular refurbishment and perpetual new builds mean that many hints of the Shōwa era (1926–1989) and the current Heisei era can be found as well.

West of Tokyo Station, in Chiyoda, Marunouchi's Naka Dōri is a small, peaceful haven. Cut off from traffic, the mock-cobbled streets let you amble at your own pace, shopping, lunching or admiring the regularly changing themed sculptures. Shopping and dining is easy and breezy, spilling out onto the streets in the form of food and coffee carts, or filling the twisting halls of seemingly endless complexes. Not far from here, everything goes green: the Imperial Palace (where the Emperor still resides today, p. 340) and its gardens take up a hefty plot of land where you can easily drop a day strolling the grounds and exploring the treasures that it holds. A picnic, an afternoon of tea and *wagashi* (traditional sweets; p. 124) in the gardens, or a day of appreciating nature will get you back in balance.

Imperial Palace Gardens (above and opposite)

With the glamour of Marunouchi and Ginza at your fingertips and the Imperial Palace Garden's swathe of perfect greenery on your doorstep, the area around Ōtemachi Station is a delight for explorers, shoppers and high-end diners. The East Gardens of the Imperial Palace and the spectacular Kikyo-mon Gate are some of Tokyo's most impressive sights and are an easy stroll from the area's hotels. Ginza's shopping paradise and popular Tsukiji Fish Market (p. 206) are a few stops away, or a bracing walk if you're feeling energetic. Ōtemachi's broad streets boast some of Tokyo and the world's most upmarket brands in exquisite stores. It's no wonder the Diet, Japan's Governmental Headquarters, set up in Ōtemachi's sphere, on the lip of the impressive gardens; the area is home to some of Tokyo's most beautiful hotels, ryokans, dining and 'wa' (Japanese) experiences. If you're looking for a honeymoon experience or a luxe Tokyo break, you can't go past elegant Hoshinoya Tokyo Ryokan (1-9-1 Ōtemachi, https://www.hoshinoresorts.com/en/sp/nihonryokan/). Pamper yourself in the *onsen* (hot spring), take part in a traditional tea ceremony and enjoy memorable cultural adventures. Location and spectacular views add to the allure.

South of Tokyo Station, things are decidedly different. Broad streets give way to Yurakūchō's narrow lanes, public squares and rail tunnels that bubble with life: a vibrant economy of sizzling, smoky yakitori joints with crates for chairs; bars that spill out onto the street with regular happy hours; and hole-in-the-wall takeaways where those with local knowledge will queue for the specialties. The Muji flagship store (p. 212) is here – a goldmine for fans. Their 'no brand' brand of clothes, stationery, food and homewares fills three manic floors, and you'll be hard-pressed to leave the store without armfuls of purchases. From here it's just a wander through the station eateries and shops before spying Ginza in the distance.

North of Tokyo Station, Nihonbashi stretches toward Akihabara (p. 224) and Sumida. Nihonbashi ('Japan bridge') takes its name from the wooden bridge, constructed circa 1603, that connected Tokyo with the road to Kyoto. The current stone bridge that spans the Nihonbashi River is more than 100 years old, and is one of the few remnants of prewar Tokyo to survive the 1945 bombing. A major trading area, Nihonbashi is home to Japan's first modern department store, Mitsukoshi (1-4-1 Nihonbashi, mitsukoshi.mistore.jp/store/nihombashi), which was established in 1904 by the Mitsui family and still operates today. Old-world department store Takashimaya (2-4-1 Nihonbashi, takashimaya.co.jp) can also be found here. Nihonbashi's history means that there's a touch of old Tokyo in its backstreets and hidden corners. One of its fortes is pickles – preserve aficionados should scour the area for lunch sets and pickle packages that elevate the cured vegetable to pure excellence.

An arterial network of discoveries tendrils out from Tokyo Station. Using the public transit system, you can reach several Tokyo hotspots quickly. Kyōbashi, Nihonbashi, Yurakūchō and Ōtemachi are each only one stop away – all you need to do is jump on a train. That is, if you manage to get out of Tokyo Station in the first place!

Hoshinoya Tokyo Ryokan (top left, middle right, bottom); East Gardens of the Imperial Palace (top right)

MARUNOUCHI WALK

If you are in Marunouchi at the right t you can attend the Oedo Antique Mar which is held on the first and third Sun of each month. It's the largest vintage market in Tokyo, so you may want to arrive early to work your way through 250 stalls, fossicking for vintage koke dolls, notebooks, stamps and kimono. *For other vintage markets, see p. 308.*

Tokyo Station; Marunouchi Naka Dōri; Train *ekiben*; Vendors at Oedo Antique Market (clockwise from top left)

A relaxing Sunday stroll along Marunouchi Naka Dōri, Marunouchi's main street, to Tokyo Station Gallery (1-9-1 Marunouchi, www.ejrcf.or.jp/gallery/english.html) is the perfect antidote to the big-city blur. Get off at Yurakūchō Station and exit using the D5 Exit or International Forum Exit. Head north towards Marunouchi Naka Dōri, stopping at impressive Café 1894 (Mitsubishi Ichigokan Art Museum, 2-6-2 Marunouchi, mimt.jp/english/cafe1894) for your kickstart coffee.

Once outside Café 1894, make a right turn and then another to Marunouchi Naka Dōri to stroll down the very European cobbled thoroughfare (continuing straight ahead rather than turning into Marunouchi Naka Dōri will take you to the East Gardens of the Imperial Palace, p. 340, if that appeals to you more than shopping). The streets are regularly closed to traffic on Sundays, making it the perfect place to walk and shop or kick back with a vino and people-watch. If you need more caffeine, grab a coffee from one of the tiny food trucks that pop up on the weekend. There is plenty of food and fashion. Inspect the range at chic Plain People (3-4-1 Marunouchi, one-be-one.com) before heading into Kanazawa prefecture sake vendors Fukumitsuya (3-1-1 Marunouchi, fukumitsuya.co.jp/english). Choose between take-away sake ice cream and hot matcha (green tea) *amazake* (sweet fermented rice drink), or pull up a stool at the bar and try the tasting set of three regional sakes. From here it's across to Comme des Garçons (3-4-1 Marunouchi, comme-des-garcons.com), the first of two CDG stores on this street, for some artfully designed clothing. Further up is Wakuden (3-4-1 Marunouchi, www.wakuden.jp/tenpo-marunouchi), an elegant *wagashi* (traditional sweets, p. 124) store that has an unmissable sister tea house (p. 129) around the corner. Across from Wakuden is a branch of Kyoto's treasured tea house Ippodo (3-1-1 Marunouchi, ippodo-tea.co.jp).

Over the intersection, the European flavour really kicks in. Brick Square (2-6-1 Marunouchi) is an enclave hosting the likes of patissier Joël Robuchon, parfumier Jo Malone and a host of French, Italian and Japanese eateries. A little further up, chic Japanese store Kagure (2-5-1 Marunouchi, kagure.jp) has stylish and relaxed fashion. The second Comme des Garçons store houses The Rose Bakery (2-1-1 Marunouchi, rosebakery.jp). You'll also find Tomorrowland (2-5-1 Marunouchi, tomorrowland.jp), Adam et Ropé Wild Life Tailor (2-2-3 Marunouchi, wildlifetailor.adametrope.com), and a giant Beams store (2-4-1 Marunouchi). The stylish Kitte building (2-7-2 Marunouchi) and the Marunouchi (2-4-1 Marunouchi) and Shin-Marunouchi (1-5-1 Marunouchi) buildings have serious shopping and dining experiences. Keep an eye out for the street's sculptures, treasured pieces of outdoor art on loan from the Hakone Open-Air Museum in Kanagawa prefecture. In the winter months, the trees in the street are illuminated, creating a fairy wonderland. From here, walk east until you see the big open square that announces the entrance of Tokyo Station (p. 198). ⊗

TOKYO STATION & EKIBEN

Built in 1889, Tokyo Station is an astoundingly impressive biosphere of commuting, shopping and dining. The frontage at the North Marunouchi Exit is strangely at odds with its surrounds, looking more like the home of the Hogwarts Express than the futuristic Astro Boy jet-off point that would befit one of the main hubs for the Shinkansen (bullet train). Architect Tatsuno Kingo designed the facade with restraint in mind after Japan won the Russo-Japanese War of 1904–05 but suffered heavy financial losses in pursuit of victory. The station was firebombed during the Second World War, and the subsequent rapid but faithful rebuild accounts for the still very conservative nature of the building. An angled roof replaced the previously impressive domes, reducing the entrance building to two levels instead of three.

The Shinkansen, Japan's world-famous bullet train, first connected Tokyo and Osaka in 1964 (just in time for the Olympic Games) and expanded from there. It's rightfully legendary, whisking passengers from one stunning destination to another, running with precision and at speeds that other trains can only dream of. Between the Shinkansen, the Narita Express airport link and the spaghetti tangle of JR and other rail network lines that make up the station's bustling and complicated underworld, people from all over the city and country are getting on and off, and Tokyo Station happily competes with itself to entertain and feed them.

For the ramen devotee, the station is home to one of the city's must-try noodle destinations – even the purist will want to experience Ramen Street, a modern lantern-strewn walkway featuring eight of Japan's best ramen-makers. There will almost certainly be queues of hungry travellers snaking out of every door at lunchtime. You'll just have to make like a local and wait patiently – *shōganai*, as the Japanese would say: it can't be helped. Lines move fast; ramen is a slurp-and-run affair; and patience here is duly rewarded. Fukuoka specialty *tonkotsu* (pork-bone broth) ramen (or as it is known in Fukuoka, *hakata* ramen) is served up at Oreshiki Jun, and lovers of a thick, rich broth will find it decadent and irresistible. Hirugao is the master of *shio* (salt) ramen, a thinner, extra-tasty broth with chewy hokkien noodles. Fans of *tsukemen* dipping noodles will want to wait (for some time) outside popular Rokurinsha, where Ryosei Mita, a disciple of the dish's creator, Kazuo Yamagishi, proudly provides perfectly cooked noodles for you to swish through delicious sauce. Soranoiro serves Edo-style ramen, which includes – non-meat-eaters rejoice! – a vegan ramen. Vegan or vegetarian diners can also head over to Keiyo Dōri in the eastern quadrant of the station to T's TanTan, a popular ramen joint for those who don't want any meat products in their soup. Vegetarians can add an egg for extra flavour and protein (see p. 118 for more information on being vegetarian or vegan in Tokyo).

These options are just the tip of the sliced seaweed atop the noodle bowl, so pick a queue and commit to waiting for that perfect slurp. If you're in the mood for something else, check out Kitchen Street, a labyrinth of eateries on the first floor near the Yaesu North Exit. *Izakaya* (pubs; p. 41), standing sushi bars, rice bowls, tempura – it's all good and all within reach. Alternatively, stumbling full-bellied out of Ramen Street will bring you to Okashi Land, a Willy Wonka–like tour of Japanese sweets. Glico, Calbee and Morinaga make confectionery treats to delight kids and adults alike.

Food isn't the only thing worth your attention at Tokyo Station, either. Character Street, with its rows of pop-up stores and cartoonish riot of noise and lights, is a must for anyone into Tokyo cute (p. 256). Danger: children underfoot! Although you're likely to hear them coming first, squealing with delight as they nudge parents out of the way and rifle through shelves and racks selling toys relating to twenty-one (at last count) of Japan's best-known children's characters.

All of the greats are here: Hello Kitty, Ultraman (complete with lycra tights and Metropolis-style retro robot helmet – Steve's favourite), Kapibara-san (so cute!), NHK's awesome Domo-kun, Pokémon and Godzilla – just to name a few. All are available as keyrings, biscuits, badges, figurines, comics, sweets and swap cards, and range from small and affordable to huge and pricey. Essentially a tiny amusement park without the rides, Character Street is one of the most fun places you'll ever visit – and to think, it's inside a train station!

If the maze-like twists and turns of Tokyo Station become a little too confounding, perhaps a good approach is to concentrate on branching off and returning to the central thoroughfare, a straight line that runs from the North Yaesu Exit to the North Marunouchi Exit.

EKIBEN

For anyone about to board a train for a long journey, there are plenty of snack opportunities, ranging from moreish crackers to try-me-if-you-dare dried squid and tiny honey-glazed crabs. But a true must-have – to go with your beer or *chūhai* (*shōchū* highball), of course – is an *ekiben*. A portmanteau of the word for train station, *eki*, and a shortened form of the word *bentō*, *ekiben* are convenient boxed lunches that come in many varieties, setting you back as little as 700 yen or as much as a 'deluxe' 1800 yen. No matter what you choose, you'll find yourself itching to open your selection as it sits perched in front of you on the train's fold-down tray.

Naturally, Tokyo Station has many places to grab *ekiben*. A great one-stop shop is Ekiben Matsuri, just inside the Yaesu North Exit. At busy times (i.e. most of the time) it is a crush of people sorting through, deliberating over and selecting various *ekiben* as though making the wrong choice could spoil their trip (hint: it can). You'll have to dodge *bentō*-blind people with boxes stacked ten-deep in front of their faces.

Ekiben include culinary specialties from all over Japan and have brightly coloured illustrated covers, some with plastic peekaboo windows offering tantalising glimpses of the contents inside. As you are buffeted by the crowds, pin-balled from one stage to the next in a stream of eager shoppers, you might find that your palms get sweaty and your head starts to spin. Once the wide selection of drinks is also thrown into the mix, you're bordering on overwhelmed, and on top of that your train is due to arrive. Decisions, decisions! This list of *bentō* types will hopefully go some way towards reducing *ekiben*-related stress.

Meat Yazawa Kuroge Wagyu Hamburg Bentō

Look for a brown cover with 'Gotanda Tokyo' written on it. It's one of the more expensive *ekiben*, and only features one hamburger patty. It's a wagyu beef patty, though, made from exceptional quality beef from Yazawa Meat in Shinagawa. The accompaniments are also choice.

Niigata Ebi Senryou Chirashi

Another culinary excursion for the adventurous, this time featuring the not-to-everyone's-taste *unagi*, or eel, sitting on a bed of vinegared rice and covered with a blanket of delicious omelette.

Shinkansen E7 Bento

Perfect for kids (or kidults), this *ekiben* comes in an actual Shinkansen – well, a small plastic model of the E7 bullet train. Inside you'll find a small vegetarian selection and some *onigiri* (rice balls), great for small appetites. It may also set you off on a hunt for other Shinkansen-themed *ekiben*, which can be found in various locations around Japan. You can keep the container and reuse it.

Tokyo Bentō

One of the most expensive *ekiben* (for good reason), the Tokyo Bentō offers a bejewelled selection of delightful morsels created by some of Tokyo's best-known chefs. You'll find fish from Tsukiji Fish Market (p. 206), beef from Asakusa, seasoned omelette and braised vegetables, all tasters of signature dishes from iconic eateries. Look for the vintage illustration of Tokyo Station and 'Tokyo Station Lunch' written in English on the box.

Yonezawa Beef Domanakka

Sukiyaki, wagyu beef and regional specialties: they're all represented. Yamanaka prefecture's favourite *ekiben* is a bright yellow box with a small window shaped like a smile. Perfect, really, as this is one of the most popular *ekiben* of all time. The quality *sukiyaki* beef over rice won't disappoint, especially when consumed with your favourite beer.

Zeitaku Mille-feuille

For the adventurous among you – and those wanting the full Japanese experience – you can't go past this deep, multi-layered box that offers a surprise at every stratum. Salmon and herring roe, crab, minced fish and wasabi make up the elegant top layer, and then you can work your way down through the layers of rice, sashimi and vegetables.

The wall of possibilities at Ekiben Matsuri (opposite)

えび千両ちらし
深川めし
幕之内弁当
鯛めし
金目鯛西京焼弁当
牛べん
特撰かにめし
牛めし
伝承 鰺の押寿司
会津蔵出弁当
バーベキュー弁当
だるま弁当
いかめし
牛肉どまん中
BEEF DOMANNAKA
東京弁当
雪だるま弁当
村上牛しぐれ
平泉うにごはん
神奈川牛肉弁当
Kanagawa Yamayuri Beef

GINZA

——— Named after the silver mint that stood here in the early 1600s, Ginza is still the moneyed-up town where the wealthy go to shop and the less wealthy go to get a taste of how the other half live. If the central Tokyo area around the station is where Tokyoites make money, then Ginza is where they come to spend it. It wasn't always this way; a great fire tore through the town and razed everything to the ground in 1872. The subsequent rebuilding, however, made sure that Ginza emerged as Tokyo's first truly modern (and in many ways, Western) city. European-style buildings went up in what seemed like the blink of an eye. Few remain now, but the iconic Wako Building (4-5-11 Ginza, www.wako.co.jp/en) still holds court on the corner of Ginza's main intersection, a reconstruction of the Hattori Clock Tower perched proudly on top.

After rebuilding, Ginza quickly became Tokyo's luxury-shopping capital, and still retains this status today. High-end retail around the world has nothing on Ginza. The wide thoroughfares glitter with bright retail jewels. European and Japanese fashion houses look down their noses at you from lofty, conceptual towers. Some of the buildings here are truly awe-inspiring: architectural masterpieces that seem to strut down the expansive swathe of Ginza Dōri. Facades compete to out-design each other, vying for your attention. Monolithic, super-styled walls with swooping curves, structured design elements, glimmering panels and emblazoned logos make for endlessly photographable frontages – temples to the new gods of shopping and consumerism. Among it all you'll find a living slice of Taishō-era (1912–1926) Tokyo, with well-dressed, well-heeled shoppers cruising the boulevards and slipping into Dior, Gucci, Valentino or Shiseido before relaxing in retro coffee houses, upmarket cafés, expensive sake bars or high-end tea houses serving perfectly hand-crafted *wagashi* (traditional sweets; p. 124).

Wako's Hattori Clock Tower (above); Ginza architecture (opposite)

But don't worry – you don't have to be rich to shop in Ginza. There are plenty of budget-friendly opportunities among the sprawling department stores and the plethora of retail outlets. Small, charming backstreets hold many surprises. Quality eateries, food halls and chain stores are plentiful, and Ginza holds some excellent art secrets as well: stand-out galleries that you'll want to visit again and again. As an added bonus, the main streets are blocked off to traffic on weekends, giving everyone a chance to amble down the mighty promenades at a casual pace, taking in the grandeur. Order a beer and plant yourself at one of the many outdoor tables shaded from summer sun or shielded from winter rain by colourful umbrellas. Sunday is the perfect day to people-watch. Keep an eye out for ladies shopping, lunching and strolling the boulevard looking impossibly chic in brightly coloured kimono.

Yamaha Building (above); Ginza shopping, including Fujiya and paper products from Kyūkyōdo (opposite)

ExcelHuma
EH株式会社
MITSUKOSHI

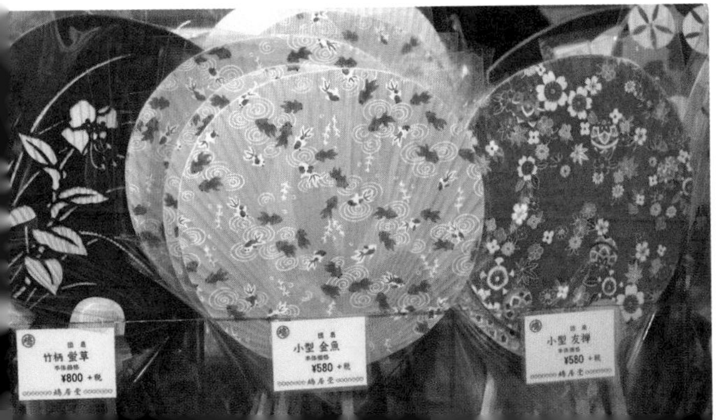
竹柄 蛍草
¥800 +税
小型 金魚
¥580 +税
小型 友禅
¥580 +税

FUJIYA

TSUKIJI FISH MARKET

The world-famous Tsukiji Fish Market can be found just southwest of Ginza, outside Tsukiji Station on the Tokyo Metro Hibiya Line. The market's frenzied appeal is legendary: a cacophony of shouted orders and numbers; gumbooted, uniformed market-workers in a mad flurry of activity; and rows of polystyrene crates stuffed with an array of aquatic oddments, soon to become seafood. The amazing range of fresh sushi and sashimi eateries in the surrounding area is another major magnet for tourists, both domestic and international.

Visitors used to be able to walk freely through the auction rooms – an activity definitely not for the squeamish, with all manner of magnificent ocean creatures on display. You can still get a sense of this, even though the auction rooms are now a no-go zone. Lovers of seafood will be in heaven here. You won't get fresher sashimi anywhere else – unless it's by the sea. Visitors swear by Sushi Dai, which has garnered a reputation over the years for serving up the best sushi in the world. Queue up with the tourists to wait an hour (or four) before having some amazing sushi if you like, or hit one of the other joints around the area. It's all fresh from the market, wonderfully prepared and absolutely delicious.

5-2-1 TSUKIJI, TSUKIJI-MARKET.OR.JP

Also swam …

Kagura
4-14-13 Tsukiji
Chūō 104-0045
tukijikagura.jp

Sushi Zanmai
3-11-9 Tsukiji
Chūō 104-0045
kiyomura.co.jp

Tsukiji Sushi Sei Honten
4-10-9 Tsukiji
Chūō 104-0045
tsukijisushisay.co.jp

Sushi Dai

5-2-1 Tsukiji
Chūō 104-0045

The queues here are legendary – honestly, we think that's part of the draw. We're talking queue at 3.50 am, wait for them to open and then wait some more; total wait-time can get up to four or five hours. If that sounds good, or if you are the type to queue overnight for the latest Apple device or concert tickets, Sushi Dai might be for you. The sushi is excellent.

Daiwa Sushi

5-2-1 Tsukiji
Chūō 104-0045
tsukijigourmet.or.jp

Another queue-fest, Daiwa has gained the reputation of being the Sushi Dai you go to when you can't be bothered waiting in line for Sushi Dai. As a result, you'll wait in line here as well – just not quite as long, which is better. It's much of a muchness; both are excellent. Neither are super cheap, but they are reasonably priced (depending on your exchange rate) and offer that Tokyo experience you will always remember.

Tempura Tenfusa

5-2-1 Tsukiji
Chūō 104-0045

Not everything at the fish market has to be about sushi and sashimi. If you find yourself thinking about fish gently fried in the lightest of batters and placed on a bed of fluffy rice or in a rich, hot soup, then this is the place for you. Tempura for breakfast might seem odd, but believe us, it hits the spot at any time of the day. An old-school vibe with a bustling crowd of market-workers and locals lets you know that it's the real deal. Vegetarian options are available, and – pescetarians rejoice – the prawns are spectacular.

GINZA WALK

If you're meeting up with friends, the lion statues out the front of the Mitsukoshi department store (4-6-16 Ginza, mitsukoshi.mistore.jp/store/ginza) are a good place to do it. Inspired by the lions of London's Trafalgar Square and cast by British sculptors, the Mitsukoshi Lions were erected in 1914, and the rendezvous point is almost as popular as Hachikō Square's eponymous dog statue. From here you can head into the store, shop the many levels, brave the food hall and marvel at the store's survival of fire, bombing and internet shopping. Take a moment to muse on its humble roots as a kimono shop established in 1673, and perhaps buy something – if only to have it wrapped in their famous red-and-white packaging.

One of the newest additions to the Ginza landscape is Ginza Six (6-10-1 Ginza, ginza6.tokyo). Nearly 250 of Tokyo's best brands nabbed their own piece of Ginza Six, so there's plenty of variety. Ubiquitous 'best bookstore in the world' Tsutaya has a spacious, airy sixth-floor shop here. There's even a *Noh* theatre (p. 368) on the third basement floor, so stop by and take in a four-hour show or two. The stage, and the troupe that goes with it, were relocated from Shibuya.

Having moved from the home it once shared with the Muji in Yūrakuchō, the Ginza branch of lifestyle superstore Loft (Ginza Velvia-kan 3–6F, 2-4-6 Ginza, loft.co.jp) has received an upgrade befitting its new, swish surroundings. You can still get all of the things that Loft does so well, including stationery, homewares, luggage and assorted kitchenalia, but now it's in a shiny new space with all of the mod cons. Don't forget to check out the Pencil Bar, where stationery-lovers will become intoxicated by the vast array of graphite implements. The notebook and washi-tape selections often feature limited-edition creations, and a host of cute and stylish 'reprints' of vintage stationery items are also a standout.

A stone's throw away you'll find the Wako Building (4-5-11 Ginza, www.wako.co.jp/en), the epitome of traditional Tokyo elegance that featured in Ozu Yasujirō's timeless masterpiece *Tokyo Monogatari* (*Tokyo Story*; 1953). Designed and built in 1932, the department-store building has a neoclassical feel to it, with nods towards Art Deco. Wako sits in the centre of Ginza and acts as a beacon to help you get your bearings. The Westminster chimes of the Hattori Clock Tower (a recreation of the original tower that stood here until 1921) will tell you exactly how long (but not how much) you've spent shopping. Window-shop the high-end foreign products; watches, handbags, jewellery and porcelain are all specialties of the store.

By now you'll need a coffee, and Café de l'Ambre (p. 143) is a Ginza institution, encapsulating both the town's history and its sophisticated character. Since 1948, this *kissaten* (European-style coffee house; p. 142) has been re-inventing coffee – so much so that its creations are a revelation to its Western visitors. The coffee jelly here is one of those Tokyo must-haves: a petite dessert glass with jellied coffee and cream – a sweet treat and a pick-me-up in one! The frontage echoes the glory days of Ginza, when the Taishō era (1912–1926) ticked over into modern Shōwa (1926–1989) and traditional Japanese elegance gained a Western flavour. The exterior signs and interior decor of Café de l'Ambre are still of the era; stepping through the doors is like a trip back in time. There's so much to love here: tiny ashtrays with logos, coffee that takes longer to make than it does to drink, and baristas who were making coffee before baristas were a thing. Owner Ichiro Sekiguchi was there when it all started. He was 104 when he passed away in 2018 and still worked in the café! That's a lifetime of experience. (He also invented his own coffee kettle). Premium filters, coffee weighed out on old-school scales and long-time patrons lounging around the coffee bar like they own the place (they do in a way; they have been coming here for half a century): this *kissaten* is culture in a cup.

Further up the street and one right turn later, you'll find one of Tokyo's great '70s relics, the Nakagin Capsule Tower (p. 349). This concrete sliver of space pods is the epitome of retro-futurism – a capsule hotel made up of actual capsules, slotted into one another like Tetris blocks. For the Metabolist (p. 348) or Brutalist architecture obsessive, there are not many sights that will satisfy you like Nakagin. The tiny *2001: A Space Odyssey* sleeping capsules are exactly the kind of thing that you wish for when you're drunk and unable to get home in Japan, knowing that you have to get up for work the next morning. On the verge of demolition in 2006, Nakagin received a stay of execution. At times, one or two of the capsules can be rented through Airbnb. Open the pod bay doors, Hal.

If you fancy a spot of art, the gallery in the Shiseido Building (p. 365), opened in 1919, is thought to be the oldest gallery in Japan still exhibiting. You will always find something that excites and challenges you here. The nearby Ginza Graphic Gallery (p. 362) shows the very best of graphic art, past and present, at always breathtaking one-off shows.

Ginza also features the stunning Kabuki-za theatre (p. 368), and is a short walk to the Tsukiji Fish Market (p. 206). For a bit of Ginza rough, hit the Ginza Lion beer hall (Ginza Place B1F, 5-8-1 Ginza) for a stein and a schnitzel. ⊗

STATIONERY, PAPER & ART SUPPLIES

For stationery nerds, Tokyo is a dream destination. If, like Michelle, you can spend hours looking at washi tapes, textured papers, sticky notes and envelopes, you may need to factor in two extra days in Japan's capital.

Tokyo has everything, from old-school Edo-period printed paper and items made by hand using centuries-old techniques to the boldest and brightest contemporary designs. We're in Tokyo every three months and there is always an interesting new colourway or a classic design with a twist. If you are there around New Year, check out the festive cards; yet again the seasons play a part in bringing beauty to everyday items.

Apart from book and stationery stores, all kinds of outlets stock stationery ranges relating to their specialty, so keep your eye out for some interesting and unusual buys. (Even convenience stores get in on the act.) Post offices have a great selection of postcards and paper items, and one of the most incredible ranges of stamps you'll find anywhere in the world. Shop the selection; you'll want to get creative with your purchases and send off some snail mail.

ART SUPPLIES

When it comes to art supplies, Tokyo has it all and more, from beautiful handmade brushes to sketching and tracing papers, easels, a vast array of paint colours and all manner of things to help you create the perfect art moment. If you're artistically inclined, you won't be able to contain your excitement when you find familiar things that have been elevated to the next level.

BOXES & BAGS

You can find many cute boxes and bags in Tokyo, and they come in all shapes and sizes. Polka dots, stripes and designs with French text are popular, and you can buy bows, ribbons, twine and colourful stuffing to match. Box and Needle (p. 212) offers some of the most beautiful patterned boxes you are ever likely to see.

DIARIES

In a world where many have moved to an online diary, Tokyo still holds a torch for the paper kind. Diaries come in all shapes and sizes and you'll have fun choosing stickers and accessories to match.

ENVELOPES

If you like posting off snail mail or need a way to store stamps or postcards, envelopes are a necessity. Check out the range of patterns and paper textures and look out for embossing, letterpress and risograph-printed examples.

ERASERS

Erasers rise above their function in Tokyo. Animals, fruit and Japanese food shapes are popular, and you won't want to erase anything for fear of ruining them. Michelle loves the retro-looking ones with vintage type and old-school faded colours. A warning: if you buy more than one, you've started a collection.

LABELS

Tokyoites (and Michelle) are big fans of buying quirky address labels to put on packaging or handmade envelopes. The Midori brand makes great self-sticking labels, but you can also cheat a little and buy non-adhesive cards and a glue stick to make your own labels if you really love the shapes or patterns.

NOTEBOOKS, JOURNALS & PLANNERS

Travel journals are wildly popular in Tokyo, as are books made especially for bullet-point journalling. If this is your thing, Traveler's Factory (p. 212) is a must-visit, or look out for Hobonichi – the Filofax of Japan – which has the kind of cult following that can often mean long queues.

ORIGAMI PAPER

A favourite paper product to buy in Tokyo, origami paper comes in many designs, from traditional to contemporary. Great for folding origami hearts to post home envelopes. They also make excellent presents, especially if you include a little tutorial in the package.

PENCIL CASES

How retro, storing pencils in a case! Having pencils at all, in fact. But the sense of nostalgia is keen here, and one manifestation of this is making the most perfect little pods in which to store pens and pencils. Slip your set of HBs into a Hello Kitty or Ultraman-themed holder, or select a tasteful Shōwa-era design that has been reworked and reborn from Tokyo schooldays gone by.

PENS & PENCILS

A popular unisex purchase – after all, everyone needs a good-looking pen or pencil that writes beautifully. An overwhelming selection of colours and thicknesses are available in Tokyo stores. Choose from old-school ink pens with nibs, pencils of all textures from soft to hard, brightly coloured character ball-points or sophisticated pens with beautifully flowing ink.

STICKERS

You'll find stickers everywhere in Tokyo. Tiny stickers, puffy stickers, flat stickers, animals, cute faces, jumbo shapes with crazy-fun themes and bright colours ... Grab some sheets and start showing off how much you 'heart' various things, give some hard copy a thumbs-up or a thumbs-down, or express your emotions with a smiley or sad face – stickers were the original emojis.

STICKY NOTES

We all need reminders, so make them as cute as possible. Patterned notes rule, and pick up some *kawaii* animal stickies for your fridge or whiteboard. Animal-head bookmarks that peek from the pages of a book are a must.

TRADITIONAL WASHI PAPER

Washi paper is handmade and uses centuries-old techniques, embellished by hand with colour or patterns. If you are looking for paper to frame or to use to create your own Tokyo artwork, the city has some amazing options.

Ozu Washi
(p. 379)
This traditional washi store opened in 1653. They also operate a gallery and run paper-making classes.

Gekko-So
Eiju Building BF–1F
8-7-2 Ginza
Chūō 104-0061
gekkoso.jp

Isetatsu
2-18-9 Yanaka
Taitō 110-0001
isetatsu.com

WASHI TAPE

Paper tape is a phenomenon in Japan. There are hundreds of different colours and patterns, some transparent or opaque. Inexpensive and useful, a couple of rolls are a must-buy for any stationery-lover. MT is the market leader, but small brands are also making a name for themselves.

PERENNIAL FAVOURITES

Bingoya
10-6 Wakamatsuchō
Shinjuku 162-0056
bingoya.tokyo

Itōya Ginza
2-7-15, Ginza
Chūō 104-0061
ito-ya.co.jp

Kyūkyodō
5-7-4 Ginza
Chūō 104-0061
kyukyodo.co.jp

Loft Shibuya
21-1 Udagawachō
Shibuya 150-0042
(Also at other locations)
loft.co.jp

Muji Yūrakuchō (flagship store)
3-8-3 Marunouchi
Chiyoda 100-0005
(Also at other locations)
muji.com

Pack Mate
Nakamichi Dōri
Kichijōji Honcho
Musashino 180-0004

Tegamisha 2nd Story
2F 1-17-5 Kikunodai
Chofu 182-0007
tegamisha.com

Tokyu Hands Shibuya
12-18 Udagawachō
Shibuya 150-0042
(Also at other locations)
www.tokyu-hands.co.jp/en

ART SUPPLIES

Bumpōdō
1-21-1 Kanda-Jimbōchō
Chiyoda 101-0051
bumpodo.co.jp

Pigment
Terrada Harbor One
Building 1F
2–5–5 Higashi-Shinagawa
Shinagawa 140-0002
pigment.tokyo

Sekaido
3-1-1-Shinjuku 1–5F
Shinjuku 160-0022
sekaido.co.jp

BOXES & BAGS

Box and Needle
3-12-11 Tamagawa
Setagaya 158-0094
boxandneedle.com

ENVELOPES & LETTERPRESS

Winged Wheel
4-5-4 Jingūmae
Shibuya 150-0001
winged-wheel.co.jp

Exceptional letterpress gift cards and stationery. Michelle particually loves their vast array of envelopes in different colours and paper varieties.

NOTEBOOKS

Kakimori
1-6-2 Misuji
Taitō 111-0055
kakimori.com
You can make your own custom notebook here. A dream workshop and store for anyone into journalling and documenting.

TOBICHI
4-25-14 Minami-Aoyama
Minato 107-0062
1101.com/tobichi/tokyo

Traveler's Factory
3-13-10 Kamimeguro
Meguro 153-0051
travelers-factory.com

Why not get your own Japanese-language name stamp made? Michelle once spent hours at Itōya in Ginza (opposite) choosing her *hiragana* and *kanji* stamp – they even filmed it for Japanese television. It was an interesting experience, as every name can be spelt in many different ways, so you can choose the prettiest or most meaningful character that suits you. You can also choose the type of case that houses your stamp. Japanese people often use these personalised stamps to sign documents, especially those relating to finance and insurance. You'll come away with something unique.

JIMBŌCHŌ

Do you love heading down to your local second-hand bookstore and perusing the shelves for a classic or two to add to your collection? Now imagine a town where you can find an estimated 160–200 shops (around one-third of all second-hand bookstores in Japan) selling new and pre-loved books. Some books are very old – dusty tomes with price tags to match. Others from more recent times, like science books from the sixties with cool modernist covers, classic manga from the seventies and eighties, children's books, pop-culture and fashion magazines and assorted textbooks, can sell for as little as 100 yen. Most stores are wall-to-wall books, shelves crammed with barely enough room to sidle past, browsing bibliophiles and teetering piles of pulp-fiction books and magazines blocking your every turn. Books spill out onto the streets in stacks and on trolleys, pages turning in the wind as if some ghostly book-lover is leafing through the yellowed sheets, recalling an old literary love.

Anyone who adores books but doesn't speak Japanese (or hasn't quite mastered the language yet) will be happy to know that many bookshops in Jimbōchō sell English books and also dabble in a variety of other languages (Italian and German feature prominently). As an added bonus, Jimbōchō is well known as a place to buy amazing Japanese paper, and if you like vintage hunting in general you'll find many other stores selling retro bits and bobs. The junction of Yasukuni Dōri and Hakusan Dōri is home to one of the biggest second-hand book markets in the world, and along the south side of Yasukuni Dōri, away from the scorching glare of the afternoon sun, you'll find a string of bookstores that have walls of over-stuffed bookshelves or bargain bins outside (hence the sun protection).

Keeping with the theme, there are many publishing houses set up in the area (the Iwanami Shoten publishing house, which publishes the Japanese dictionary Kōjien, was established in Jimbōchō in 1913 and has its own renowned bookstore, p. 217). Additionally, five of Japan's major universities are just a stroll away from Jimbōchō Station: Nihon, Meiji, Hosei, Juntendo and Senshu circle the area, creating a central well of intelligence, a confluence of brainy students that helped form Jimbōchō into what it is today.

All that thinking is hungry work, and the influx of students and philosophers to the area necessitates a local specialty that is fast, cheap and filling. In the case of Jimbōchō, curry is the dish of choice, and dotted among the bookstores you'll find many highly rated curry houses who will gladly serve you something to eat while you peruse your latest literary purchase. All the knowledge contained in those books has seeped into the very fabric of Jimbōchō, and intellectuals and students like to gather in its bars to discuss the topics of the day over a drink.

CAHILL
ビッグケーヒル
映画ドラえもん
團菊以後
伊原青々園著
相撲昭和史 激動の軌跡
明治商賣往來
仲田定之助著
續明治商賣往來
絵本落語長屋
新宿裏町三代記
野村敏雄著
明治商賣往來
HISTORICAL GEOGRAPHY
Philosophy of ART & BEAUTY
THE GREEKS AND THEIR GODS
Ryle The Concept of Mind

BOOKSTORES

Isseido Shoten
1-7 Kanda-Jimbōchō
Chiyoda 101-0051
isseido-books.co.jp
Isseido's antique books and scrolls and rare Japanese collectibles come in three categories: the affordable, the once-in-a-lifetime purchase, and the museum piece you can only look at in wonder. This store is almost a museum exhibit in itself. There are plenty of other book-buying opportunities to be had in the general stock that fills the shop's shelves, outdoor bins and narrow aisles.

Nauka Japan
1-34 Kanda-Jimbōchō
Chiyoda 101-0051
www.naukajapan.jp
Nauka means 'science' in Russian, so this is the place to go if you're looking for cool mid-century molecular science covers with a Soviet twist. Nauka's tottering piles of books are a ramshackle rifle-fest that could see you lose track of time.

Ohya Shobō
1-1 Kanda-Jimbōchō
Chiyoda 101-0051
ohya-shobo.com
If old maps are your thing, then you'll be in heaven when you see this impressive collection of topographical elevations, tracings and delineations from various eras. The art books here are premium and there are some great finds – or perhaps just great eye candy, depending on your budget – among the old Edo-period texts.

Sanseido
1-1 Kanda-Jimbōchō
Chiyoda 101-0051
jinbocho.books-sanseido.co.jp
The flagship store of what has become a successful Japanese chain, Sanseido in Jimbōchō is a multi-storey bookshop where no category is left out. In addition to the absurd range of new and old books, you'll also find lifestyle products, local crafts and stationery. For Anglophiles, the fifth floor is dedicated to English books.

Tokyodo
1-17 Kanda-Jimbōchō
Chiyoda 101-0051
tokyodo-web.co.jp
You wouldn't know that this bookshop dates back to 1924 just by looking at it. Its current contemporary design and clean lines have made it a popular drop-in for locals and visitors. The refillable 180-yen coffee and the free wifi at the Paper Back Café might also have something to do with that. History books, magazines, posters, postcards and a large selection of religious material, especially Buddhist, are the store's specialties.

Yaguchi Shoten
2-5-1 Kanda-Jimbōchō
Chiyoda 101-0051
yaguchi.movie.coocan.jp/eigo
Cinema books are the big deal here. That being said, Yaguchi Shoten, housed in one of Jimbōchō's oldest buildings, is also home to architectural digests, scientific pamphlets, pre-loved novels, textbooks, dusty yellowed paperbacks and hulking doorstoppers.

OTHER RECOMMENDATIONS

At Wonder
Kaitakusha Building 2F
2-5-4 Kanda-Jimbōchō
Chiyoda 101-0051
Sci-fi and pulp with a side of coffee.

Jimbōchō Book Centre with Iwanami Books
Iwanami Shoten Annex 1–3F
2-3-1 Kanda-Jimbōchō
Chiyoda 101-0051
Scientific and other academic texts, plus postcards and prints.

Kitazawa Shoten
2-5 Kanda-Jimbōchō
Chiyoda 101-0051
kitazawa.co.jp
Great selection of Japanese children's books.

Komiyama Shoten
1-7 Kanda-Jimbōchō
Chiyoda 101-0051
book-komiyama.co.jp
Photography, philosophy and art books, as well as great changing photo exhibitions.

Oshima Shoten
Kurata Building 1F
1-1 Kanda-Jimbōchō
Chiyoda 101-0051
Known for its reasonable prices and well-sourced paperbacks, Western books, language books, and texts on history, religion and science.

Scenes from Jimbōchō (opposite)

CURRIES

Bondy
2-3 Kanda-Jimbōchō
Chiyoda 101-0051
bondy.co.jp
One of Jimbōchō's stalwarts. Expect to queue, but expect it to be worth it. Slightly pricey for the area, most curries come in between 1100–1300 yen, but at Bondy they are very bounteous with portion and flavour.

Dylan
3-3-3, Kanda-Surugadai
Chiyoda 101-0051
Cool name, good curry. One of the newer places serving a very punctilious curry meal. Great if you are feeling undecided, as you can order the half-and-half: two different types of curry in one.

Mandala
2-17 Kanda-Jimbōchō
Chiyoda 101-0051
westindia-group.com/mandala
Cooked by Indian expat chefs, Mandala's curry is authentic and popping with flavour and spice. Choose from more than twenty different kinds of curry, including excellent vegetarian options. Don't forget to soak it up with some excellent, pillowy naan bread.

Manten
1-54 Kanda-Jimbōchō
Chiyoda 101-0051
For the truly hungry among us. What Manten lacks in refinement it makes up for with heavy-hitting curries topped with larger-than-life extras like *tonkatsu* (fried pork cutlet), sausage, egg or Chinese *shaomai* dumplings. Perfect for those with a big appetite and only 1000 yen in their pocket. If you're slightly more cashed-up and even hungrier, go for the *zenbu-nose* option, where they throw on all the toppings. Worth a try once, surely?

Perusona
Matsumoto Building 2F
1-28-9 Kanda-Jimbōchō
Chiyoda 101-0051
Highly rated for their deeply flavoured curries and range of ingredients. They serve 'European' curry here, a milder, sweeter curry. Check out the retro interior and carnival masks on the walls (hand-decorated by the owner).

Udon Maruka
3-16-1 Ogawamachi
Chiyoda 101-0052
The marriage of udon noodles with curry is a joyous feast – and an eye-opener to anyone who always has their curry with rice. Japan's curry *nanban* (sometimes known as curry udon) is an unctuous curry noodle soup where thick udon noodles soak up the flavour and spice of the broth, forming one irresistible melange. Udon Maruka's silky curry is delicious. You'll be slurping the moreish soup long after the noodles have gone.

OTHER RECOMMENDATIONS

Chantoya
Shoryukan Building 1F
3-28-7 Kanda- Ogawachō
Chiyoda 101-0052
chantoya.com

J. Tipple Bar
1-64 Kanda-Jimbōchō 2F
Chiyoda 101-0051
witchcraft.co.jp/jtipple

Shahi Dawat
2-2-11 Kanda-Nishikichō
Chiyoda 101-0054

Shinsekai Saikan
Shinsekai Building
2-2 Kanda-Jimbōchō
Chiyoda 101-0051

大辞林
国語大辞典
模範六法

Match
avec
MAO
BREJNEV
HEATH
5
jours
qui
changent
le
monde

ROCK SHOW
PIN-UP BOOK '84
ROCK SHOW
MONTHLY

ろしあ亭
CLOSED

JIMBŌCHŌ WALK

Leave Jimbōchō Station via the A7 Exit. To your left is a tiny street featuring the unique *kissaten* (European-style coffee house; p. 142) Sabouru (1-11 Kanda-Jimbōchō); its frontage is buried under a tangle of foliage and overseen by a huge Tiki carving. Pop inside for a coffee or strawberry juice and admire the oddball collection of clocks and pictures covering the walls. Next door is Sabouru 2, popular for its *Naporitan* pasta – a very American take on spaghetti, with tomato sauce, Tabasco, bacon, sausage and various vegetables – which came to Japan after the Second World War. Further down on the corner, don't miss Big Boy (1-11 Kanda-Jimbōchō, jazzbigboy.sakura.ne.jp), a café and curry house that also sells records. Cool jazz refrains leak out onto the street.

Head right for Suzuran Dōri. Turn left and find Magnif Zinebocho (1-17 Kanda-Jimbōchō, magnif.jp), where they specialise in Japanese, French and American magazines from the fifties and sixties. Vintage music and magazines can be found down the street at Rock on King (Fujimoto Building 3F, 1-19-1 Kanda-Jimbōchō, www.rockonking.com). Opposite is design, art and architecture book specialist Bohemian's Guild (1-1-9 Kanda-Jimbōchō, natsume-books.com). Slip up the small street opposite Ueshima Coffee (1-1-13 Kanda-Jimbōchō, ueshima-coffee-ten.jp) to find Jimbōchō Kagetsu (1-23 Kanda-Jimbōchō, yoshimoto.co.jp/jimbocho), a fractured metal shell that houses a theatre hosting plays and storytelling. Things go from highbrow to lowbrow when you cross the street: Book Dash (1-1-25 Kanda-Jimbōchō), specialises in retro magazines and manga with a soft glamour porn theme.

Back on Suzuran Dōri, you'll find Bumpōdō (p. 212), a mecca for art supplies with several floors dedicated to paints, pencils, woodblock print tools, paper and sundries. Opposite is Sanseido (p. 217), one of Jimbōchō's biggest bookstores, where you can find new books, magazines, souvenirs, second-hand books and books in English.

Head out and turn left down Yasukuni Dōri, which will bring you into contact with a hefty chunk of Jimbōchō's best second-hand book stores. Early on you'll encounter Ohya Shobō (p. 217). This museum of a bookstore is incredible: hand-written *kanji* labels poke out from rows of old tomes, making for an impressive sight; old maps will set you back hundreds or even thousands of dollars. Further down, Bunken-Shoin (2-3 Kanda-Jimbōchō, bunken-shoin.co.jp) is keeping music-magazine culture alive. If you long to acquaint (or reacquaint) yourself with old editions of *Vox* and *The Face*, poodle-rock, hair-metal and teen-idol magazines, and pop-culture pamphlets and paraphernalia from the fifties to the nineties, Bunken-Shoin makes for a crazy, fun and colourful peruse. Komiyama Shoten (p. 217) specialises in art, fashion and photography. Stacked volumes block your way at every turn and teeter hazardously on staircases. The wall of books on the side street is one of Jimbōchō's most snap-happy moments. Meirinkan Shoten (1-19 Kanda-Jimbōchō, meirinkanshoten.com) is a jumbled maze of books with a leaning towards paperbacks – but it's only a slight leaning; anything goes here.

You will be back at the station now, but there is plenty more to explore in this amazing town. ⊗

Jimbōchō Kagetsu (top left and right); Book Dash (bottom left)

BEST PHARMACY BUYS

Great packaging, a vast array of brands, overstuffed shelves: the Tokyo pharmacy has it all and more. The Japanese obsession with beauty products is legendary and the range is staggering. Manscaping is a thing as well, so guys won't miss out on the fun. Look for products with Japanese ingredients like *tsubaki* (camellia seed) oil, yuzu citrus, rice – anything out of the ordinary. If you've overdone it the night before, grab a liver tonic, some nausea powder and headache tablets with added muscle relaxants. Bath salts, eye drops, high-SPF sunscreen, sheet masks … it's all here. Discover your new favourite brand and find some true gems in the Tokyo pharmacy. A warning: you might have planned to visit a gallery today, but spending hours in the pharmacy instead is a very real danger.

BEST BEAUTY BUYS

Blotting paper to reduce facial oil and shine

Eyelash curlers

Sheet masks and whipped-cream-style face cleansers

Tsubaki (camellia seed) hair products

Water-based SPF creams (SPF 50 and very light on the skin)

BEST PHARMACY BUYS

Anti-nausea and hangover cure powders

Bath salts (look out for scents like yuzu citrus, hinoki cypress, and pine)

Eye drops

Heated eye masks

Liver tonics for hangovers (look for the liver pics)

Pocket warmers or coolers

BONUS BUYS

Bug repellent stickers (stick them on, keep bugs off – great for picnics)

Extra-soft face brushes

Foot sheets to massage your feet

Kawaii character Band-Aids to cheer up any boo-boo

Milk soap and charcoal soap (the latter used since the Edo period for its medicinal qualities)

1.

2.

3.

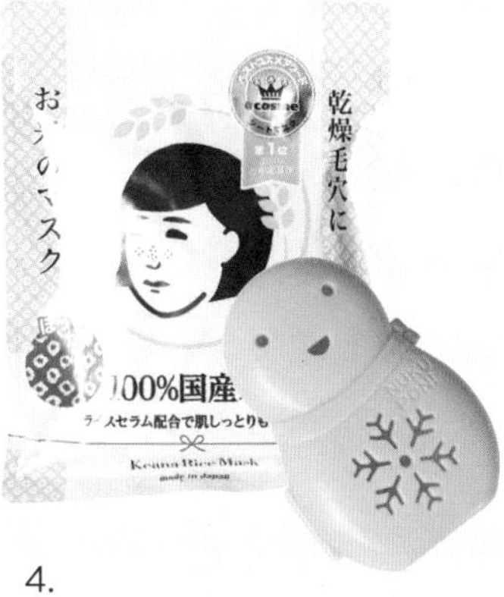

4.

5.

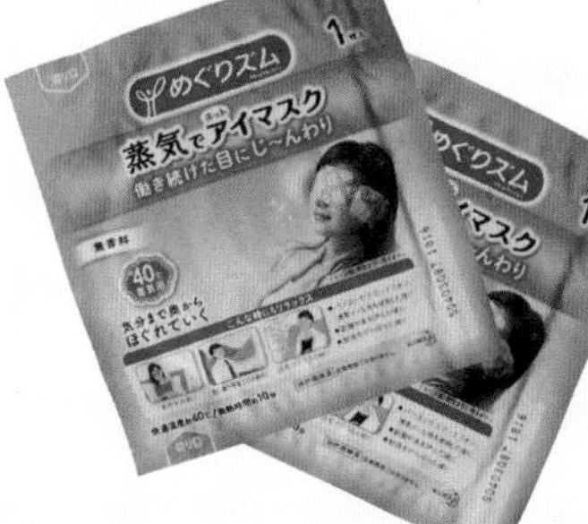

6.

7.

8.

9.

1. Face brush
2. Foaming cleanser and SPF
3. Moisturisers
4. Face mask pack
5. Pocket warmers
6. Heated eye masks
7. Bath salts
8. Face masks
9. Eye drops

SEGA
HIROSE
您好！欢迎！
货比三家
安心购物
价格优惠
优质服务
愛客国際免税店
DUTY FREE
激安販売の専門店
もっと強い奴と戦いたい
CLUB SEGA

AKIHABARA

——— Akihabara has long been the *otaku* (obsessive fan) capital of Tokyo, and nerds of all stripes gather here to scoop up armfuls of toys, games and manga. A major freight transit point during the Meiji era (1868–1912), Akihabara was home to a thriving fruit and vegetable market, and later became a public transport hub once the railway line was opened to the public. These three factors, along with the absence of a stable government, allowed for a highly successful black market to operate during and after the Second World War. It was this established market infrastructure and entrepreneurial spirit that facilitated Akihabara's postwar turn to the future, and soon American and European electrical goods flooded its markets, earning it the moniker 'Electric Town'.

Akihabara still holds this reputation as the best place in Japan to buy your gadgetry, and it is an essential stopover for many Westerners wanting to catch up with the latest in technology. Robots, personal buddies, high-tech drones, virtual reality: everything that's happening now was already happening back then in Akihabara. Along with the tech came the tech-obsessed, and Akihabara became the area where geeks, or *otaku* as they came to be known in Tokyo, gathered. Obsessives of all nerdish persuasions – comic-lovers, hardcore gamers, computer-builders, model-makers, figurine-collectors – came by the trainload, as did a few unsavoury habits, including the penchant for maid cafés and risqué manga.

All this aside, anyone into model-making, gaming (retro or futurist), manga, figurines or junk food has a kind of utopia waiting for them in Akihabara. Ramshackle geek oddment superstore Mandarake (3-12-11 Soto-Kanda, mandarake.co.jp) has its flagship here, a multi-storey trip through everything that grown-ups shouldn't still be playing with but most definitely are. The quality is what makes its range truly stand out. Retro dolls are a big deal and can fetch some eye-watering prices. Rows of growling vintage Godzillas and robots in all shapes, sizes and eras peer from musty shelves. Floors of containers with manga ranging from wholesome to 'Christ, don't let the kids see this' will keep any Japanese-comic enthusiast landlocked for hours.

Long-term fans of video games will think they have died and gone to heaven at Super Potato (p. 226). It must be one of the few megastores in the world that sells retro gaming equipment, including old-model hardware from the likes of Nintendo, Sega, Amiga et al. Consoles and games are restored to perfect working order, and their popularity is a reflection of the endurance of gaming culture in the twentieth and twenty-first centuries.

Things have changed in Electric Town over the past two decades, but it hasn't lost its edge; even though there has been a seismic shift in how it is perceived. In keeping with new technology, the imagined futures of manga are now reality. *Otaku* has crawled out of the subterranean darkness and into the light, rising at a blistering pace from subculture to ruling class – and with it, Akihabara has moved from underground to above board.

FIVE NERD WONDERLANDS

Animate

1-20-7 Higashi-Ikebukuro
Toshima 170-0013
animate.co.jp

For anime and manga it's unlikely that you'll find a store with such a broad and eclectic range anywhere else. This towering monolith of pop-culture retail has more than 100 stores in Japan alone, but the Ikebukuro store is the one you're most likely to get lost in. Unless you have a particular manga, show or film in mind, you really won't know where to start. Most of us just end up looking at the pretty colours and covers, piled high on shelves or arranged neatly in seemingly endless rows. Hours will go by until eventually you'll hear your name called out over the loudspeaker as if you're a lost child and realise that you've wandered off down your own magical manga rabbit hole.

Gachapon Hall

3-15-5 Soto-Kanda
Chiyoda 104-0061
www.akibagacha.com

For anyone with a capsule-toy (p. 228) obsession, the Akihabara Gachapon Hall is a source of infinite temptation: rows and rows of machines dispensing an ever-evolving range of small toys sealed in plastic balls. Prices vary, depending on the intricacies of the toy. Some machines are stocked with models so complex that they command 500 yen or more, while the ever-popular *Naruto* body stickers can be nabbed for just 100 yen. With *gachapon*, not knowing which toy you're getting is always part of the fun and frustration. Glass cases tease us with previous capsule toys no longer for sale; you can only window-shop these rare and enticing novelties. Disturbingly for the capsule-toy addict, half of the contents of the machines in Gachapon Hall are replaced monthly, meaning some of the purchases are truly one-off experiences. CTA (capsule-toyholics anonymous) meeting, anyone?

Gojira-Ya

3-67-1 Kōenji-Minami
Suginami 166-0003
www1.plala.or.jp/GODZILLAYA

The mother lode for the retro-character collector, Gojira-Ya, or Godzilla House, has overstuffed its shelves with classic and rare models of the famous monster. Keeping him company are plenty of other characters that pack a similar nostalgic punch. Marvel at ultra-rare Ultraman figurines. Gasp as Astro Boy, Kamen Rider and Gigantor seek out shelf space while their most powerful adversaries battle them for attention. Quality ranges from small, static, plastic figurines to die-cast wonders with intricate moving parts. If it all gets too much, hit the bar downstairs to drown your sorrows over that one Godzilla model that you couldn't afford. The bar is Godzilla-themed, with television screens playing the famous monster's greatest and most wobbly-costumed moments.

Nakano Broadway

5-52 Nakano
Tokyo 164-0001
nbw.jp

Perfect for the *otaku* on the go, this mall is a one-stop shop. There are 27 different Mandarake stores here alone, so it's no wonder that Nakano Broadway is often referred to as 'the collector's haven'. It's not a safe haven, that's for sure: crowds of other obsessives, like human bumper-cars, will be constantly nudging you out of contention for game consoles, anime character toys, manga, magazines, CDs and DVDs, all spread out over four colourful, riotous floors.

Super Potato

Kitabayashi Building 3F–5F
1-11-2 Soto-Kanda
Chiyoda 101-0021
superpotato.com

A true gaming mecca, Super Potato stocks vintage game consoles, computers, cartridges, floppy disks, Nintendo handheld devices, arcade games … if you once wasted hours on it, it's here. Super Mario high-fives Donkey Kong and Pacman in this multi-storey haven. If you think that three dimensions are overrated, that jumping platforms is way better than taking the stairs, and that a handful of pixels is all the visual information you need, then bleep and bloop your way through the store's levels, tackling bosses and discovering newly refurbished gizmos that will take you back to some of your most precious moments of alone time.

Chūō Dōri; Akihabara 'maid'; Tokyo toddler transport; Blythe dolls (opposite, clockwise from top)

MANGA

The Japanese obsession with manga, or comics, remains unabated, even with the advent of digital media. You will see more mobile phones on crowded trains now, but manga is still widely read on public transport as a way to unwind or pass the time. Manga has its origins in twelfth-century scrolls, but came into prominence in the late eighteenth and early nineteenth centuries. Katsushika Hokusai (p. 20) had great success with his work *Hokusai's Manga* as far back as 1814. For those who don't read Japanese, you can now easily access English versions of classics like *Oishinbo (The Gourmet)* by Kariya Tetsu and Hanasaki Akira.

Aoyama Book Center
Cosmos Aoyama Garden Floor B2F
5-53-67 Jingūmae
Shibuya 150-0001

Daikanyama T-Site/ Tsutaya Books
17-5 Sarugakuchō
Shibuya 150-0033
real.tsite.jp/daikanyama/english

Kinokuniya
3-17-7 Shinjuku
Shinjuku 163-8636
www.kinokuniya.co.jp/contents/en

Maruzen and Junkudo
Tokyu Honten Department Store 7F
2-24-1 Dōgenzaka
Shibuya 150-0043

Yaesu Book Center
2-5-1 Yaesu
Chūō 104-8456
yaesu-book.co.jp

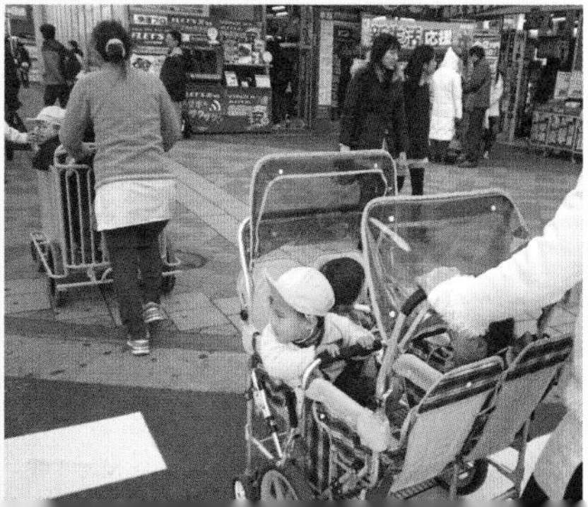

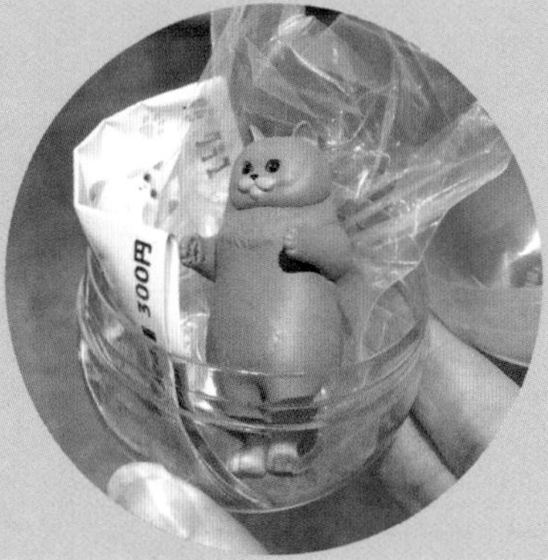

TOKYO VENDING MACHINES

The world still has a long way to go to catch up with Tokyo's vending machines. Introduced to keep visitors happy during the 1964 Tokyo Olympic Games, vending machines have since become a regular (and often very welcome) sight on Tokyo streets. On hot days you can pick up cold drinks: cold green tea, iced coffee, water with electrolytes – everything you need to keep you going. In the chill of winter, hot coffee or tea from a vending machine is a blessing. Small coffee shots in the morning or afternoon are the perfect pick-me-up.

Tokyo's vending machines don't just sell drinks, however; they stock an awesome (and sometimes disturbing) variety of things. Whether it's snacks, booze and oddly flavoured junk food or a complete change of clothes, vending machines are more like mini convenience stores. Pasta in a can, tiny toys, sex toys, tiny sex toys, technology, model kits … the list goes on, and often what you can get will depend on where you are. For example, if you're in Akihabara (p. 224), the machines are more likely to have things for *otaku* (obsessive fans). If you're in Ameya-Yokochō (p. 175) or Kabukichō (p. 250), you can find the more, er, racy items. Of course, capsule-toy machines (p. 226) are vending machines as well. Found all over Tokyo, they are full of great gifts for friends … or great keepsakes for yourself!

かわいいかわいい
ねこランド
ねこランド
かわいい
キャンディちゃん
全6種300円
この水族館
全6種300円
かわいいかわいい
ねこのかぶりもの
サンリオキャラクターズ
全6種400円

AKIHABARA WALK

You don't have to be *otaku* (p. 225) to walk Akihabara, but it helps. There's plenty here for families and for small and big kids alike: impressive toy stores (some for children, others more ... adult), surprisingly good ramen and a variety of animal cafés and themed bars that should satisfy even the most die-hard pop culture fan.

Most of the action is in and around Chūō Dōri, so head out of Akihabara Station's Electric Town Exit. To the left are a plethora of stores for gamers, collectors and model enthusiasts, like Volks Akihabara Hobby Tengoku (1-15-4 Soto-Kanda, www.volks.co.jp), Card Kingdom (1-14-7 Soto-Kanda, cardkingdom.jp), Sega Akihabara (1-15-9 Soto-Kanda, tempo.sega.jp/am/akiba-eki) and the Akihabara Gamers Main Store (1-14-7 Soto-Kanda, www.gamers.co.jp).

To your right, you'll find a small Gundam Café (1-1 Kanda-Hanaoakachō, g-cafe.jp/akiba). Fans of the giant-robot manga and anime franchise might want to tick this off their list. The AKB48 (p. 320) café, shop and ticket lottery counter is here, so try your luck. Multi-storey Bic Camera (4-1-1 Soto-Kanda) and Yodabashi (1-1 Kanda-Hanaoakachō) stores also flank the station.

M's Pop Life Adult Department Store (1-15-13 Soto-Kanda, ms-online.co.jp) has what must be the world's most extensive and eye-opening range of sex toys over seven gasp-inducing floors. Add nearby tobacco store Mimatsu to the mix and it's no wonder that the Akihabara Medical Clinic is nearby.

If all that misbehaving is making you hungry, delicious Yasubei noodle house (1-15-11 Soto-Kanda) is also in this cluster. Alternatively, you can grab an organic treat at the Mother Farm Milk Bar (Atré Akihabara1 1F, 1-17-6 Soto-Kanda) or hit nearby Komaki Syokudō (8-2 Kiraimakichō) for a vegetarian lunch. A quick jaunt across the river will get you to Obscura Coffee Roasters (1-25-4 Kanda-Sudachō), where you can pick up your afternoon jolt.

Head out to Chūō Dōri and slip into Adores Akihabara (1-13-1 Soto-Kanda).

This store combines two of Akihabara's obsessions: karaoke *and* cosplay. Dressing up and singing songs: does anyone ever grow out of that? No, they don't, so put on a Pokémon costume and belt out a chorus or two of 'When Will I Be Famous?' The answer is 'never', but don't let that stop you from having a good time. If video-game players find themselves getting fidgety at this point, there's a Taito Station arcade (4-2-2 Soto-Kanda) nearby.

Anime fans will want to pop in to Animate Akihabara (4-3-2 Soto-Kanda, animate.co.jp/shop/akihabara) for an extensive range of manga and anime that spills out of overstuffed shelves. From here, capsule-toy heaven Akihabara Gachapon Hall (p. 226) is just around the corner.

Akihabara is also the home of animal cafés and themed cafés. The Final Fantasy Eorzea Café (1-1-10 Soto-Kanda 2F) lets you live out your gaming dreams. Decked out with notable Final Fantasy vistas (and some of the game's legendary weapons), it is still the Moogles, those cute little floating balls of fluff, who steal the show.

Little TGV (Isamiya Dai 3 Building 4F, 3-10-5 Soto-Kanda) is a café where cosplay waitresses serve up train-inspired food in an interior that is decked out like a bullet train.

And for anyone who is intrigued by the idea of maid cafés, there's Maidreamin Café (3-16-17 Soto-Kanda), where character-themed food and cute décor are served by waitresses dressed as maids. Doubters may find it more playful than confrontational and more tourist than sexist.

The area's animal cafés include Owl no Mori Café (4-5-8 Soto-Kanda), MoCHA Cat Café (4-5-8 Soto-Kanda) and Cheese Hedgehog Café (4-4-3 Soto-Kanda), although animal treatment can vary from place to place.

Finally, Akihabara boasts some quality ramen. Check out Motenashi Kuroki (p. 109), Ramen Shokudo Ika no Issho (1-27-2 Soto-Kanda) and Kyushu Jingara Ramen (3-11-6 Soto-Kanda).

MODERN TOKYO

While Tokyo Station and its surrounds are the heart of twentieth-century Tokyo, in many ways the Shibuya–Shinjuku hub is the centre of twenty-first century Tokyo. It's all here, bigger and more impressive and evolving as each year passes, pushing itself further up on the scale of one to *Blade Runner*. Shibuya is the modern face of Tokyo, neon-lit at night, impossibly crowded on afternoons and weekends, the enduring image of contemporary Tokyo as thousands of workers and visitors cross the iconic scramble and snap pictures of crowds meeting up by Hachikō Square's famous dog sculpture. These areas are the definition of the Tokyo Vortex, places where you can lose hours or days – even weeks.

SHIBUYA; SHINJUKU; OMOTESANDŌ, HARAJUKU & AOYAMA; ROPPONGI; CREATIVE NEIGHBOURHOODS

SHŌWA ERA (1926–1989), P. 40; HEISEI ERA (1989–2019), P. 48

——— If Shibuya is the hip young thing obsessed with fads that come and go before the West has even noticed them, then Shinjuku is the brash older sibling who just doesn't understand its pop-culture leanings. Probably the largest of Tokyo's mini-cities, and definitely the most concentrated in population, Shinjuku is up-late Tokyo, where you go to shop and then drink. Nearby Roppongi, a cluster of nightclubs and a haven for expats, is where you head afterwards to dance and drink and miss the last train home. Roppongi is on the rise again and starting to challenge its messy reputation, however, and its art triangle and Midtown shopping complex are making it shine in the light of day. To Shibuya's northwest, Omotesandō has a reputation for architecture and fashion, and connects vibrant Harajuku with the sophisticate to the east, Aoyama.

These areas flourished in the Shōwa era, but earthquakes, the Second World War and constant modernisation have meant that few examples of the era's architecture remain. That said, Golden Gai in Shinjuku (p. 247), Nonbei Yokochō in Shibuya and Harmonica Yokochō in Kichijōji (p. 303) are some of the finest examples of early twentieth-century Tokyo.

Both Shinjuku and Shibuya stations are legendary, with Shinjuku Station holding the world record for ushering the most people through its ticket gates each day. As manic as these stations are, they act as gateways to some of Tokyo's most picturesque towns. The Tōkyū Tōyoko, Keiō Inokashira and Tōkyū Den-en-Toshi lines from Shibuya, and the Chūō Sobu Line from Shinjuku will transport you from the frenetic to the peaceful. Daikanyama, Ebisu and Nakameguro is a walkable triangle of great eating, drinking and shopping. Further out, Shimokitazawa, Kōenji and Nishi-Ogikubo are an absolute mecca for vintage fans. And Kichijōji and Chōfu provide more of a sleepy atmosphere, with beautiful parks, the Ghibli Museum (p. 362), the Fudatenjin shrine (p. 334) and a glimpse of verdant, outer-suburban Japan.

SHIBUYA
suumo
スーモ
永谷園
日本のお茶づけ
永谷園の
お茶づけ海苔
寿司
しゃぶしゃぶバイキング
しゃぶ葉
9F
1,199円
1,599円
コンタクト
Caféレストラン ガスト
7F
6F
AEON 英会話イーオン
eyecity
美容外科
渋谷駅前ビル

——— Shibuya is a playground for new ideas, fashions and experiences. It is Tokyo's youthful laboratory, where something is always bubbling above and below the surface.

Young Tokyoites have headed to Shibuya for many years to get a sense of what's in and what's coming. Whether you want to shop the latest looks, head for a date at a honey toast or pancake joint, or flip through coming-of-age books, records and manga in a multi-storey boutique, Shibuya has it all. Hit the backstreets to scour the up-and-coming young designer labels or fossick through a dizzying array of homewares and everyday goods in some of the world's best department stores. The whole town throbs with a vibrant energy.

Crowds gather to meet friends at the overwhelmingly busy and over-photographed (yet still charming) Hachikō Square, which ebbs and flows under the watchful eye of the statue of Hachikō the Akita. Hachikō was a dog who met his master, a university professor named Ueno Hidesaburō, at Shibuya Station every day after work. When Ueno died during a lecture and failed to come home, Hachikō continued to make his way to the station every day for nine years, until his own death. Hachikō and his unwavering devotion became something to emulate, and he is still held up as an example of loyalty to this day.

Hachikō dog sculpture (above); Hachikō Square (opposite)

Since the twentieth century, Shibuya has been a browser's paradise, a shopaholic's Achilles heel, and nirvana for the crowd-watcher. Despite many changes, it continues to give you the feeling of a city that is both at the centre of the world, reimagining commerce and reinventing itself day by day according to global trends, and also wholly separate from the world, doing everything on its own terms.

In the new millennium, however, Shibuya is growing up, and growing up fast. It's putting away childish things, knocking down its long-standing, pre-millennial prefabs and replacing them with mountainous glass towers of Babel with multiple floors dedicated to shopping, eating and the creative arts. These superstructures are the face of a new Tokyo, grand statements of prosperity and rebirth, at once frightening and exhilarating.

The 109 building (2-29-1 Dōgenzaka, shibuya109.jp) is still making a defiant stance, waywardly predicting future fashion: yesterday it was high-tech sci-fi fabrics woven and warped into ultra-chic dresses and jackets; today it's a bondage-glam fairyland look that provokes a hint of outrage even in savvy parents who lived through and absorbed the fashion shocks of punk. The soundtrack at 109 is consumer pop music and the visuals are flashing lights and gaudy colours – a migraine waiting to happen – further underscoring Shibuya's status as the place where youth culture is born kicking and screaming. Between Harajuku and Shibuya, all youth-culture bases are well and truly covered. Anyone wanting a glimpse of what Tokyo kids are up to need not look further, as these two neighbourhoods are the latitude and longitude of cool (although for good measure, you may as well drop in on Akihabara or Ikebukuro, too).

A friend of ours recently remarked, 'I went to Tokyo for a week and couldn't get out of Shibuya.' If you're hoping to see a lot of Tokyo, it's a very real danger. Loft (p. 212), Tokyu Hands (p. 212) and Hikarie (2-21-1 Shibuya, www.hikarie.jp/en) alone could take up two days – at least. Loft is legendary: a superstore showcasing the latest and best products – from souvenirs to household goods to beauty. Tokyu Hands is Loft's handy cousin who's good with tools and crafts. Between them they are a great introduction to Tokyo shopping for first-timers, providing unmissable experiences that astound and excite across two destination buildings that define modern Tokyo. Repeat visits will still yield many delights. The backstreets heading out to Harajuku and Omotesandō are an adventure in themselves: Tower Records, Mandarake, HMV, Disk Union, Bic Camera ... there's another day lost among them. Dōgenzaka has its chic, sharp and up-to-the-minute fashion retailers; Beams, Margaret Howell, Ragtag (for upmarket retro), and fabric mecca Toa are all opportunities to shop till you flop. Cramped alleys filled with smoky yakitori joints and standing sushi bars may be on the decline, but they are still plentiful enough to ensure that you have the fuel to keep going. Of course, you will have plenty of chances to try out Tokyo's take on 'junk' food, too, with Mos, JS and Freshness Burger all popular options.

Shibuya by night

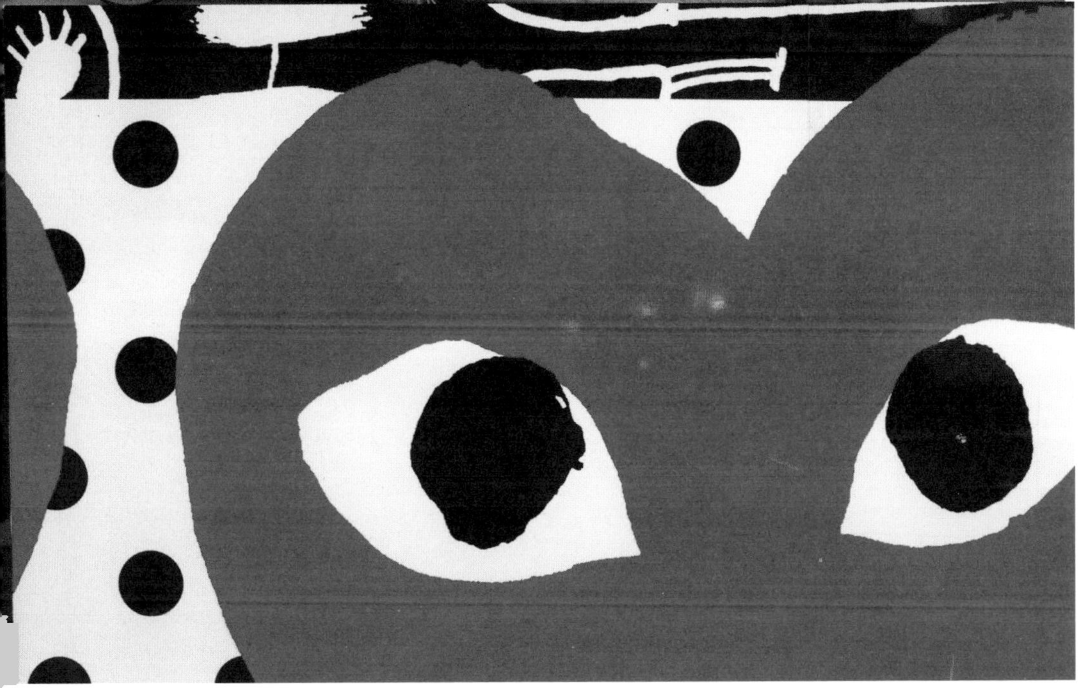

Shibuya vintage signage (top); Comme des Garçons, Seibu (bottom)

Where else would you start a Shibuya walk but at the statue of Hachikō the Akita dog (p. 353) in Hachikō Square (2-1 Dōgenzaka)? Line up with visitors from all over the world to have your pic snapped next to the famously faithful pooch.

Next up is another unmissable photo opportunity: the Shibuya scramble, a five-way pedestrian crossing where you can walk in whichever direction you choose. The crowds that cross here are voluminous to say the least, and at any given time you'll see visitors taking snapshots and videos of a tide of people ducking, weaving and dodging their way across the vast intersection.

From here, stroll up towards the 109 building (2-29-1 Dōgenzaka), which will also take you to Don Quijote (28-6 Udagawachō) and the Bunkamura arts complex (2-24-1 Dōgenzaka). Alternatively, Center Gai ('centre street') is the narrow, crowded street you will see at the northwest end of the scramble. You'll find infamous club Gaspanic (Fuji Building B1F, 21-7 Udagawachō, gaspanic.co.jp) here, as well as sushi-go-round favourites Genki (Leisure Plaza Building 1F, 24-8 Udagawachō, genkisushi.co.jp/en) and Uobei (Dairoku Central Building 1F, 2-29-11 Dōgenzaka) and a plethora of cheap shops and Japan-only experiences.

Wander around the backstreets to get a feel for the real Shibuya. Statement department stores Loft and Tokyu Hands (both p. 212) are home to a legendary mix of homewares and handicrafts, while record stores Disk Union and HMV (both p. 244) are sure to give the vinyl fiend several hours of crate-digging and bin-flipping. From here, head north into Jinnan to explore the smaller maker stores like Beams (1-15-1 Jinnan, https://www.beams.co.jp/global/shop/s) and United Arrows (Parkway Square 2 B1–2F, 1-19-11 Jinnan, www.united-arrows.co.jp). Fabric obsessives can pop into Textile World Toa (1-19-3 Jinnan, www.toa-ltd.com) to sift through their rolls and rolls of material, buttons, ribbons, thread, wool, beads and patches – a heaven for anyone wanting to create their own fashion line. Well-stocked designer vintage store Ragtag (1-17-7 Jinnan, ragtag.jp) offers a premium vintage fix, and adjacent Kōen Dōri features an extensive and popular Muji (B1F, 21-1 Udagawachō).

Strolling back down towards the station, you will find Modi (1-21-3 Jinnan). Foliage covers the arched frontage

The stairway at Opening Ceremony

beckoning you into a chic, contemporary shopping complex – a one-stop shop-fest for the latest fashion, books, music, designer homewares and cosmetics.

Back on the main drag, you'll find cafés serving Shibuya's favourite sugar hit, honey toast (p. 133), a hollowed-out loaf of bread filled with cream and fruit. Gather your friends together at Pasela Resort Shibuyaten (1-22-9 Jinnan) and dig in.

Further along the road, Tower Records (p. 245) is a colourful, quirky space tower where you can sort through floors of music. It specialises in J-pop, as well as indie, world, jazz, inspirational and more. The excellent Tower Records Café and a great bookstore have opened up on the second floor.

South of Shibuya Station, Sakuragaokachō is a quiet enclave where bright pink blossoms burst into life during *sakura* (cherry blossom) season (p. 76). You can find healthy eatery Daylight Kitchen (23-18 Sakuragaokachō, daylightkitchen.jp) here, a top lunch spot for gluten-free eaters.

The east side of Shibuya station is slightly more gentrified, with wide streets that lead off to Harajuku to the north or Aoyama to the east; both destinations in turn link up with each other. Relatively new builds are changing the shape of this side of the station. Shibuya Hikarie's multi-storey shopping complex (2-21-1 Shibuya) boasts brilliant destination shopping, eating and art, including D&Department's gallery, designer homewares store and café, a great spot to get a bird's-eye view of the Shibuya scramble and snap a few choice pics. Boutique hotel Claska has a chic, floaty design store here, and there are pop-up-sized shops, including designer utility-ware specialists Smith, as well as many other opportunities to empty your wallet over eight floors.

Walk along Meiji Dōri toward Harajuku and you'll soon deviate right onto Cat Street, which connects Shibuya to Omotesandō. A peaceful wander, it is not busy so much as bustling. The Roastery by Nozy Coffee (p. 143) will give you the energy you need to tackle approaching Omotesandō. Young, independent fashion labels like Bulle de Savon, I Am Hole and Pulp 417 Édifice, and American darlings Opening Ceremony, line the strip. If you get hungry, the WaraTako *takoyaki* stand (5-11-3 Jingūmae) will serve you the famous octopus snack. ⊗

Girls texting in front of Shibuya scramble poster (left); I Am Hole signage (right)

RECORD STORES

Tokyoites are passionate about music. People queue around the block for the latest J-pop releases, in-store promos, signings and Tokyo-only limited editions. People are fanatical about classic jazz, soul, funk or hip hop, and often open cafés and specialist stores based around their obsessions. Tokyoites appreciate the inherent value of a one-off recording, special packaging and other oddities; CD and record sleeves are often must-have graphic and sculptural works of art. Tokyo is also at the vanguard of the rebirth of the cassette tape, in line with the city's deep-rooted interest in vintage music formats.

Retro vinyl and Tokyo are best friends, and the dedicated trophy hunter can scout some glorious finds in stores run by vinyl enthusiasts. Shinjuku has at least twenty second-hand record stores, so walk around and look up, down and around. If any sign looks like it might be for a music store – for instance, if it has vinyl or musical notes on it – it probably is. The ramshackle nature of low-rise buildings with rabbit-warren-like pathways and twisting staircases spiralling up behind unremarkable facades has given rise to some seriously good hidden vintage vinyl and music stores. Some can be as hard to find as the records themselves, but winkling out those gems is part of the process for the crate-digger. Often, the further down a dingy backstreet or deeper inside the echoing corridors of a seedy seventies building, the better.

For anyone wishing to spend a day browsing, music monoliths like Disk Union, Recofan, HMV or Tower Records have extensive selections packed into long aisles over many floors. For the visitor, there are plenty of international records, imports and Japanese versions of world classics that can be hard to find anywhere else. More often than not, the condition is good to mint, and frequently the company will be exceptional: like-minded hunters squirrelling through tightly packed record flip-bins, hoping to root out that precious vinyl gem or new release intricately packaged and featuring three extra tracks and a bonus live CD. Genres are broad, and though jazz, reggae and soul are a staple feature of most stores, pop, classic rock, ambient, soundtracks, progressive, house, disco and hip hop are well catered for. One thing is certain: you'll lose hours, days, and possibly your friends and family, but new and vintage record buying is a religious experience, and Tokyo is the spiritual capital.

BE-IN RECORD

3-57-8 Kōenji-Minami
Suginami 166-0003
bein.co.jp

Kōenji's Look Street is one of the world's ley-lines for vintage hunters, and Be-In Record is one of the major stops. Tokyo is famous for its standing bars; you could view this as a standing record store. There's certainly no room to do anything else among the store's packed record bins and matchstick-thin aisles. You'll be there for hours hunting through endless treasures: rock albums you thought were lost, vinyl treasures you've seen on the internet and now can hold in your hand. Prices vary, but you can get hold of that long sought-after platter for a decent price if you spend the time to look for it. Elsewhere it's pretty much a masterclass on Stones and Beatles rarities, and there is some premium vinyl window-shopping with bootlegs, live records and first pressings.

BIG LOVE RECORDS

Houei Building 3F
2-31-3 Jingūmae
Shibuya 150-0001
bigloverecords.jp

Defiantly indie, Big Love was into the cassette revival before it was popular. Nestled upstairs in a hush-hush building on a secluded street within wandering distance of Harajuku's mad centre, Big Love is the secret vinyl hangout you've come to Tokyo to find. It's a mixtape, analogue record player, retro-music love-in of a store that the holier-than-thou vinyl aficionado can go to without fear of being let down. Classic house is represented with labels like XL, while 4AD, Rough Trade and Creation bring the choice indie/alternative pop. The craft aesthetic extends to the small bar where you can grab a beer while you look over your rare indie-label purchase or ponder which vinyl you absolutely have to have in your collection.

TIP: *If cassette tapes and decks are your thing, Waltz in Nakameguro specialises in both.*

DISK UNION

3-31-4 Shinjuku
Shinjuku 160-0022
diskunion.net

This used vinyl and general music behemoth somehow manages to remain down-to-earth. It almost feels like your local, and it achieves this by splitting its stores up into one main store and many tiny specialist shops, some up spiral staircases in shabby buildings sharing space with bars and hairdressers, and others sequestering the upper floors of faceless business buildings or crouching in wait behind a randomly unfurled roller door down a narrow alley. The main store is eight floors of music, an insurmountable selection broken up into specialty areas. Hit the vintage vinyl floor just to peruse the walls – a collector's paradise of unaffordable bootlegs and rarities that is more like a record museum than a record store. The range of styles and merchandise is staggering. A good challenge would be to try and get through all of the Shinjuku Disk Unions in a day. The best way to do this is to grab the store's vinyl map, which will also tell you the best record stores across Tokyo. Your ears will thank you; your wallet not so much.

DISK UNION SHIBUYA

Antena 21 Building 2–3F
30-7 Udagawachō,
Shibuya 150-0042
diskunion.net

Low-key little cousin to Shinjuku, Shibuya's spiral staircase of five specialist retro-vinyl and CD floors snakes up into the Antena 21 building in busy Udagawachō. Credit cards at the ready, you can flip through soul, jazz, indie, sixties rock (Beatles and Stones, anyone?) and an ever-growing range of progressive rock and ambient. Rare-as-seventies-rock-bands'-teeth bootlegs and first pressings will have you salivating. Crates and bins are crammed with records; racks are stuffed with CDs and related merchandise. You'll have to crabwalk sideways down most of the aisles. Shinjuku might have the breadth, but the Shibuya store has the depth and you'll find yourself looking up eventually, having forgotten what city you're in and what day it is with a crick in your neck and a beaming smile on your face.

TIP: *If you love Disk Union, there are five stores in the Ochanomizu area near Jimbōchō.*

HASSHODO KOSHOTEN

5-2-10 Nishi-Ikebukuro
Toshima 171-0021

Starting as a second-hand bookstore in 1960, Hasshodo Koshoten has since expanded into records. This is one of the biggest selections you'll find outside of Shinjuku and Shibuya, and is worth the trip out if only to graze through their Japanese *enka* rarities. This style of prewar Japanese pop, based on traditional music with a hint of Americana, is a genre in its own right. The covers can be the best thing about the records, especially the ones from the seventies. Elsewhere, the store has a great selection of jazz, rock and soul, and some cool retro music magazines.

HI-FI RECORD STORE

6-19-17 Jingūmae
Shibuya 150-0001
hi-fi.gr.jp

A little gem hidden on the third floor of a nondescript store on Meiji Dōri, Hi-Fi offers an old-school flip through packed crates and boxes arranged artlessly in a small square of some of Tokyo's most valuable real estate. You'll be rubbing elbows with your fellow crate-diggers as you flick through rare vinyl finds looking for that fabled pop, jazz or folk record that doesn't seem to be on eBay. Chances are you'll find it as well; this selection is not as haphazardly put together as the store, but carefully and lovingly sourced so you don't have to do the footwork.

HMV

36-2 Udagawachō
Shibuya 150-0042
hmv.co.jp

The UK's HMV gave up the ghost in 2013 when it went into receivership. Luckily their selection and democratic, grassroots approach to music continues in the Shibuya store, opened in 2014 in Udagawachō. Audio equipment and merchandise line shelves and retro records are stacked in bins on a bare concrete floor, giving you the feeling that you are digging for gold at your favourite record fair. Genres are heavy on indie, rock, pop and progressive. Head upstairs for some good finds among the ubiquitous jazz, reggae and soul on the second floor. The ever-expanding selection of colourful cassette tapes against the wall brings the eighties screaming back.

LIGHTHOUSE RECORDS

Seijutsu Building 4F
2-9-2 Dōgenzaka
Shibuya 150-0043
lighthouserecords.jp

Dōgenzaka's must-visit record store for anyone hunting out dance, house, techno and beats, Lighthouse is the cooler-than-cool destination that is happy to downplay its status by hanging a huge mirror ball from the ceiling and stocking the occasional Fun Boy Three record. DJs who want floor fillers from the days when music ruled discos, house parties and raves will find an armful of high-energy power-fuelled classics, low and slinky downbeat and knife-edge funk and hip hop among this selection, which is updated weekly. Anyone who still throws around words like Balearic, acid jazz or deep house will find themselves very at home here.

RED RING RECORDS

Nakagawa Building 2F-B
7-8-2 Nishi-Shinjuku
Shinjuku 160-0023
redringrecords.com

Nishi-Shinjuku is well known for a plethora of second-hand record stores, but they can often be pricey and obsessed with bootleg recordings. If bootlegs are your thing, definitely head to Blind Faith (7-15-8 Nishi-Shinjuku) with a shopping trolley full of cash and you'll come away with some serious rarities. For anyone looking for a well-curated selection of progressive and hard-rock records, plus a general selection at good prices, Red Ring comes up aces.

TOWER RECORDS

1-22-14 Jinnan
Shibuya 150-0041
tower.jp

Tokyo does the preservation of long-faded international record stores better than anybody. California's late lamented Tower Records opened in Tokyo in 1979, became independently owned in 2002, and survived the advent of digital music and the collapse of the parent company in 2006. Seven floors of music, books, audio equipment, stationery and a café are housed in a retro-futurist block of Lego, a grey-and-yellow monolith of bricks and external plastic tube elevators that looks like Paris's Pompidou Centre on a sci-fi acid trip. Yet to expand into vintage vinyl (although there is a smattering of new 180 g releases), Tower Records is still a place where you can easily drop hours sifting through the Japanese and international music on offer. There's plenty of pop and blaring screens and busy attendants to ensure that selling 'physical' music looks as vibrant now as it did in the glory days.

OTHER CHOICE STORES

City Country City
Hosozawa Building 4F
2-12-13 Kitazawa
Setagaya 155-0031
city-country-city.com/about-en

Coconuts Disk
3-22-7 Nishi-Ikebukuro
Toshima 171-0021
coconutsdisk.com

Daruma-ya
Sasaya Building 2F
1-36-5 Higashi-Ikebukuro
Toyoshima 170-0013
darumaya.to

Jet Set Records
Yanagawa Building 201
2-33-12 Kitazawa
Setagaya 155-0031
www.jetsetrecords.net

Manhattan Records
10-1 Udagawachō
Shibuya 150-0042

Recofan Shibuya
Shibuya Beam 4F
31-2 Udagawachō
Shibuya 150-0042
recofan.co.jp

Record Sya
2-26 Kanda-Jimbōchō
Chiyoda 101-0051

Warehouse/Nat Records
Shinmei Building 2F
7-7-33 Nishi-Shinjuku
Shinjuku 160-0023
natrecords.shop-pro.jp
warehouse.shop-pro.jp

SHINJUKU

——— Shinjuku is a modern-day phenomenon: a thriving, bustling city that is a collection of striking department stores, towering hotels and state-of-the-art buildings, yet is still glued together by faded posters and small whispers of pre-millennial, alleyway Tokyo – the Tokyo where the proprietors of traditional stores, cafés and eateries rail against the seemingly unstoppable march of skyscrapers and ubiquitous chain stores. If you ever feel the need to get lost, Shinjuku is a good place to do it. This vast city within a city is frenetic and crowded – confusing and exhilarating in equal measure. It is home to the biggest and busiest train station in the world, featuring a staggering 200 exits and more than 50 platforms. An estimated 3.5 million people, possibly more, flood through its gates on any given day. Shinjuku somehow manages to accommodate the sheer volume of people spilling out into the city, catering to starving diners hunting out eateries, thirsty office-workers in need of a good bar, and tourists looking for great shopping or sensory experiences.

As a major commercial district, there are faceless business centres best avoided by the thrill-seeking traveller, but even here there is value to be found: design enthusiasts looking for interesting new structures are bound to appreciate some of Shinjuku's proud new towers, architectural marvels pulling the area even further into the future. Now, in true Tokyo form, Shinjuku is starting to put on a fresh face. The Yayoi Kusama Museum (p. 363), opened in 2017, is just the beginning of its transformation.

Nevertheless, a large part of Shinjuku's charm will always be the remnants – squashed between looming modern monoliths – of an older, more rustic time, charming enclaves down narrow backstreets that are small relics of Shinjuku's colourful past. No matter your preference, whether it's the ramshackle Golden Gai's mouse-in-a-maze adventure of retro watering holes (1-1 Kabukichō, goldengai.jp), the upmarket Isetan (3-14-1 Shinjuku, isetan.mistore.jp/store/shinjuku) and its ocular overload of a food hall, or the vinyl hunter's holy grail, Disk Union (Antena 21 2–3F, 30-7 Udagawachō), expect a joyous assault on the senses.

View over bridge, Shinjuku Station East (opposite)

新宿区

LOVE

情熱ホルモン
KIRIN
キリンビール
ラーメン
餃子
岐阜屋
焼
かっぺ亭

ねこ膳

¥500

Cocoon Tower (above); Astro Boy mural at Takadanobaba Station; *LOVE* sculpture; Shinjuku izakaya; NEWoMan; Omoide Yokochō (opposite, clockwise from top left)

SHINJUKU WALK

You have a big day ahead of you in one of Tokyo's most over-the-top areas, so start early – around 10 am – with a little bit of calm at Bingoya (p. 212), a multi-storey Japanese handicrafts store. Slightly out of the public eye on Shinjuku's outskirts, Bingoya has the feel of an old-school souvenir store rather than a tourist target. You'll find quality *kokeshi* dolls, *noren* curtains, kimono fabrics, children's toys, stationery, ceramics, cookware and more.

From here, walk southwest towards central Shinjuku; it's about two kilometres to the station. Or, if you want to save your energy, catch the train to Higashi-Shinjuku from Wakamatsu-Kawada Station on the Toei Ōedo Line. From Higashi-Shinjuku Station, walk south down the main street until you find Shinjuku's main spiritual enclave, Hanazono Inari Jinja (p. 334), a Shinto shrine and your last patch of peace before heading into the madness. Stroll the grounds before heading west into the heart of Golden Gai (1-1 Kabukichō, goldengai.jp).

At night this ramshackle hive of (mostly drinking) activity truly comes to life, but during the day it's still a treat. Make a note of any bars that take your fancy for your evening's refreshments. Bear in mind that some of these establishments are members-only, although you can try to work your way in with a winning smile. Just next door is Kabukichō, a rough, slightly creepy and *slightly* dangerous place. Unheard of in Tokyo! It's fine to walk around during the day, but be a little more wary than usual at night, and sidestep the hawkers (unless you're out to misbehave).

As midday approaches and you start thinking about lunch, stroll southwest towards Isetan (3-14-1 Shinjuku, isetan.mistore.jp/store/shinjuku), one of the world's oldest and best department stores. There's quality dining at Eat Paradise on the seventh floor, but grabbing a *bentō* and some *wagashi* (traditional sweets; p. 124) from the seriously good food hall and devouring them in the rooftop garden is a real treat.

Bingoya handicrafts

If you want to try the local gems, Ramen Ichiran (Peace Building B1F, 3-34-11 Shinjuku, en.ichiran.com), Menya Musashi (K-1 Building 1F, 1-2-6 Nishi-Shinjuku, menya634.co.jp/storelist/shinjuku) or Fuunji (p. 108) are rated soup establishments. If you're vegan, Ain Soph Journey (p. 115) is a good stop for lunch. Vinyl hunters can't miss Disk Union (p. 244) and the tech-obsessed who like a side of fashion with their electronics should hit BicLo, an unholy megastore alliance between Uniqlo and Bic Camera. If you're on the hunt for something to read, Kinokuniya (p. 227) has an astounding range. Alternatively, if you feel the need for some pampering at this stage, head back to Kabukichō, where you'll find chic local *onsen* (hot spring) Thermae-Yu (1-1-2 Kabukichō, thermae-yu.jp).

For a snapshot of how old Shinjuku lived, visit Omoide Yokochō ('memory lane') on the west side of Shinjuku Station. Snap some pics of the picturesque alleyways before readying your camera for one of Shinjuku's statement photos. Cross under the bridge and turn to face the railway line to see Shinjuku's endless stream of colourful trains speeding past in front of the concrete metropolis and its billboards by day or the quintessential neon jungle by night. From here, head west to Robert Indiana's *LOVE* sculpture (p. 353) and then south to the Metropolitan Government Building (p. 161), where panorama enthusiasts can take in the wonderful (and famously free) aerial view of Tokyo.

Head back towards Shinjuku Station, stopping at Sekaido (p. 212) for supplies if you are an artist or craft-lover. Cross to the east side of the station to NEWoMan (4-1-6 Shinjuku, newoman.jp), Shinjuku's brand-new ultra-stylish shopping destination. Department store Takashimaya (5-24-2 Sendagaya, takashimaya.co.jp) is still holding its own and boasts an excellent food hall and resident Tokyu Hands. If you have time, or if you are in Tokyo to explore the gardens, don't miss the vast patch of green that is Shinjuku Gyoen (p. 343). ⊗

Shinjuku vending machines (left); Hanazono Inari Jinja (right)

HARAJUKU & AOYAMA

OMOTESANDŌ

——— Officially, Omotesandō is the street that links Harajuku, that one-time magnet for experimental youth culture, with glamorous Aoyama. But the name has also come to refer to the whole area that flanks Omotesandō Dōri (p. 260) – that is, Omotesandō the street – which encompasses parts of Jingūmae (including Harajuku), Kita-Aoyama and Minami-Aoyama.

Since the nineties, Harajuku has been the parade ground for youthful peacocks strutting their otherness, and it still possesses the power to delight and surprise within its voluminous crowds. But the changing times and the influx of tourists has also meant that the area can slip into self-parody. Mega-companies cashed in by creating an affordable, more palatable interpretation of Harajuku kids' latest style experiments, while *Fruits* magazine took Japanese street style to the world and made what had previously been an admired and feared art form, a rebellious statement, into an accessible commodity. The influx of international brands put a few more nails in the coffin, grinding the Harajuku edge down to a nub.

In spite of all that, Harajuku is still alive with possibility. Laforet (p. 258) buzzes like a disturbed bee hive; by providing small spaces for independent and mid-sized designers it has become almost like a hawker's market for fashion – especially during sales, when the crazy really kicks in. Serious bargains bring out kids with megaphones who entice sardine-can crowds into the nooks and crannies of Laforet's expansive ecosystem. It's quintessential Tokyo: life-affirming fun and an experience not soon forgotten.

Laforet (above); Omotesandō Dōri (opposite)

Crowds in Harajuku defy logic, a claustrophobic pedestrian crush that runs along Meiji Dōri and bottlenecks into the schoolkid wonderland of Takeshita Dōri. It's 200-yen stores and bargain-basement everything here, with all of the Tokyo fashion food groups on offer, from Pokémon socks and Hello Kitty earrings, to I-heart-whatever T-shirts and ten-dollar platform shoes that Marc Bolan would have recruited for his wardrobe. The food here matches the decor; waffles and crepes with a combination of familiar and unfamiliar flavours. Takeshita is nothing more than a local laneway, but its location in one of the city's main hubs, flowing down from Harajuku's perpetually busy station, as well as its plethora of cut-price shops, has made it one of the world's busiest and most colourful streets – an experience not to be missed. Launching headlong into the seething mass of humanity is like an amusement park ride; the multitudinous madness of it all is one of Harajuku's consistent drawcards.

The Sunday 'freak parade' outside the station has long since dwindled, moving into Yoyogi Park (p. 342). There's still plenty to photograph: mid-life-crisis Elvises striking the king's legendary poses; gothic Lolita dolls with far-off looks and I-dare-you stares; doily-clad *dolly-kei* enthusiasts; warped nurses with makeup smears and torn, bloody clothing; and waif-like, ghostly creatures who would happily be misfits in any crowd. Westerners hoping to capture some of the essence that has made Harajuku so intriguing over the years can dress up and join in – you'll almost certainly come off as an uber-nerdy wannabe, but that's part of the fun.

Laforet (above); Omotesandō Hills at Christmas time (opposite)

KAWAII CULTURE

Kawaii ('cute') culture is loved all over Japan, but its heart lies in Tokyo – the home of emojis, Hello Kitty and Pokémon. It would be unusual to spend a day in the capital and not see a life-size character promoting something, a brightly coloured truck pumping out a jingle, food shaped as animals, or products adorned with smiley faces. Miniature dogs sporting designer outfits, sitting in special dog prams, is par for the course. Cute splinters into different groups, too: there is creepy *kawaii*, dolly *kei*, fairy *kei*, Lolita, *mori* girl and a whole host of other variations on the theme of *kawaii* culture.

Peak cuteness is mostly centred around Shibuya, Harajuku and Sunshine City in Ikebukuro, as well as Akihabara, where *kawaii* comes in all manner of guises. Surprisingly, Ginza (the home of luxe and chic, p. 202) has some great *kawaii* stores and activities. The Kit Kat store (p. 135), the Fujiya chocolate shop (p. 258), the Sanrio World shop (p. 258) and Loft (p. 208) can be found here, and it's a quick train ride to Tokyo Station's Character Street (p. 199). Shimokitazawa (p. 317) is also a good spot for cute stores and cafés.

The cliché Harajuku-girl image of *kawaii* may have ended with the nineties, but cute itself will never go out of style; the trend just keeps turning over and reinventing itself again and again. Just be warned: if you're travelling with small children, don't be surprised if you have to queue with teens or even single adults for seats at a character-related event.

Our sections on cats (p. 186), kids' hangouts (p. 268) and Akihabara (p. 224) are also great resources for your *kawaii* needs.

Crazy Kit Kat flavours; Kiddy Land dolls; *Kawaii* street scene (clockwise from top left)

ANIMAL ACCESSORIES & DOG-WASH VIEWING

Claska Kiokuh
Claska 2F
1-3-18 Meguro
Chūō 152-0001
claska.com/en

Green Dog Tokyo Midtown
Tokyo Midtown Galleria 1F
9-7-4 Akasaka
Minato 107-0052
green-dog.com/store/tmt/

Kojima in Roppongi
3-18-12 Roppongi
Minato 106-0032
pets-kojima.com/shop/0092/

ANIMAL CAFES

Cat cafés
(p. 188)

Cheese Hedgehog
Tokyo Ogiso Building 2F
4-4-3 Sotokanda Chiyoda-ku,
http://fureai-harinezumi.com

Fukurō Sabō Owl Café
3-15-1 Higashi-Motomachi
Kokubunji 185-0022
hukurousabou.sakura.ne.jp

Kotori Bird Café
6-3-7 Minami-Aoyama
Minato 107-0062

Ms Bunny
Iwahori Bldg 3F
6-7-2 Roppongi, Minato-ku
http://www.harinezumi-cafe.com

CHARACTER CAFÉS

Café de Miki with Hello Kitty
DiverCity Tokyo Plaza 2F
1-1-10 Aomi
Kōtō 135-0064
cafedemiki.jp

Cinnamoroll Café
Shinjuku Marui Annex
3-1-26 Shinjuku
Shinjuku 160-0022
cinnamorollcafe.com

Plus Secret (Monchhichi)
1-17-5 Asakusabashi
Taitō 111-0053
plussecret.shopinfo.jp

Pompompurin Café
Cute Cube Harajuku
1-7-1 Jingūmae
Shibuya 150-0001
pompom.createrestaurants.com

Sailor Moon x My Melody Candy Parlour
Ikebukuro PARCO Honkan 7F
1-28-2 Minami-Ikebukuro
Toshima 171-0022

CUTE DESTINATIONS

Fujiya Ginza
Crystal Building 2F
4-2-12 Ginza
Chūō 104-0061
fujiya-peko.co.jp

Kit Kat Chocolatory Ginza
(p. 135)

Sanrio Puroland
(p. 188)

Sanrio World Ginza
Nishi-Ginza Department Store 2F
4-1 Nishi-Ginza
Chūō 104-0061

CUTE FOOD

Frozen popcorn at Sweet XO Good Grief
Harajuku 77 Building
1-16-6 Jingūmae
Shibuya 150-0001

Honey toast
(p. 133)

Kakigōri at Ice Monster
6-3-7 Jingūmae
Shibuya 150-0001

Technicolour fairy floss at Totti Candy Factory
RYU Apartment 2F
1-16-5 Jingūmae
Shibuya 150-0001

Kawaii chocolate packaging
- Chocolate by Meiji
- Gudetama by Furuta
- Karamel Corn by Tohato
- Kinoko no Yama and Apollo

HARAJUKU KAWAII

Café Crepe Strawberry House
Laforet Harajuku 1F
1-11-6 Jingūmae
Shibuya 150-0001
cafe-crepe.co.jp

Gram Café & Pancakes
1-9-30 Jingūmae
Shibuya 150-0001
cafe-gram.com
Sky-high, ultra-fluffy pancakes.

Harajuku Bridge, Yoyogi Park
6-6 Jingūmae
Shibuya 150-0001
Head here on Sunday to see groups of kids in costumes.

Kawaii Monster Café
YM Square 4F
4-31-10 Jingūmae
Shibuya 150-0001
kawaiimonster.jp
If you're a fan of popstar Kyary Pamyu Pamyu's psychedelic aesthetic, this café is designed by her art director, Sebastian Masuda.

Kiddy Land
(p. 270)

Laforet
1-11-6 Jingūmae
Shibuya 150-0001
laforet.ne.jp/en
For teen fashion.

Takeshita Dōri
(p. 254)
1 Jingūmae
Shibuya 150-0001
For people-watching, and inexpensive stores.

Design Festa; NHK bus; Takeshita stairs; Pompompurin Café signage; Ghibli cat bus toy; Cheese Hedgehog (clockwise from top left)

OMOTESANDŌ DŌRI WALK

——— Omotesandō – the street. The connective thread that links tranquil Meiji Jingu (Meiji Shrine, p. 334) and its forest glade in the north to Harajuku and Aoyama in the south, terminating at the serene Nezu Museum (p. 352). Omotesandō Dōri is one of Tokyo's premiere destinations. A vast boulevard, Parisian in style and scope, it is Tokyo's equivalent to the Champs-Elysées. Trees line the expansive avenue, draped in

Ikubundo Aoyama Dōri building

fairy lights that flick on at night and make the entire street sparkle. A cluster of inventive, monolithic buildings showcase the work of some of Japan's best-known architects – extraordinary structures that announce their occupants as the pinnacle of haute couture. The neighbourhood of Aoyama continues the 'top end of town' feel, leaving a trail of upmarket bread crumbs that lead down to the Nezu Museum's beautiful gardens and tea house. It really does go from serene to crazy to serene in a short, exhilarating distance.

Omotesandō Dōri is wider than Takeshita Dōri and other surrounding streets, but you will still find yourself bumper to bumper with your fellow humans, especially during holidays, sale times or when school gets out and students flock to the area to shop until they drop.

The Jewels of Aoyama

Looking down from Harajuku into the human soup – a blur of colourful figures milling along the sidewalks – you'll be daunted, but not enough to stop yourself from joining the throng, becoming part of the experience.

High-end brands make Omotesandō Dōri a luxe destination for big spenders, while more accessible stores like Kiddy Land (p. 270) and Oriental Bazaar (5-9-13 Jingūmae, orientalbazaar.co.jp/en), boutique shopping centres like Omotesandō Hills (4-12-10 Jingūmae, www.omotesandohills.com) and Gyre (5-10-1 Jingūmae, gyre-omotesando.com), and Louis Vuitton's wonderful, free top-floor gallery space (p. 365) mean that everyone has plenty to do. Kiddy Land is the perfect distraction for unruly children and equally unruly adults, a multi-storey building with themed floors crammed with Tokyo's cutest character toys and models. An hour per floor might just cover it, and *kawaii*-hunters will leave laden with bags of the latest and greatest toys. Nearby Oriental Bazaar might literally be the most touristy store on one of the most touristy strips in Tokyo, but there are some seriously good purchases here, with something to suit every budget. Various items of Japanalia, from kimono and ninja outfits to ceramics, statuettes and textiles, are spread over two floors. The range is excellent in terms of quality and design, and is perfect for gift-hunters.

The trick to Omotesandō Dōri is to go with the flow. You'll find yourself strolling past long queues of people lining up for the latest chocolate-popcorn vendor, European chocolatier or Hawaiian-themed café, and admiring the many pets on leads or in strollers out for some fresh air. Take on Laforet's multi-storey youth-fashion

mecca (p. 258) – make sure you visit the small Zen garden at the back, opposite the Ōta Memorial Museum of Art (p. 362) – and if you aren't shopped out from that, cross the road and explore Tokyu Plaza (4-30-3 Jingūmae, omohara.tokyu-plaza.com). The main attraction is a ride up the escalator, then an about-face to see the 'hall of mirrors' entrance that reflects the outrageous passing parade of shoppers. This relatively new building is home to tasteful, contemporary Western and Japanese fashion stores, eateries and a rooftop with a captivating view.

All along the thoroughfare are architectural marvels, many belonging to the biggest of the big names in international fashion. Brands like Louis Vuitton (5-7-5 Jingumae, jp.louisvuitton.com), Yves Saint Laurent (4-3-10 Jingūmae, ysl.com) and Dior (5-9-11 Jingūmae, dior.com) flaunt themselves in spectacular displays of wealth and design. You don't have to be a fashion obsessive to appreciate what's on show here: window displays are like gallery installations; buildings are works of art in themselves; and mannequins and shop assistants alike pose for imaginary cameras. Don't miss the Tod's (p. 351) and Hugo Boss (5-1 Jingūmae) stores, delightful architectural triumphs standing side by side. The Tadao Ando–designed Omotesandō Hills shopping centre still manages to stand out, an almost Escher-like twist of escalators, stairways and paths with a cavernous central space that is often used to good effect (especially at Christmas), showcasing musicians or startling displays.

Use Omotesandō Dōri as your base and weave in and out, popping down any of the narrow backstreets that branch off like capillaries, filled with small fashion stores and tiny cafés and remnants of pre-millennium

Vintage kimono (above); Prada Epicenter (opposite)

Tokyo where many treasures can be unearthed. Buried behind Omotesandō Dōri in a stylish bunker is the Fred Perry store (5-9-6 Jingūmae, fredperry.jp); its Japan-only range is a must for mods and the mod-inclined. Head to the upper level to check out the carved wooden desk with the brand's laurel-wreath logo; it's magnificent. If you find yourself on Cat Street (p. 241) and it's suiting your mood, cross directly over Omotesandō Dōri and head past Ralph Lauren (5-17-13 Jingūmae, ralphlauren.co.jp/en) and Journal Standard (6-7-1 Jingūmae, journal-standard.jp), where the street continues. It has been home to the Airstream Garden (4-13-8 Jingūmae, airstream-garden.com/en) pop-up coffee and food pitstop for years now, so refuel before hitting vintage nerve-centre Chicago Inc. (4-26-26 Jingūmae, chicago.co.jp) or any of a number of independent Japanese and international fashion stores. Maisen (p. 123), one of Tokyo's best *tonkatsu* (fried pork cutlet) joints, is further down Omotesandō Dōri and to the right, as well as one of the world's best coffee stores and a shrine to the coffee bean, Koffee Mameya (formerly Omotesandō Koffee, p. 143). Stop in at Galerie Doux Dimanche (p. 365), a charming gallery and craft shop, to see some of the work of Tokyo's best local illustrators and designers, and to stock up on exquisite handcrafted items.

If Omotesandō Dōri is pure Paris, then the crossroads where Omotesandō Dōri meets Aoyama Dōri is pure New York: a huge open space with looming fashion billboards. In summer there's nowhere to hide from the blistering sun; in winter this is surely one of the coldest street corners in the world. As exposed as it may be, the intersection is the perfect point from which to marvel at the breadth of Tokyo while getting your bearings. If you are walking down Omotesandō Dōri away from Harajuku, turning right into Aoyama Dōri will take you into the heart of Shibuya – a much shorter walk than you might expect. You'll arrive at Shibuya Hikarie (2-21-1 Shibuya, www.hikarie.jp/en) in around fifteen minutes. Shop at Spiral (5-6-23 Minami-Aoyama, www.spiral.co.jp) or Found Muji (Nakajima Building 1–2F, 5-50-6 Jingūmae), then stop to admire the warped portholes of the Ikubundo Aoyama Dōri building and the playful mosaic statue *Kodomo no Ki* (*Tree of Children*) by Taro Okamoto along the way.

Continuing straight on Omotesandō Dōri will deliver you into the heart of glamorous Aoyama. Omotesandō Dōri narrows significantly here to become a chic shopping strip. Issey Miyake disciples will be in heaven here, with a plethora of stores – all aimed at different markets, with varying themes and design directions – dotted along the ribbon of road like small galleries showing micro-pleated, distressed and evolutionary works of fashion art. Comme des Garçons (p. 352) breaks the Miyake monopoly. Pop into this otherworldly dimension and see how the other half (eighth? tenth?) dresses. Kawakubo-sama's gothic-space-noir-pod-alien-hobo chic is unlike anything you've seen or worn – the stuff of your dreams, or possibly nightmares. The prices befit the custom-made artworks that these garments are, but mere mortals can always grab a fragrance or the classic Comme des Garçons Play heart motif T-shirt. Age makes no difference to the employment

Omotesandō Dōri lanterns (top left); Aoyama Cemetery (top right); Galerie Doux Dimanche (bottom)

SunnyHills; Nezu Museum garden; Nezu Museum (clockwise from top left)

practices of this store. You could be served by a sharp twenty-year-old in a sleek, dark suit, or a septuagenarian space-age bohemian Dracula, a walking-on-air piece of performance art pretending to arrange racks of clothes to avoid noticing that you exist.

Effete and elegantly wasted though they are, Issey Miyake and Comme des Garçon's powerhouse stores are still overshadowed by Prada's bottle-green bubble obelisk (p. 352), one of the world's most arresting pieces of pop architecture. Designed by Swiss architects Herzog & de Meuron, the Prada Epicenter is a leaning tower of neo-futurist cool, a warped cubist shape covered in myriad 'contact lenses' that expose the building's internal workings, making it one of Tokyo's most photographable facades. On any given day you will see people observing it from different vantage points, trying to find the building's best profile. For your continued high-end shopping delectation, Stella McCartney, Thom Browne and Acne are just around the corner from the Prada building. A multi-storey Cos, H&M's chic sister brand, is also close by.

Crowds will have already thinned out by now, and once you get to the Palace Building you'll have much more room to move. Turn right to peruse the upmarket design wares in at At the Corner by Art and Science (6-1-6 Minami-Aoyama, arts-science.com/en). Several other stores in this area show beautifully curated crafts and enticing must-have ceramics and jewellery.

The beauty of these objects complements the beauty of the Nezu Museum (p. 352), which sits in a bamboo grove across the road. Rotating exhibitions of Japanese traditional crafts, as well as some wonderful permanent exhibits, make this a necessary stop. The bamboo-clad walkway is a conduit to the stunning museum and equally impressive garden. Take your time strolling the grounds, as this exquisitely kept Japanese-style garden is the perfect peaceful city escape. The tea houses here have long been a focal point for Tokyoites wanting to relive the glory of traditions past. At any given time you'll probably see a group of women looking immaculate in traditional kimono while kneeling and taking tea on the *tatami* mats overlooking the tranquil lake. For the contemporary at heart, the traditional tea ceremony is mirrored by a new café, enveloped by a shade-cloth sail that actually acts as a canvas, turning the light of day and the organic shapes of the garden outside into abstract silhouettes.

The winding backstreets of Aoyama make for a wonderful stroll and offer up many enticing surprises. Grab a delicacy from Higashiya Man (3-17-14 Minami-Aoyama, higashiya.com), the hole-in-the-wall cousin of Ginza's chic confectionery store, and explore the beautiful residential architecture and hidden shops. Pop in for some pineapple cake at SunnyHills (p. 352) and, if it's dusk, take a magical detour through Aoyama Cemetery (2-32-2 Minami-Aoyama), where famously loyal pup Hachikō (p. 235) is buried. Further into the neighbourhood of Gaienmae, Doinel (p. 365) is a charming little gallery and shop, a worthy stop on the way to the edgy Watarium Museum of Contemporary Art (p. 360). ⊗

THINGS WE LOVE

KIDS' HANGOUTS

Travelling internationally with kids can sometimes be challenging. Where do you eat? How do you find activities that both kids and adults will love? How do you navigate public transport without losing anyone? The great thing about Tokyo is that it is one of the most kid-friendly cities in the world. Tokyoites love children, and if you have a pram or heavy luggage and a couple of kids in tow, you will always find help when you need it.

One of the biggest challenges for parents is that Tokyo is a late riser. Opening hours for museums and galleries range from 9.30 am to 11 am, so make sure you check before arriving. Many cafés around town open at 11 am or later. Thankfully, free parks and gardens (p. 336) and shrines (p. 330) are always open. Grab some coffee, juice, fruit and breakfast snacks from the convenience store or from a food hall the night before and head out at your own pace for a picnic breakfast.

If you have a day planned at the Mori Art Museum (p. 357), which opens at 10 am, why not arrive early and have a wander and a play in the Mori Garden at the foot of the Roppongi Hills Mori Building? Nearby Roppongi Station has lots of great eateries so if you left your accommodation on an empty stomach you'll find some good options there.

The Yamanote Line does a loop around the city and, provided you avoid peak times, a trip on the line (jumping on and off as you please) can be a great first day. Make sure you stop at Tokyo Station at lunchtime and head to Ramen Street (p. 199) for a bowl of noodles, or alight at Ueno Station instead and have a picnic in the park and visit the zoo or ride a swan boat.

There are designated seats for pregnant women on trains and you can get a pregnancy badge from most stations. Wearing it will ensure that you are instantly looked after.

EARLY BREAKFAST

Café Kitsuné

3-17-1 Minami-Aoyama
Minato 107-0062
Open from 9 am, seven days a week.

Good Morning Café Sendagaya

Tokyo Metropolitan Gymnasium Pool Building
1-17-1 Sendagaya
Shibuya 151-0051
good-morning-cafe.com/top.php
Breakfast from 7 am to 10.45 am, seven days a week.

Ivy Place

Daikanyama T-Site
16-15 Sarugakuchō
Shibuya 150-0033
www.tysons.jp/ivyplace/en
Breakfast from 7 am to 10.45 am, seven days a week.

Nui Hostel Café

2-14-13 Kuramae
Taitō 111-0051
backpackersjapan.co.jp/nuihostel/cafebar
Open from 8 am, seven days a week.

Slow Jet Coffee

1-29-12 Senju-Azuma
Adachi 120-0025
slowjetcoffee.com
Breakfast from 7 am to 11 am, seven days a week.

Streamer Coffee Shibuya

1-20-28 Shibuya
Shibuya 150-0002
streamer.coffee
Open from 8 am weekdays and 10 am weekends.

Trunk Kitchen, Trunk Hotel

5-31 Jingūmae
Shibuya 150-0001
trunk-hotel.com
Breakfast from 7 am to 10 am and brunch from 7 am to 3.30 pm, seven days a week.

Tsukiji Fish Market

(p. 206)

Breakfast available in the outer area from 5 am, seven days a week.

LUNCH & DINNER

Lunch and dinner times in Tokyo can be quite strict, with lunch typically in service between 11.30 am and 2–2.30 pm, so plan to eat around these times and you won't be disappointed. Dinner can start anywhere from 5–6 pm, but check online before you head out the door. If the weather is nice, we recommend picking up a selection of things from the food hall at a department store like Isetan (p. 129) and having a picnic outdoors with your haul.

BURGERS (INCLUDING VEGETARIAN OPTIONS)

Commune 2nd

3-13 Minami-Aoyama
Minato 107-0062
commune2nd.com

Freshness Burger

Multiple locations
www.freshnessburger.co.jp

Mos Burger

(p. 120)

CONVEYOR-BELT SUSHI

Hamayoshi

6-12-12 Ueno
Taitō 110-0005

Midori

Multiple locations
sushinomidori.co.jp/eng

Uobei

Multiple locations
genkisushi.co.jp/en

THINGS WE LOVE

HONOURABLE MENTIONS

Muji Café & Meal
Multiple locations
cafemeal.muji.com/jp

Ramen Street, Tokyo Station
(p. 199)

Straw Hat Café
Ghibli Museum (p. 362)
ghibli-museum.jp/en

FAMILY RESTAURANTS

A somewhat weird hangover from the fifties, a handful of American-style family restaurants still operate in Japan. All now owned by Japanese companies (including Denny's), they have inexpensive set meals – mostly Japanese flavours – and are a fun option to try (especially for breakfast, as most open early). Completely retro in appearance, they include Joyfull, Gusto and Coco's. Check online for locations and precise opening hours, as they may differ from venue to venue.

Coco's
Multiple locations
www.cocos-jpn.co.jp
Generally open from 7.30 am, seven days a week.

Gusto
Multiple locations
www.skylark.co.jp/gusto
Generally open from 9.30 am, seven days a week.

Joyfull
Multiple locations
joyfull.co.jp
Generally open from 7 am, seven days a week.

TREATS

Café Crepe Strawberry House
(p. 258)

Floresta Nature Donuts
(p. 135)

Shiro-Hige's Cream Puff Factory
(p. 135)

Taiyaki in Sun Road, Kichijōji
(p. 303)

BICYCLE RENTAL

Muji Yūrakuchō
(p. 212)

Tokyobike Rentals, Yanaka
4-2-39 Yanaka
Taitō 110 0001
tokyobikerentals.com

Swan boat rental
Inokashira Park (p. 342)
Ueno Park (p. 342)

PLAYGROUNDS

Sumida Hokusai Museum playground
(p. 363)
This might seem like an odd choice, but the views of Tokyo Skytree (p. 161) from here are impressive.

Kodomo no Kuni, Yokohama
700 Narachō
Aoba, Yokohama 227-0036
kodomonokuni.org/english

RoboRobo Park
6-16-46 Roppongi
Minato 106-0032

Setagaya Park
1-5-27 Ikejiri
Setagaya 154-0001

SHOPPING

Character Street
(p. 199)

DiverCity Tokyo Plaza
1-1-10 Aomi
Kōtō 135-0064
Kids will flip over the giant Gundam robot sculpture in the forecourt (p. 353).

Kiddy Land
6-1-9 Jingūmae
Shibuya 150-0001

ANIMALS

Cat and animal cafés
(p. 258)

Sunshine Aquarium
Sunshine City
World Import Mart Building
3-1 Higashi-Ikebukuro
Toshima 170-0013
www.sunshinecity-global.com/en/facility/aquarium

Ueno Zoo
9-83 Uenokōen
Taitō 110-0007
www.tokyo-zoo.net/english/ueno

DESTINATIONS

Kidzania
North Port 3F
Urban Dock LaLaport Toyosu
2-4-9 Toyosu
Kōtō 135-0061
www.kidzania.jp/tokyo/en
Kidzania is a place where kids can play at being adults: learn to drive, learn to shop and learn to work, all in a cute environment two-thirds the size of the real world.

Sanrio Puroland
(p. 188)
Hello Kitty heaven.

Cup Noodles Museum
(Yokohama, p. 363)

Gōtoku-ji (cat shrine)
(p. 334)

Hanayashiki Amusement Park
(p. 158)

Metropolitan Government Building Observation Deck
(p. 161)

Tokyo Disneyland, Chiba
1-1 Maihama
Urayasu, Chiba 279-0031
www.tokyodisneyresort.jp/en

Tokyo Skytree
(p. 161)

Toshimaen Amusement and Water Park
3-25-1 Kōyama
Nerima 176-0022
www.toshimaen.co.jp

Toshimaen Niwa-no-Yu
3-25-1 Kōyama
Nerima 176-8531
www.niwanoyu.jp

This amusement and water park offers a great kid-friendly pool experience, while the Toshimaen Niwa-no-Yu *onsen* is the place to go for a great traditional (naked) Japanese bath experience.

GALLERIES & MUSEUMS

Edo-Tokyo Museum
(p. 360)

Ghibli Museum
(p. 362)

Legoland Discovery Center
Decks Tokyo Beach Island Mall
1-6-1 Daiba
Minato 135-0091
legolanddiscoverycenter.jp

Meguro Parasitological Museum
(p. 363)
For kids who love to go, 'Eeeew, that's gross …'

National Museum of Emerging Science and Innovation
2-3-6 Aomi
Kōtō 135-0064
miraikan.jst.go.jp

Tokyo Toy Museum
Yotsuya Hiroba
4-20 Yotsuya
Shinjuku 160-0004
goodtoy.org

Toto Tokyo Center Showroom
(p. 365)
Kids and toilets: a great combination.

TOKYO TIPS FOR KIDS, BY A KID

NINA LARKINS, AGE 7, PRIMARY SCHOOL STUDENT

What do you like about Tokyo?
There is good food and good stuff you can do. And they invented Pokémon there.

Favourite places to visit?
The Pokémon Center, Kiddy Land (p. 270) and the sushi train (Uobei; p. 269).

Best memory?
My best memory was when we went to the sushi train. Because the food went zip ... ta-da! And you order it on a screen. I like it, it's yum.

Favourite Japanese food?
Easy, sushi! I mostly order *inari* sushi and *nigiri* sushi – all sorts of *nigiri*. It's just very yum somehow. I like it.

Favourite shops?
Pokémon Center and Kiddy Land. They're both toyshops. The Pokémon Center has just Pokémon stuff. Kiddy Land has got a bit of Pokémon, a bit of Hello Kitty, a bit of Rilakumma.

Do you like riding on the trains?
Yes, it's fast. It's sometimes busy. I have to stay close to my mum every time. I like that I get my own Pasmo card there. Also, I met a new friend on the train. We showed each other what games we were playing.

Favourite character?
Totoro. And Vulpix.

Best present you've bought for someone in Tokyo?
Cooking chopsticks for my dad from a market. The big fish market (Tsukiji; p. 206). There were lots of fish there and I got a fan. Someone made me tiny sushi – I love tiny sushi. And there was a cat that looked like my friend Pepper.

Favourite Japanese words?
Neko (cat), *sumimasen* (excuse me), *konnichiwa* (that's hello), *arigatō gozaimasu* (thank you). *Kawaii* is cute. Pikachu!

Do you like to do more Japanese things now?
Yes. I eat sushi and make sushi. And watch *Totoro*.

0120-853-174

ROPPONGI

——— Tokyo is very good at reinvention, and clawing back the reputation of its fallen cities is Tokyo's forte. Roppongi's seedy reputation is now seriously under threat. The art triangle (p. 357) hub of the Suntory Museum of Art, the Mori Art Museum and the National Art Center has brought some decorum to the chaos. Add to this the 21_21 Design Sight museum (p. 362), the amazing Fujifilm Square (a world-class photography gallery crossed with a store crossed with a camera museum; p. 365) and the Design Hub, all in and around Tokyo Midtown (9-8-1 Akasaka, www.tokyo-midtown.com/en), and you have a major destination in your sights.

Yes, there are still dive bars, late-night clubs with shadowy dealings, people asleep in train stations because they've missed the last train home, and hordes of drunken expats trying to shake off the week's hefty work schedule all add up to no good. Vomit on the streets, shifty characters lurking in alleyways, broken windows: it simply isn't the Tokyo we know and love. Like Kabukichō in Shinjuku, Roppongi is where Tokyo can get a little messy. You'll find discount chain Don Quijote's most run-down yet possibly best-stocked store here, as well as a plethora of Western-themed eateries on the grimy main streets.

Midtown's handicraft stores, quality homewares outlets, well-rated eateries and Toraya's simply beautiful *wagashi* (traditional sweets; p. 124) store (p. 129) make it a must-visit destination. With the 21_21 Design Sight on its grounds, Fujifilm Square as part of its street frontage, and the nearby Mori Art Museum showing fascinating, cutting-edge exhibitions against a backdrop of the Tokyo skyline through its sky-high windows, Midtown is now a pretty formidable compass point. Even the Roppongi Hills complex (6-11-1 Roppongi, roppongihills.com) a stone's throw away, with its oddball Louise Bourgeois spider sculpture crouching menacingly over the main square and its disorienting cul-de-sac corridors, has somehow arranged itself into a happening space.

Additionally, Roppongi is home to a lot of embassies, and the restaurants in the area reflect this multicultural clientele. Fans of mid-century architecture can find some fine examples dotted about the streets. Tokyo Tower (p. 161) looms large in the distance; although superseded by the Skytree (p. 161), it's still a sentimental favourite. Azabu-Jūban, a charming enclave with rice-cracker and sweet stores and older-style eateries, is just a fifteen-minute walk from Roppongi.

Picnickers around Tokyo Midtown Park's *Fragment No.5* sculpture (opposite)

ROPPONGI WALK

Roppongi Station is a convoluted rabbit warren that facilitates the ebb and flow of thousands of commuters each day. Exits will deposit you in a variety of different places, and because of this, you can run this walk forwards or backwards. It won't really make a difference; you'll see stunning art and do some amazing shopping either way.

When you exit the station gates, you can follow the signs to Tokyo Midtown, the National Art Center or the A1 Exit. For the purposes of this walk, start at the National Art Center (p. 357). Exit 7 from the Toei Ōedo Line or Exit 4A from the Hibiya Line will get you there. The Art Center's many rooms play host to a variety of exhibitions – some contemporary Japanese art, some international spectacles – and the building is a work of art in itself, so take your time and admire all that creativity.

Exiting the Art Center, turn left and walk straight until you arrive at Tokyo Midtown (p. 275). Keep walking and you'll see 21_21 Design Sight (p. 362), an honorary member of the Roppongi art triangle (p. 357). Take in a smartly curated show of local and national design, then cross back over the bridge to Tokyo Midtown. Pause to admire the dog grooming in session at Green Dog (p. 258) – it's pure *kawaii*. (You can buy premium dog accessories and foodstuffs here as well.) Midtown itself is a multi-storey shopping complex with a European flavour, catering to Roppongi's expats and embassy-dwellers. Paradoxically, however, it's the Japanese stores in Midtown that pack the punch. Toraya's *wagashi* (traditional sweets; p. 124) store, its tiny gallery (with an ever-evolving and informative exhibition on the nature of agriculture, creation, festivals and Japanese sweets) and the café next door are all worth a visit.

Tokyo art lover at Fujifilm Square

Stop off at Sadaharu Aoki for the epitome of East meets West: the *matcha* (green tea) éclair. Kayanoya sells premium dashi broths, mirin, sauces and miso, and showcases them through regular tastings in a small café, which is an excellent spot to stop for lunch (also recommended is the fish restaurant Suzunami). Nihonbashi Kiya on the third floor sells state-of-the-art knives, cutlery and cookware in a stunning gallery-like space. Peruse the other stores on this level to find an impressive range of homewares and Japanalia.

Attached to the front of Tokyo Midtown is Fujifilm Square (p. 365), which has a gallery that is not to be missed. Head in and catch the latest photography exhibition or peruse the beautiful range of vintage Fujifilm cameras on display. If you are using a Fujifilm camera, the workshop upstairs will be able to troubleshoot any problems you might be having.

Once you're back out on the main drag, look for Tokyo Tower (p. 161) in the distance and head in that direction. When you pass Roppongi Station, you have the option of two different routes. It's possible for the keen walker to cover both in one go, but if time or energy are not in your favour, you can choose to visit either Tokyo Tower and the suburb of Azabu-Jūban, or the popular Roppongi Hills (p. 275) and the Mori Art Museum (p. 357).

If you opt for Tokyo Tower, continue straight down the main street towards the spire of the tower, which you will see in the distance. Along the way, pop into the rough-and-tumble Don Quijote (3-14-10 Roppongi) and spend a few hours buying up cheap and cheerful items. Stop off at the Axis Building (5-17-1 Roppongi) and check out the homewares at Living Motif, then peruse the books at Bibliophile. Textile obsessives: don't miss Nuno. Cross over the major intersection and take the next right

for a quick detour down the sleepy backstreets to find beautiful handicrafts and design-wares store UGUiSU, the Little Shoppe (p. 282). Back out on the main drag, it's a short walk to Tokyo Tower. Snap a few shots of the icon and head up for a sweeping view of a broad section of Tokyo.

Once you're back on terra firma, return to the main intersection near the Axis Building and turn left down the winding street headed south, which will take you past some picturesque eateries bubbling over with the chatter of expats and locals; you will soon be deposited in strollable Azabu-Jūban. Walk around Azabu, soaking up the neighbourhood atmosphere, watching locals and embassy workers buying *senbei* crackers and *wagashi* (traditional sweets; p. 124) or popping into any one of a host of international restaurants. Line up at Naniwaya Sōhonten (1-8-14 Azabu-Jūban), who have been making delicious *taiyaki* (fish-shaped pastries with a sweet filling) since 1909 – in fact, they are thought to be the original makers of the delicious snack. Their *taiyaki* are still handmade using traditional methods, as is their red-bean filling, a process that can take up to eight hours. From here, head back to the main drag to end up at Tokyo Tower.

Alternatively, if you opt for Roppongi Hills, turn right after Roppongi Station and you will soon find yourself at the impressive shopping and art enclave. Take a few pictures under Louise Bourgeois' creepy giant spider *Maman* and her equally creepy egg sac, then master your vertigo and ride the elevator up to the fifty-second floor to the Mori Art Museum, which offers a stunning view of Tokyo. If you're doing a Tokyo view experience, make sure you take in both Tokyo Tower and the Mori Art Museum in one day. Don't miss Tsutaya's huge corner bookstore (6-11-1 Roppongi, real.tsite.jp/ttr/english), where you can peruse books, get coffee or set up your own workspace for the day. It's a central hub that connects Roppongi with Azabu-Jūban and the Tokyo Tower district.

National Art Center (top); 21_21 Design Sight (bottom)

Roppongi overpass

REGIONAL SOUVENIRS

HIKI KOMURA, CURATOR OF UGUISU, THE LITTLE SHOPPE

Japanese crafts and products can now be seen and obtained more easily outside of Japan, but because small makers and individual artists can often only produce in limited quantities – and with the language barrier – it is not easy for many of them to sell overseas. I knew that there were so many people who appreciated and wanted to purchase Japanese products, but didn't have a way to do so, which is why I started my online store in 2009 – making these products available to the world was the main purpose of UGUiSU at the beginning.

UGUISU, THE LITTLE SHOPPE, WAROU FLAT 4, ROOM 7 3-3-23 AZABUDAI, MINATO-KU
WWW.UGUISULITTLESHOPPE.COM

I like things that are thoughtfully and carefully made, things that last and are loved, things that won't be thrown away. I wanted to share the stories and culture behind these products, to make them meaningful. The majority of the items I collect for my store are handmade items, and many are created using traditional techniques or materials. They might not meet trends or appear in many magazines, but they also can't be found in other stores around Tokyo. Like the items, my little shoppe is hidden away. To find it is like a treasure hunt – and I hope, once people discover the shop, they also discover a treasure inside. Something that they like, or something entirely new to them.

餃子の
30
2,860

CREATIVE NEIGHBOURHOODS

A wander through Modern Tokyo's creative hubs

EBISU

—— South of Shibuya you'll find the spiritual home of Yebisu beer and the actual home of Evisu jeans: Ebisu, a mishmash of big-town shopping and business, and small-town drinking and eating. Your first hint that you're out of the main areas is the jingle-jangle melody of the theme from *The Third Man*, which plays on the station platform. There's also the size of the station – it's much smaller than the main hubs, but there's still room for Atré, a kind of craft- and homewares-oriented department store where you can spend hours leafing through books and magazines, buying amazing bags or glasses, stocking up on stockings and socks, or buying ultra-cute kitchenalia.

From the station, stroll along the skywalk until you hit the towering Yebisu Garden Place (4-20 Ebisu, gardenplace.jp). This office-block biosphere has several unique selling points, but chief among them is the glorious view from the thirty-ninth floor. A vast and spectacular swathe of Tokyo is laid out before you: parks and sports fields are patches of green; concrete clusters, retail jungles, crowded residential blocks and rail lines are a tangle at your feet. In the distance, lining the horizon, are mountain ranges lightly kissed by clouds, giving Tokyo a verdant, mystical border. Standing proudly among them – if you're lucky enough to get a clear day – is Mt Fuji, the majestic, symmetrical peak that has become an enduring symbol for Tokyo. There are plenty of good eateries up here. Sipping sake and gazing out to Fuji-san: what could be better?

Tokyo Metropolitan Museum of Photography (opposite)

At the base of Yebisu Garden Place, you'll find Famima, a *kombini* (convenience store) that redefines the concept of convenience stores. Slick graphic design illuminates the aisles; the shelves are stocked with choice products; and if you need to work or relax, there is a small room with wifi access that you can slip into. This is what all convenience stores should aspire to be: well-stocked, designed with attention to detail, and actually convenient. Just outside the *kombini* you'll find the Tokyo Photographic Art Museum (p. 363). Recently renovated, it is one of Tokyo's premium galleries, showcasing new and challenging work, as well as classic photography from Japan and around the world.

Instead of taking the skywalk back to the station, head left and into Ebisu's backstreets to find some of Tokyo's most interesting boutique stores. This is the home of the cult clothing brand Yaeca (2-20-15 Ebisu-Minami, yaeca.com), as well as Maison Margiela (2-8-13 Ebisu-Minami, maisonmargiela.com) and eyewear store Continuer (2-9-2 Ebisu-Minami, continuer.jp). These backstreets are an interesting walk just for the glimpse into residential Tokyo's fascinating architectural styles, as you'll find houses with potted gardens spilling into the streets, tiny coffee shops and restaurants.

Continue wandering until day turns into night to see Ebisu really come to life. Roller-shutters clatter in the dusk air as they reveal their hidden treasures. Tiny stand-up or eight-seat eateries bubble and steam to life. Ebisu's winding lanes by evening are home to an abundance of riches, and are perfect for anyone on the hunt for slurpable ramen, crisp tempura or conveyor-belt sushi. The only problem is which one to choose. Start at Ebisu Yokochō (1-7-4 Ebisu, ebisu-yokocho.com), a mini lantern-lit all-in-one with tiny bars, eateries and hangouts.

From Ebisu's broad main street you can head northwest, and before long you'll find yourself on the outskirts of Daikanyama (p. 295), a favourite weekend hangout for locals and visitors alike. Alternatively, if you maintain a more westerly direction, you'll find yourself floating into the canal district of Nakameguro (p. 299), a vibrant hotspot in *sakura* (cherry blossom) season and a peaceful stroll at any time of the year.

Ebisu architecture (left); view from Yebisu Garden Place (right); Ebisu street details (opposite)

MM,Tokyo
MM,Los Angeles
メゾン マルジェラ
MM,Omotesando
MM,Montpensier Women
MM,Montpensier Men
MM,Grenelle
MM,Hong Kong

まとや

薄皮餃子専門

COME IN! WE'RE OPEN

YOYOGI & TOMIGAYA

——— Walking directly up Kōen Dōri in Shibuya will bring you to Yoyogi Park, a broad patch of greenery that meanders eastward to Meiji Jingu (Meiji Shrine; p. 334), Harajuku (p. 253) and the top of Omotesandō Dōri (p. 260); northward to Yoyogi and Shinjuku; and westward to Tomigaya's streets, a strollable haven away from the bustle of the big city. Yoyogi Park is huge – two kilometres long and nearly as wide – and there is plenty to do, including watching the Sunday cosplayers and Elvis clones put on a show, packing a picnic lunch and drinking sake under the trees, visiting flea markets or going to pop-up festivals.

A right turn when you reach the NHK building at the southern end of the park will transport you back to the late Shōwa era (1926–1989) as you come face-to-face with the stunning Yoyogi National Gymnasium (p. 351), a mid-century and almost Brutalist piece of architecture that was built for the 1964 Olympic Games. It's a national treasure and a symbol of the birth of a new Japan. It still looks great today: a flowing, undulating structure that beautifully mimics the lines of the athletic physiques that performed within. From here Harajuku comes into view; the Meiji Shrine is just a short walk through the dense trees; and Omotesandō beckons (p. 252).

One of the best walks towards Yoyogi and Tomigaya starts at Loft (p. 212) in Shibuya. At the junction of Inokashira Dōri, head west to where the streets have no name. The Tiger Gyoza Hall (37-35 Udagawachō), which has vegetarian options, and the super-cool Shōwa-era *izakaya* (pub; p. 41) Baka Musuko Chonan (35-4 Udagawachō), with its vintage posters and colourful lanterns, will provide any sustenance you might need.

Shibuya will start to give way to Tomigaya and things get decidedly more local. You'll pass an enclave of small punk bars and photographable eateries. ØL by Oslo Brewing Company (37-10 Udagawachō, oltokyo.jp) will satisfy your craft-beer cravings and rated *teppanyaki* restaurant Onnadojo (41-23 Udagawachō) is nearby. There are plenty of delicious food options, including take-out *onigiri* (rice ball) stores for picnics in the park.

Bars (like the ultra-cool cocktail and coffee bar Fuglen; 1-16-11 Tomigaya, fuglen.no), publishing houses, second-hand bookstores and smaller shops that thrive on handicrafts all conspire to give Tomigaya the feeling of being close to the action, but somehow removed from it at the same time. Flower shops spill into the streets, and an assortment of indie stores and boutiques, as well as the stylish Coffee Supreme (grab a toasted sandwich; 42-3 Kamiyamachō, coffeesupreme.com), appeal to passers-by. On the western fringe of Yoyogi Park, Little Nap (5-65-4 Yoyogi, littlenap.jp/loc) brews premium coffee.

This is also the place that the Monocle Shop (1-19-2 Tomigaya, monocle.com/shop) chose to call home. We always aim to visit the Case Gallery (p. 365); their curation is impeccable and there is always something interesting to see, even if that's just the gallery's exterior, which looks like a pyramid squeezed between two of the area's faceless towers like a flower pushing up through the pavement. Pop into the attached sweets store with its powder-blue exterior. From here you have lots of choices. Head east into Yoyogi Park for an afternoon of nature; walk southwest towards the genteel suburb of Yoyogi-Uehara; take the Odakyū Line from Yoyogi-Hachiman Station to Shinjuku or the Chiyoda Line from Yoyogi-Uehara Station to Omotesandō; or cross the park to JR Yoyogi Station and jump on the Yamanote Line to Harajuku and beyond.

Baka Musuko Chonan (above); Case Gallery (opposite top left); Coffee Supreme (opposite top right)

La Fuente

DAIKANYAMA

——— After the hustle and bustle of Shibuya or Shinjuku, popping out into Daikanyama Station, just one short stop from Shibuya on the Tōkyū Tōyoko Line, will feel like chaos has given way to calm. This train line also has other worthy stops along its length – Nakameguro (p. 299), Gakugei-Daigaku and Jyūgaoka – and as an added bonus it terminates at Yokohama, for anyone wishing to head to Japan's second-largest city. Alternatively, you can make your way to Daikanyama by wandering the slender backstreets from Shibuya (p. 234) or Ebisu (p. 287). Irresistibly walkable, packed with 'son-and-daughter' stores (a contemporary twist on mom-and-pop, these are young locals who have inherited shops and made them their own) and pleasant, watch-the-world-go-by cafés, Daikanyama is a destination where you can chill out and see township Tokyo in action without straying too far from any main hubs. Not only that, it's just a short walk from Nakameguro, with its canal-side shopping, bars and Sakura Museum (p. 363).

Grab your first coffee of the day from the Motoya Express van outside Daikanyama station. Head towards Hachiman Dōri where you'll spy the *Sunflower* sculpture (p. 353), which is great for a photo opportunity. There is a Frenchie vibe going on in Daikanyama and Japano-francophiles will feel at home with the Café Le Cordon Bleu (28-13 Sarugakuchō, cordonbleu.edu/japan/home/ja), fashion stores such as Nîmes (26-11 Sarugakuchō), L'Atilier du Savon (2-8-3 Sarugakuchō) and men's (25-2 Sarugakuchō, apcjp.com) and women's (11-9 Sarugakuchō, apcjp.com) stores from French stalwarts A.P.C., plus Bonjour Records (24-1 Sarugakuchō, bonjour.jp).

Sunflower sculpture by Piotr Kowalski (opposite)

You'll find cafés with champagne and French pastries, café au lait, chic brunch venues and cosy spaces.

Tsutaya bookstore has made its presence felt all over Tokyo (and elsewhere), but T-Site (p. 227), the Daikanyama branch of the phenomenal bookstore, is still its proudest achievement. Here you'll find well-stocked bookshelves, a café, a music library and a workstation hub that you could actually live in – well, at least spend a whole day in. It's not called the best bookstore in the world for nothing, and you can while away many hours just perusing shelves, flicking though magazines, reading a purchase over a lazy lunch or typing frantically on your laptop while sipping on a latte. T-Site stocks pretty much everything when it comes to books, DVDs, music and associated bits and bobs. If you're travelling with kids, take them to the children's book section; the huge range, in both Japanese and English, is enough to entertain the most easily distracted minds. The retro magazines and vinyl are a treat; the cooking section is a culinary dream; and the Leica Store will make any photography enthusiast drool and dream about being able to afford some of the stunning classic

T-Site (left and top right); Nîmes (bottom right)

Leica cameras on display. There is even a dog-washing facility, not to be missed for a glimpse of some of Tokyo's most pampered pooches. Ivy Place on the grounds is a popular spot for locals to grab an early breakfast or brunch (their fluffy pancakes are legendary; p. 269), especially on weekends, when you should expect to queue.

On the way up to T-Site is an unmissable retail experience for anyone in love with textiles and design. The inimitable Minä Perhonen has a flagship store (p. 372), with clothing, textiles and accessories housed in a beautiful interior full of offshoot rooms and corridors. The delicate beauty of this brand is magical and perfectly represents Japanese creative culture. Along the train tracks heading towards Shibuya, you'll find a plethora of vintage and *zakka* (handicraft; p. 372) stores and small cafés with more of a student vibe. Did somebody say brunch? Bird (9-10 Daikanyamachō, bird-daikanyama.com), Chano-ma (Za House 2F, 1-34-17 Ebisu-Nishi) and Blu Jam (20-20 Daikanyamachō, blujamcafejapan.com) make brunch an essential weekend meal, more important than breakfast, lunch or dinner.

Ivy Place; A.P.C.; Bonjour Records (clockwise from top left)

鮮馬刺し 980
角ハイボール 390
ウーロンハイ 400
中ジョッキー 550
干物
本日の逸品
ねぎ間 160
ハツモト 180
ハツ 180
上レバー 180
上ささみ 190
上もも 200
本日のお刺身 480～
〆さば 580
たこぶつ 650
まぐろ中おち 650
いかり屋の刺盛り 980
居酒屋
釜揚げ桜海老 480
菜の花のナムル 420
鮮馬刺し 980
いかり屋の刺盛り 980
平塚
漁港直送
いかり屋の刺盛り
大辛口

NAKAMEGURO

——— Nakameguro is easily reached on the Tōkyū Tōyoko Line from Shibuya, and is in walking distance of Ebisu, Daikanyama and Meguro. A casual stroll canal-side, a break from city living, a spot of shopping and a leisurely drink or two: this is what Nakameguro is all about. Cherry blossoms are a feature of the area, with thick boughs adorned with colourful petals forming a pink marquee over the canal in the short, treasured week of bloom. Fittingly, you'll find the Sakura Museum (p. 363) here.

This suburb is all about the lazy wander. Take your time and amble through the backstreets, which are a mix of tiny stores, clever residential architecture and snug eateries. Along the canal you might waft into Cow Books (1-14-11 Aobadai, www.cowbooks.jp/english.html), still so cool after all these years; a survivor of encroaching digital media. Revolutionary tomes from the sixties, underground treatises, classic works of literature and philosophy, and weighty doorstops on art, architecture and design line the shelves. Pop into Plain People (1-16-10 Aobadai, jaho.com/pages/jaho-tokyo) to shop and enjoy the beans at Jaho Coffee, or try Sidewalk Stand (1-23-14 Aobadai, sidewalk.jp), Onibus (2-14-1 Kamimeguro, onibuscoffee.com) or Blue Bottle (3-23 16 Nakameguro, bluebottlecoffee.jp/cafes/nakameguro) – all cementing Nakameguro's reputation for being home to some of the best new coffee joints. Pop in and out of the canal-side shops and eateries and enjoy cake and coffee, booze and lunch, shopping and people watching.

Have a quiet lunch at Café Red Book (1-3-2 Kamimeguro) or visit the charming Aoya (1-15-10 Aobadai, aoya-nakameguro.com)

Nakameguro Canal (opposite bottom)

for a delicious Japanese rice set lunch. Across the road from Red Book and up the stairs you will find a mini collection of ever-changing vintage and oddity stores, and SML (AK-1 Building 1F, 1-15-1 Aobadai, sm-l.jp) near Aoya is a longstanding local eatery.

On the other side of the station, away from the canal, is the hidden Traveler's Factory (p. 212), an amazing store that sells stationery and supplies perfect for the traveller, such as books to record adventures, packets and pockets to store travel writing, and iconic travel emblems. From here, make sure you stroll up around the station, as there are some skinny backstreets that have all kinds of excellent food stops, craft stores and bars. As the sun sets, head over to the beautifully designed *sentō* (public bathhouse) Kohmeisen (1-6-1 Kamimeguro, kohmeisen.com). The top floor *rotenburo* (outdoor onsen) alternates every five days between sexes, so if you're lucky enough to visit when it's your turn, an unmissable rooftop bathing experience awaits your aching body. Join the queue at Tonki (p. 123) for a crispy pork *tonkatsu* dinner or cram yourself into one of the standing *oden* (fish cakes and vegetables simmered in a soy broth) bars or small eateries that make this area so loved. Nakameguro is also a famous suburb for pizza so if you feel like a bit of J-Med try Da Isa (1-28-9 Aobadai, da-isa.jp), Seirinkan (2-6-4 Kamimeguro, theseirinkan.com) or ask your local barista for their recommendation.

Sakura from Nakameguro Station (top); Sidewalk Stand (bottom); Sakura Museum and Aoya (opposite)

KICHIJŌJI

——— Head to Shibuya Station West, find Hachikō Square, then hot-foot it across the road towards the Shibuya Mark City mall. There you'll find a steep escalator descending to the correct platform. Follow the signs for the Keiō Inokashira Line, then take the Keiō Inokashira Line all the way to the last stop, Kichijōji. Catch the express service for a faster, more direct route to Kichijōji's charms. You can also take the JR Chuo Line here from Shinjuku Station: this train stops at Kōenji and Nishi-Ogikubo, so if you want to make a big day out and visit all three places, start with Kichijōji and wind your way back to the city. If you find this slice of Tokyo attractive, nearby Mitaka is also worth a visit. It's the place to catch the cat bus to the Ghibli museum (p. 362) and home of the Reversible Destiny Lofts (p. 354).

An area populated by students, young families and left-of-centre thinkers, Kichijōji is bordered by Inokashira Park to the southwest and the Sun Road shopping arcade to the northeast. Wedged in the middle is Harmonica Yokochō, a magical Shōwa-era cluster of tiny bars and eateries, a relic of earlier times. It's a great place to chill out at night and grab a drink and a bite to eat. The Sun Road arcade, which skirts Harmonica Yokochō, has some excellent food stops. Pickle and tea specialists and Satou, the meat shop with the permanent queue, can all be found in the covered walkway. Old-school cavernous *kissaten* (European-style coffee house; p. 142) Kugutsusō (p. 143), still resolutely living in the seventies, is the perfect place for a hit of the addictive bean. Also worth a visit is the store on the outer perimeter of Harmonica Yokochō, which fills sweet fish-shaped pastry with custard, sweet potato and other glorious fillings. Just walk past the queue at Satou and towards the station.

Ghibli Museum (opposite)

Not far away, Nakamichi Dōri is a shopping strip fringed by small maker stores, craft shops and tiny food stalls. You may find yourself dodging bicycles, cars and rampant shoppers. Small design, fashion and homewares stores line this popular street. Craft and paper suppliers and specialist stores give anyone with a creative streak the chance to buy all the bits and bobs needed to make a statement. Curry houses (with great vegetarian options), dumpling purveyors: you'll find it all on Nakamichi Dōri. Toward the end of the street, Light Up Coffee (p. 143) and Hara Donuts (p. 135) sit temptingly side by side. Tiny stores pack the laneways in and around Nakamichi. Look out for Bondo (3-3-6 Kichijōji-Honchō, bondo.co.jp), Cinq (Greeny Building 1F, 2-28-23 Kichijōji-Honchō, cinq-design.com), Markus (2-18-15 Kichijōji-Honchō, marku-s.net) and Outbound (Shop 110, 2-7-4 Kichijōji-Honchō, outbound.to) – all have wonderful homewares and handmade items. Sublo (Hara Building 2F, 2-4-16 Kichijōji-Honchō, sublo.net) and Paper Message (4-1-3 Kichijōji-Honchō, papermessage.jp) have your snail mail needs sorted and Natural Laundry (2-18-15 Kichijōjimoto-machi, naturallaundry.com) has the cutest range of knitwear. This is an area for indie stores, so things are always moving and changing.

Sprawling, tranquil Inokashira Park was opened to the public in 1917; lazing peacefully across the border of Musashino and Mitaka, it features a central lake (established in the Edo period) girded by cherry blossoms, azaleas, and cypress and pine trees. In summer the lake is sprinkled with colourful swan boats ferrying giggling couples out into the hot afternoon sun. In *sakura* (cherry blossom) season, the boughs of the cherry trees thicken and bend, forming bright pink sprays over the water. As the pastel swan boats glide along the river, street-food stalls appear with cherry blossom–themed food and picnic groups populate the park, giving it the most wonderful festive atmosphere.

The park is also home to the famous Ghibli Museum (p. 362), so if you want to visit, pre-book your tickets at Lawson convenience stores or online. You must choose an exact entry time and tickets are limited, but if you have to wait, there's always plenty of park to stroll around in. It is also home to the endearing red-and-white Benzaiten shrine (p. 334), a small petting zoo and many winding paths to walk, stroll or cycle. On the weekend, buskers continue the creative feel. So head down to Sun Road or to one of the basement food stalls in Atré at the train station, grab some picnic food and stroll to the park for a relaxing Tokyo day out.

Kichijōgi's Autumn Festival is legendary. Part of the Matsuri festival, Kichijōji's celebration is a rambunctious, bubbling party in which small portable shrines are ferried around on the shoulders of riotous youths and over-confident elders. The main celebration takes place on Sunday in early September at the Musashino Hachimangu shrine.

Inokashira Park (opposite)

一圓

バナナ
280
さくらんぼ
680
茨城県産
秀
2L
SMC

400円

国産大豆
こうや豆腐

SUNROAD
いい店
いい街
サンロード♪
一店逸品街

Details from Sun Road, Harmonica Yokochō and Nakamichi Dōri (opposite and above)

VINTAGE MARKETS

If rummaging for vintage kimono and fabrics, books, *kokeshi* dolls, ceramics, toys and ephemera is your thing (it's certainly ours), then you definitely won't be disappointed by Tokyo's vintage markets. Although some of the biggest markets are monthly or even bi-monthly affairs, there are a few markets that are on weekly, so chances are good that fans of vintage finds will be able to scratch that antiquarian itch, even on a short trip.

Always check online for opening hours and changes in schedules, as these can happen quite often. If it's raining, most outside markets are likely to be cancelled, so ask if your hotel concierge or Airbnb host can look into opening hours if the weather looks dodgy, or use an online translation service like Google Translate to navigate websites without an English-language option. As with any other market, if you are serious about taking home the perfect find, getting in early is recommended.

AKASAKA ANTIQUE MARKET

1-12-32 Akasaka
Minato 107-0052
facebook.com/akasaka.nominoichi
Open Sundays, from 11 am to 5 pm.

AOYAMA WEEKLY ANTIQUE MARKET

5-53-70 Jingūmae
Shibuya 150-0001
thejmp.com
Open Saturdays, from 10 am to 4 pm. Also has a bonus farmers' market.

NOGI SHRINE MARKET

8-11-27 Akasaka
Minato 107-0052
www.nogikotto.com
Open on the fourth Sunday of every month, from 9 am until evening. A petite market in a lovely setting.

OEDO ANTIQUE MARKET

Tokyo International Forum
3-5-1 Marunouchi
Chiyoda 100-0005
antique-market.jp
Open on the first and third Sunday of every month, from 8 am until 4 pm.

SETAGAYA BOROICHI

Boroichi Dōri
1 Setagaya
Setagaya 154-0017
city.setagaya.lg.jp/setagaya/11000/11004/d00125000.html
This huge market (made up of around 700 stalls) is open twice a year: mid-January and mid-December, from 9 am to 8 pm. Check online.

SHINJUKU MITSUI BUILDING FLEA MARKET

55 Square
Shinjuku Mitsui Building
2-1-1 Nishi-Shinjuku
Shinjuku 163-0401
shinjukumitsui55info.jp/event
Open one weekend a month; dates vary, so check online.

TOKYO CITY FLEA MARKET

1-6-26 Katsushima
Shinagawa 140-0012
trx.jp/static/en/tcf
Open most Saturdays and Sundays, from 9 am to 3 pm.

YOYOGI PARK FLEA MARKET

2-1 Yoyogikamizonochō
Shibuya 151-0052
yoyogikoen.info
Open one weekend a month; dates vary, so check online.

Kokeshi dolls at Oedo Antique Market

Poubelle (bottom left and right) and Nishi-Ogikubo eateries

NISHI-OGIKUBO

——— Board the Chūō Line headed west from Shibuya Station West and alight at Nishi-Ogikubo, or catch the Chūō Line from Kichijōji. A quiet neighbourhood with a reputation for vintage and handmade items, Nishi-Ogikubo is a great place to start for any retro enthusiast or collector. Pick up the vintage shopping map – yes, it's an actual piece of paper – at the station, *koban* (police box) or one of the local shops and discover more than 60 boutiques and thrift stores specialising in vintage and pre-loved items.

You will find quality versions of the usual vintage fare in Nishi-Ogikubo, but it's the unique antique stores that are the real drawcard. These dark, cramped spaces are full of relics that have been lovingly collected and restored: industrial lights, old-school desks haunted by ghosts of students past, papier-mâché bowls with faded newspaper headlines poking bleakly through the patina of time. Refurbed hand-crafted cabinets sit alongside tools that long ago hammered or winkled their last. Odd objects made from unrecognisable materials, rusted with time, are perfect for hanging on walls or displaying on your coffee table, and new works from emerging arts-and-crafts people complete the picture. Some of our favourite shops are Poubelle (3-42-5 Nishi-Ogikita) and Fall (3-18-10 Nishi-Ogikita, fall-gallery.com), but you will be sure to discover your own. When your feet are tiring, head to the lovely local *sentō* (public bathhouse) Bunka-yu (4-3-10 Nishi-Ogikita) for a soak.

If that isn't enough to get you hooked, many stores will give you *ocha* (tea) for free, part of an event known as *chasampo*, or 'sample tea', where you can sip on a delicious brew (cold or hot, depending on the season) while you wander among trinkets and objects imbued with the spirit and narrative of bygone decades. It's a perfect opportunity to go for a stroll and uncover the Tokyo of yesteryear in all its used, pre-loved glory.

JOHN
03-4503-5255

PARIS CONTINUED
Sequins on a space-age style
and a double ruffled flounce
LIFE Magazine Poster
1960年代から70年代頃のアメリカ
ライフマガジンの中に掲載されていた
広告です。一冊から1枚しか取れないので
希少です。台紙に入ってるのでこのまま
飾れて便利です。
1poster 400yen

KŌENJI

Home to no less than thirteen temples and shrines and famous for its vintage wares, Kōenji is a brilliant little suburb around 15 minutes from Shinjuku on the Chūō Line. It's best known in Tokyo for its Awa Odori traditional dance festival, but its reputation as an eclectic suburb makes it a destination not to be missed for anyone with an eye for Shōwa-era (or mid-century) items, pop culture, music, *kissaten* (European-style coffee houses; p. 142) or anything rock and underground.

Kōenji has long been synonymous with vintage, similar to Shimokitazawa (p. 317) but further out, with stranger finds and stranger opening hours. The vintage here is scattered all around the north and east sides of the district: clothes, shoes and records are all lovingly sourced and brought back to life in small boutiques. Stretching down the southern length of Kōenji Station is a plethora of eateries, standing bars and yakitori joints serving up grilled meat and beer for the worker – a place where visitors can truly slip into the culinary vernacular of the region.

A leftover 1960s to punk vibe still defines Kōenji. If '60s and '70s fashion finds are on your radar, then this is the place to dig. You may find the store owner wore the piece you just bought to a Stones gig in the late '60s. If your fashion angles more to a mod vibe, you'll go home with a new wardrobe that will be the envy of everyone at the next scooter run. Lover Soul (3-35-15 Kōenji-Minami), Chart (Misato Building 1–2F, 4-30-8 Kōenji-Minami), Small Change (3-45-16 Kōenji-Minami, smallchange.jp) and UK Extra (Kobori Building 1F, 4-25-2 Kōenji-Minami, uk-extra.com) are all brilliant, but there are hundreds of highly rated places here.

Kōenji vintage shops (opposite)

Things kick off later in Kōenji so arrive at lunch or mid-afternoon for a wander, and make sure you stay for a drink or a bite to eat. Under the station tracks you'll find many tiny places to get a food or booze fix. Kōenji is the home of live houses, so if you're arriving for dinner plan to stay and catch a local act – maybe some punk/jazz metal fusion band or an impossibly twee and completely loveable indie duo. Make sure you memorise the last train home, though, or have enough yen for a cab ride back to your digs. Check out tokyogigguide.com for what is on when you're visiting.

A NIGHT OUT IN TOKYO

KENTA SATO, FRED PERRY & TOKYO BAR ENTHUSIAST

Where do you live in Tokyo?

I'm currently living in Hikawadai, Nerima. It's a family-friendly residential part of Tokyo. People love to walk along the Shakujii River during *sakura* (cherry blossom) season. We get stunning views looking down from our flat. It's definitely a hidden spot.

What areas have your favourite bars?

I do enjoy *nomiya* (family-owned small restaurants and bars) hopping in Kōenji or Kichijōji with a bunch of friends. Martha in Ebisu is a good jazz bar.

What is your favourite alcoholic drink?

Highballs, Mojitos and some Scotch!

Favourite craft beer?

Anything Japanese would do me well.

Do Tokyo kids still drink sake?

I suppose so. They seem to be ordering frozen sake or sparkling sake now, though.

Do you have a favourite music festival?

Labyrinth, Rainbow Disco Club or Fuji Rock.

Do you go to live houses? If so, what are your favourites?

I go to clubs a lot. Contact or Vent are my usual choices for techno. DBS night at Unit is a must-go-to for all the Sound System lovers ... and don't go home before you hit the Oath's after party.

Do you have favourite bands and performers that you like to go and see?

Oasis, Warlocks, The Beta Band, Black Angels, Biffy Clyro and Electric Wizards!

Look Street (opposite)

SHIMOKITAZAWA

——— Still somehow managing to resist the march of modernity, this rabbit warren of students, vintage emporiums, hookah-pipe lounges, cheap eateries and a perpetual sepia-toned feeling of lazy summer days, buoyant springtime walks or drizzly winter op-shop hops remains one of Tokyo's most popular 'out-of-town' destinations.

Americana from days gone by stuffs the racks of vintage stores with names like Ruby Tuesday (5-36-15 Daizawa) and Flamingo (2-25-12 Kitazawa, tippirag.com). There are major retro toy and manga finds to be had among the crowded shelves of places like Sunny (2-12-1 Kitazawa) and Swing (2-25-4 Kitazawa). Barely navigable, wafer-slight aisles are stacked with precariously balanced piles of Astro Boy comics (usually with a flexi-vinyl bonus), vintage Peko-Chan or Hello Kitty figurines and money boxes, and assorted collections of old stamps, stickers, collectors' cards and graphic matchboxes.

Coffee shops like Bear Pond Espresso (p. 143), Coffea Exlibris (5-8-16 Daizawa) and Bookends Coffee Service (2-11-17 Kitazawa, blog.livedoor.jp/vw1975) will satisfy your hometown cravings.

Elsewhere, Jet Set Records and City Country City (both p. 245) have the retro-vinyl angle covered, with classic platters just waiting for the enthusiast to grab that sought-after slice of cool. Food in Shimokitazawa tends to be fast and cheap for the younger set who drift about these hallowed streets; yakitori, burgers, curry and good vegetarian options are plentiful. Bio Ojiyan (5-35-25), Sama (2-26-18 Kitazawa, hb-sama.com), Kate Coffee (2-7-11 Kitazawa, katecoffee.jp) and, for dessert, Shiro-Hige's Cream Puff Factory (p. 135) or Cup Cake Coffee (2-16-2 Kitazawa) are irresistible. We like to visit on a weekday, when Shimokita is less crowded.

Shoko Seko on the 'Shimokita' streets (opposite)

SHIMOKITAZAWA
下北沢にて
ピュアロード
高圧ガス

質
ショッピングと買入
この先
アベビル1F
3414-4940
殻付き牡蠣の
カン缶焼き
数量限定
1,200yen
SAPPORO

Shirohige's Cream Puff Shop
髭のシュークリーム工房

Nina Larkins at Shiro-Hige's Cream Puff Factory (opposite bottom right); Shimokitazawa details (above and opposite)

TOKYO MUSIC

If you're anything like Steve, your night may be ruined when you arrive at an interesting-looking bar only to find that a less-than-interesting soundtrack is playing. Fear not, though: just a little bit of research will drop you into some of the coolest and most interesting nightspots that Tokyo has to offer. If your ideal musical night out doesn't involve getting lost in a massive crowd, you can rest easy knowing it doesn't have to be big; most of Tokyo's best live experiences happen in tiny, sweaty basement dives where bands bang out high-octane punk or vibrant jazz–rock fusion, small indie bands play the cutest plink-plonk melodies, and experimental electronic artists create new, warped soundscapes using modified analogue equipment.

Clubs can be raging all-night techno parties in youth capitals like Shibuya (p. 234) or Roppongi (p. 274) and small bars can help soak your troubles away with a heady dusk-till-dawn brew of well-curated jazz or sixties rock and well-selected booze. J-pop (and K-pop) is everywhere. If it's not playing in shops and cafés, you'll hear it blaring from brightly coloured trucks trawling the streets. Fans of J-pop can get their fix in Akihabara (p. 224). Apply for tickets to see cult idol group AKB48, or head into Akihabara's Don Quijote (4-3-3 Soto-Kanda, donki.com/en) to catch performances from new teen idols on the eighth floor.

At the other end of the live-music spectrum, you're also spoiled for choice: high-end traditional performances grace large concert halls and international bands tour stadiums, arenas and smaller venues, sometimes going onstage at 7.30 pm to polite (but rapturous) applause.

Music is everywhere in Tokyo, and it won't always be what you're used to – that's a good thing. So go crate-digging in vintage record stores; wander into a late-night live house in Kōenji (p. 313), Shimokitazawa (p. 317) or Shinjuku (p. 246); or catch a traditional Koto recital or an experimental music piece in one of Tokyo's vibrant arts hubs.

TOKYO MUSIC TIPS

Disk Union (p. 244) has a helpful vinyl map to the city's best record shops available in-store, so make sure you grab a copy to see which one specialises in your favourite genre. It can get pretty diverse, with everything from metal and punk to jazz, soul and sixties rock well and truly catered for.

Flyers for gigs are a great way to get a taste of Tokyo's local music scene. If you find a music store you like and they're playing your song, they will most likely have flyers for shows that you'll enjoy.

If you're a fan of anime, there are bands who perform well-known anime songs, as well as bands who write exclusively for anime and then take the songs on the road. The same goes for gamers and game soundtracks. You can catch performances where the music of your favourite game is performed live by the band or orchestra that wrote it, accompanied by visuals.

HMV (top); Steve at Tower Records (bottom)

JAPANESE BANDS TO CHECK OUT

Japanese bands have the best names ever. Some are quirky; others feature oddball Japanese–English blends that are endlessly funny to the visitor (and sometimes even just that little bit wrong). Below is a list to get you started.

We heart

- *Cornelius*
- *Lullatone*
- *Pizzicato Five*
- *Ryuichi Sakamoto*
- *Shonen Knife*
- *Tenniscoats*
- *The 5.6.7.8's*
- *Thee Michelle Gun Elephant*
- *Yellow Magic Orchestra*
- *Yoko Ono (you've probably heard of her)*

Popular stuff (and crazy)

- *Babymetal*
- *Exile (a genius marketing plan means that there is a young and an old version of the band, both of which still make records)*
- *Flumpool*
- *Kyary Pamyu Pamyu*
- *Mr. Children*
- *SMAP*
- *Snail Ramp*

LIVE HOUSES

20,000 Den-atsu
L-GRAZIA Building B1F
1-7-23 Kōenji-Minami
Suginami 166-0003
den-atsu.com

440 (Shimokita)
SY Building 1F
5-29-15 Daizawa
Setagaya 155-0032
440.tokyo

Club Que
BigBen Building B2F
2-5-2 Kitazawa
Setagaya 155-0031
www.ukproject.com/que

Garage
NH Shimokitazawa Building B1F
3-31-15 Kitazawa
Setagaya 155-0031
garage.or.jp

Knock Kōenji
3-48-6 Kōenji-Minami
Suginami 166-0003
knockkoenji.com

Kōenji High
4-30-1 Kōenji-Minami
Suginami 166-0003
koenji-high.com

Liquid Room
3-16-6 Higashi
Shibuya 150-0011
liquidroom.net

Mosaic
Moai Chazawa B1–1F
2-2-14 Kitazawa
Setagaya 155-0031
mu-seum.co.jp

Muryoku Muzenji
3-67-1 Kōenji-Minami
Suginami 166-0003
muzenji.web.fc2.com

Shelter
Senda Building B1F
2-6-10 Kitazawa
Setagaya 155-0031
loft-prj.co.jp/SHELTER

Shibuya Cyclone
Kokusai A Building B2F
13-16 Udagawachō
Shibuya 150-0042
cyclone1997.com/home.html

MUSIC-THEMED BARS

Art Space Bar Buena – electro
1-24-8 Hyakuninchō
Shinjuku 169-0073
buena.tokyo

Beat Café – mod and indie
Harvest Building B1F
2-13-5 Dōgenzaka
Shibuya 150-0043

Big Love Records – indie
2-31-3 Jingūmae
Shibuya 150-0001
bigloverecords.jp

City Country City – indie and soul
(p. 245)

Crawdaddy Club – blues and Led Zeppelin
K Building B1F
2-28-15 Kabukichō
Shinjuku 160-0021

DJ Bar Bridge – beats
Shibuya Parkside Kyōdō Building 10F
1-25-6 Shibuya
Shibuya 150-0002
bridge-shibuya.com

Elvis Bar
4-2-2 Nishi-Azabu 2F
Minato 106-0031

Grandfather's – funk and soul
1-24-7 Shibuya
Shibuya 150-0002
grandfather.jp

Gravity – hard rock
Seiwa Building 2F
7-4-9 Nishi-Shinjuku
Shinjuku160-0023

Hair of the Dogs – punk
Shinjuku Golden Gai
1-1-8 Kabukichō
Shinjuku 160-0021

Hammond Orgasm – Okinawan rock
Yashio Assembly Hall 4F unit B2
2-38-8 Kabukichō
Shinjuku 160-0021
progbar.jp

Little Soul – rare groove and funk
Taisei Building 2F
2-20-2 Kitazawa
Setagaya 155-0031
littlesoulcafe.com

Los Barbados – calypso and afrobeat
Papier Building 104
41-26 Udagawachō
Shibuya 150-0042
www7b.biglobe.ne.jp/~los-barbados

Millibar – reggae
J+R Building Jside 3F
33-10 Udagawachō
Shibuya 150-0042

MOD
3-4-12 Ginza
Chūō 104-0061

No Trunks – jazz
1-10-5 Naka 5F
Kunitachi 186-0004
notrunks.jp

Polka Dots – Bob Dylan
Umemoto Building B1F
3-29-3 Nishi-Ikebukuro
Toshima 171-0021

Samurai – jazz
(p. 188)

Tatemichiya – punk
30-8 Sarugakuchō
Shibuya 150-0033

Trouble Peach – rock and folk
2-9-18 Kitazawa
Setagaya 155-0031

World Kitchen Baobab – world music
Ohara Building B1F
2-4-6 Kichijōji-Minamichō
Musashino 180-0003
wk-baobab.com

TIP: *Music venues pop up, shut down, move around and reinvent themselves in Tokyo, just like the rest of the world, so check online before you go. Look out for interesting signage in areas you like hanging out in, flyers in record stores or ask for advice from shop assistants or bar staff.*

KARAOKE

If you don't really want to see a gig and you'd rather sing it yourself, you've come to the right place. Toyko is the home of karaoke, which means 'blank orchestra' in English (pronounce it properly, please: 'kah-rah-oh-keh'), and the sheer number of places where you can go and belt out a tune is staggering. They all have something different to offer, too. Some are great for groups; others are perfect for couples. Some even cater for people who are so timid they would rather be alone to croon sweet nothings to themselves. Why not? Singing is good for the soul, and Tokyoites know that if you've had a hard week, belting out a chorus or two can really relieve the tension, and that a cheeky rendition of 'I Got You Babe' with the target of your affections could help seal the deal. Drinks are usually included (everyone needs a helpful dose of liquid courage). And remember, if you don't wake up embarrassed, you didn't do it properly.

1Kara Akihabara – karaoke for one
Akiba Place 6F
3-15-1 Soto-Kanda
Chiyoda 101-0021
(Also at other locations)
1kara.jp/en

Big Echo Ginza
4-2-14 Ginza
Chūō 104-0061
(Also at other locations)
big-echo.jp

Karaoke Kan Roppongi
Roppongi B&V Building
5-1-6 Roppongi
Minato 106-0032
(Also at other locations)
karaokekan.jp

Karaoke Manekineko Shinjuku
Toyo Building 5F
1-2-5 Kabukichō
Shinjuku 160-0021
(Also at other locations)
karaokemanekineko.jp/en

Shidax Roppongi
5-2-4 Roppongi
Minato 106-0032
(Also at other locations)
www.shidax.co.jp

Studio Himawari Shinjuku
Miyata Building 5F
1-4-12 Kabukichō
Shinjuku 160-0021
(Also at other locations)
pub-kara-himawari.com

Uta Hiroba Ikebukuro
1-27-7 Minami-Ikebukuro 6F
Toshima 171-0022
(Also at other locations)
www.utahiro.com

焼き団子
目玉のおやじまん

CHŌFU

—— A fifteen-minute trip on an express train from Shinjuku Station (or a twenty-five minute one from Shibuya Station) will bring you to a secret gem called Chōfu. An unremarkable suburban landscape greets you out the front of the station, but delve a little deeper and you'll find a suburb steeped in history. From the station we always catch the free shuttle bus to the Yumori no Sato *onsen* (hot spring; 2-12-2 Shindaiji-Motomachi); ask at the *koban* (police box) or the station information kiosk for the bus's pick-up point. Having a soak in this delightful *onsen* is a great way to start or finish your Chōfu adventure. It has real hot-spring water and an *onsen* in a treehouse, among other pleasures.

If you are missing a bit of old-school Japan on your Tokyo trip, Chōfu is sure to satisfy. Prepare yourself for a day of nature, pathways lined with vendors selling street food and trinkets (*daruma* dolls, p. 80, are popular here), and one of Tokyo's most beautiful temples, all reclining in the arms of a verdant landscape. It's only a short walk from the *onsen* to Jindai-ji (p. 334), Tokyo's second-oldest temple, established in 733 AD. Jindai-ji is beautifully atmospheric, and a lazy wander through its grounds as gongs ring out and the smell of incense floats in the air will still the unquiet heart. The entrance gate alone is a sight to behold. If you are a nature-lover you will love the Jindai Botanical Garden (p 345). The water garden is a favourite of ours.

When you visit, make sure to arrive with an empty stomach so you can sample the street food and the area's famous soba (and sake) lunch. Finish a day of grazing off with tea and *wagashi* (traditional sweets; p. 124) – the grilled *dango* (rice dumplings) here are delicious.

GeGeGe no Kitarō manga series shop (opposite)

Our favourite soba restaurant is Teuchisobadokoro Yusui (5-9-1 Jindaiji-Motomachi), but there are so many good ones that you may want to hunt out your own. Look out for the wildly popular store and café based on the *GeGeGe no Kitarō* manga series – it's the building with a pair of giant wooden *geta* (sandals) on the roof. Many make the pilgrimage to Chōfu for this spectacle alone.

We love to visit in autumn, when the colour, fragrance and atmosphere on the streets is perfect, especially in the deep afternoon as the late autumn light settles on copper foliage and centuries-old buildings. If you are a canine-lover, pop into the Fudatenjin shrine (p. 334) just five minutes from the station to see their famous dog statue. After a long day, you may want to return to the *onsen* and have one last soak before riding back toward the bright lights of the big city.

GeGeGe no Kitarō manga series shop (bottom left); Chōfu street scenes (above and opposite)

CULTURE

– Temples & shrines
– Parks & gardens
– Architecture
– Galleries & museums
– Kabuki, Noh & bunraku theatre
– Traditional crafts

TEMPLES & SHRINES

——— It may surprise you to learn that a modern metropolis like Tokyo has more than 1000 shrines and temples. The smell of incense and the sounds of chanting seem at odds with the blaring of horns, the clattering of trains and the relentless pounding of construction. But the quiet corners retain their mystique, providing havens from contemporary life that bring you both a sense of inner peace and a sense of traditional Japan. Although most are reconstructions – fires, earthquakes and bombings have razed most traditional structures to the ground – they are faithful ones, and many of these spaces still retain original relics, or have since taken on their own impressive signs of age.

If you are in Tokyo for New Year's Eve, don't forget to participate in Hatsumōde (p. 73), the first Shinto shrine visit of the year. Crowds, colours, festivities and spiritual serenity all come together to make one of Tokyo's (and Japan's) most unmissable celebrations.

On weekends, at mid-morning or in the late afternoon, it's common to see traditional Shinto weddings take place at Shinto shrines around Tokyo. This kind of wedding was popularised in the Meiji era (1868–1912; p. 32) and is an extraordinarily beautiful spectacle. The procession of the bride (in a white kimono called *shiromuku* and a large, impossibly elegant white cowl), the groom (in black), shrine maidens, priests and various traditionally dressed family members is breathtaking.

An early example of the elaborate Shinto ceremony was Prince Yoshihito's wedding to Kujo Sadako, held at the Imperial Palace in 1900.

Japanese bride in *shiromuku* for traditional Japanese wedding, late Shōwa era

Jindai-ji (top left); Small shrine near Jindai-ji (top right); Nezu Shrine (middle right, bottom left and bottom right)

Jindai-ji

ASAKUSA & UENO

Asakusa Jinja (Shinto shrine)
2-26-1 Asakusa
Taitō 111-0032

Hanazono Inari Jinja (Shinto shrine)
4-59 Uenokōen
Taitō 110-0007

Kan'ei-ji (Buddhist temple)
1-14-11 Uenosakuragi
Taitō 110-0002

Sensō-ji (Buddhist temple)
2-3-1 Asakusa
Taitō 111-0032

Ueno Tōshō-gū (Shinto shrine)
9-88 Uenokōen
Taitō 110-0007

CAT-THEMED

Yes, there are cat-themed shrines, most notably Gōtoku-ji! Finally, you can pay your cat the kind of respect he believes he deserves. For more on cat shrines and other cat havens, see p. 186.

CENTRAL TOKYO

Kanda Myōjin (Shinto shrine)
2-16-2 Soto-Kanda
Chiyoda 101-0021

Yasukuni Jinja (Shinto shrine)
3-1-1 Kudan-Kita
Chiyoda 102-8246
This shrine to those who have died fighting in the name of the Emperor has a questionable reputation, due to its enshrinement of Japanese soldiers who were convicted of war crimes after the Second World War, as well as the shrine's operation of a controversial war museum. Diplomatic rancour aside, it also serves as the yardstick for the 'official' first flowering of cherry blossoms in Tokyo, and has some spectacular blooms.

CHŌFU

Fudatenjin (Shinto shrine)
1-8-1 Chōfugaoka
Chōfu 182-0021

Jindai-ji (Buddhist temple)
5-15-1 Jindaiji-Motomachi
Chōfu 182-0017

FOR ROMANTIC GOOD FORTUNE

Tokyo Daijingu (Shinto shrine)
2-4-1 Fujimi
Chiyoda 102-0071

Yushima Seidō (Confucian temple)
1-4-25 Yushima
Bunkyō 113-0034
Students pray for good grades here, too.

HARAJUKU

Meiji Jingu (Meiji Shrine; Shinto shrine)
1-1 Kamizono-chō, Yoyogi
Shibuya 151-8557

HIDDEN NEIGHBOURHOOD TREASURES

Gōtoku-ji (Buddhist temple)
2-24-7 Gōtokuji
Setagaya 154-0021

Imado Jinja (Shinto shrine)
1-5-22 Imado
Taitō 111-0024

Inokashira Benzaiten/Taisei-ji (Buddhist temple)
Inside Inokashira Park (p. 342)
4-26-1 Inokashira
Mitaka 181-0001

Kōenji (Buddhist temple)
4-18-11 Kōenji-Minami
Suginami 166-0003

Kuhonbutsu/Jōshin-ji (Buddhist temple)
7-41-3 Okusawa
Setagaya 158-0083

NEZU, SENDAGI & YANAKA

Nezu Jinja (Shinto shrine)
1-28-9 Nezu
Bunkyō 113-0031

Tennō-ji (Buddhist temple)
7-14-8 Yanaka
Taitō 110-000

TIP: *Yanaka is sometimes called Temple Town. Come here for an afternoon temple stroll and discover charming small temples and shrines off the main tourist track.*

ROPPONGI

Atago Jinja (Shinto shrine)
1-5 Atago
Minato 105-0002

Nogi Jinja (Shinto shrine)
8-11-27 Asakusa
Minato 107-0052

Zōjō-ji (Buddhist temple)
4-7-35 Shibakōen
Minato 105-0011

Atago Jinja (top left and right); Inokashira Benzaiten (middle left); Sensō-ji (middle right and bottom centre); Chingo-do (bottom left); Gōtoku-ji (bottom right)

PARKS & GARDENS

——— Tokyo is a busy modern city and it can sometimes seem relentless, with its barely organised chaos of noise and movement and its endless walls of glass, steel and concrete. Such a city can only survive if its inhabitants are kept happy and sane with some proper quiet places, and Tokyo has some of the best parks and gardens you'll ever see. Traditional Japanese gardens abound, as do modern spaces punctuated by works from renowned sculptors, with vegetation designed and planted en masse by horticultural masters. Seriously beautiful patches of green come alive with autumn colour, burst with *sakura* (cherry blossom) during *hanami* (flower-viewing) season, reward the summer sun with a technicolour palette of flowers and foliage, and make sparse, sculptural shapes in the heart of winter. The town planning of early twentieth-century Tokyo got everything right: trees, plants and flowers; places to stroll, cycle and relax; destination cafés; secret pockets hidden in the depths of sprawling parks; and galleries and museums poking their impressive heads above canopies of leaves. Some gardens are free; others have nominal fees – small prices to pay for some exquisite meandering. Tokyo is truly a perambulist's delight.

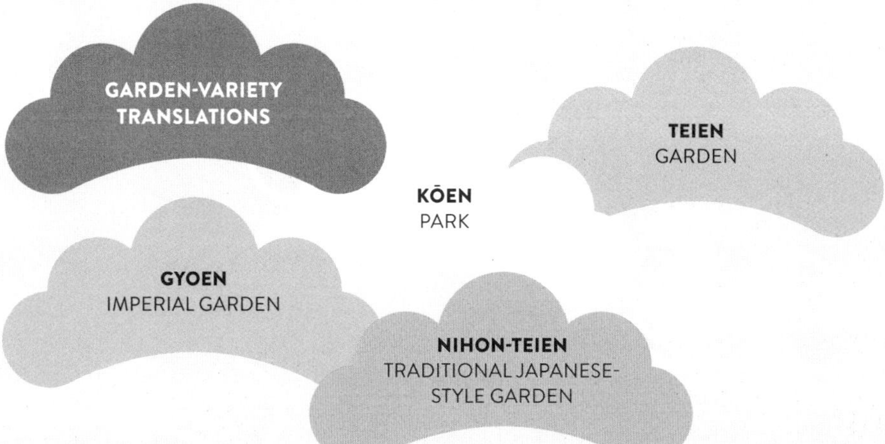

Kiyosumi Teien (opposite); Rikugi-en (pp. 338–9)

THE IMPERIAL PALACE & SURROUNDING GARDENS

Northwest of Tokyo Station you'll find old Edo's expansive swathe of greenery and its looming white Imperial Palace. The gardens were once the site of Edo Castle, residence of the Tokugawa shogun and military command post of the bustling port city. When the Tokugawa Shogunate was overthrown in 1868 and the Meiji Emperor moved to Edo in 1869, renaming the city Tokyo and making it the imperial capital of Japan, Edo Castle became the home of the Emperor. The new Imperial Palace (Kyūjō) was built in 1888, bombed in 1945 during the Second World War and then restored and reconstructed into the castle that looks over the grounds today. You can visit selected areas of the Imperial Palace grounds, but your opportunities are limited to the New Year's Greeting on 2 January, which the Emperor delivers from a balcony behind bullet-proof glass, and the Emperor's Birthday on 23 December. At other times of the year (except perhaps the rainy season from June to mid-July), the surrounding public gardens – Kōkyo Gaien, Kitanomaru Park and the East Gardens – are well worth a visit, a picnic and a lengthy stroll. In the East Gardens you'll find remnants of the old castle's moat, guardhouse, entrance gate and some sections of the original wall. Sadly, the original double bridges – ornate structures that acted as a covered walkway – no longer exist. The main entrance bridge, Seimon Ishibashi, is a beautiful stone structure. Often called the Eyeglass Bridge, its pair of curved arches rising out of, and reflected in, the water gives the appearance of eyes or binoculars gazing at you as you stand south of the gardens, which are easily accessed from Nijūbashimae Station.

One of the best treasures in the park is one of the least known: the Momijiyama Imperial Cocoonery. The cocoonery houses a rare type of silkworm, the Koishimaru silkworm, whose silk is invaluable in the restoration of ancient textiles and is used in the creation of beautiful new works. The silkworms are tended to by a small team headed by Empress Michiko, the fourth Empress to be involved in sericulture (the production of silk) since Empress Dowager Shōken, the wife of Emperor Meiji, began the cocoonery in 1871. Anyone obsessed with Japanese textiles should look out for exhibitions of the beautiful silk created by the Koishimaru silkworms, although the cocoonery itself is closed to the public.

Kudanshita Station is a good jump-off point to enter the palace's public gardens from the north. The Shimizu-mon Gate is one of the relics of old Edo and its striking wood-and-iron structure dates back to the early 1600s. The gate delivers you into beautiful Kitanomaru Park, an ideal location to take in the cherry blossoms and the home to the Science Museum, the National Museum of Modern Art and the Nippon Budōkan (all p. 354). All three would fit nicely into any Brutalist or modernist architectural itinerary.

Alternatively, Ōtemachi Station will bring you to the Kikyō-mon Gate, the iris water gardens and the beautiful Suwa-no-Chaya tea house – an easy diversion from the Marunouchi walk (p. 196). With Akihabara (p. 224) and Jimbōchō (p. 214) to the northeast, Tokyo (p. 192) and Ginza (p. 202) to the southeast, Roppongi (p. 274) and Tsukiji Fish Market (p. 206) to the south and Shinjuku (p. 246) due west, the Imperial Palace Gardens are a sizeable central hub that you can use to get your Tokyo bearings.

Imperial Palace Gardens and the Science Museum (opposite)

Japan's current emperor, Emperor Akihito, 'ascended the chrysanthemum throne' when he replaced his father Hirohito (Emperor Shōwa) in 1989. In 2017, he announced that he will abdicate the throne to his son, Crown Prince Naruhito, on 30 April 2019. As we go to press, what this era will be called is still undecided.

PARKS CONNECTED TO THE IMPERIAL PALACE GARDENS

Chidorigafuchi Park (Imperial Palace Northwest)

1-1 Kitanomarukōen
Chiyoda 102-0091
A strip of greenery runs alongside the Chidorigafuchi moat, a waterway constructed in the early Edo period. Visitors can punt around the moat.

Kōkyo Higashi Gyoen (Imperial Palace East)

1-1 Chiyoda
Chiyoda 102-0091
Historical gardens with Edo castle ruins.

SPRAWLING PARKS FOR STROLLING, JOGGING & CYCLING

Kinuta Kōen

1-1 Kinutakōen
Setagaya 157-0075
Setagaya's huge patch of green, featuring some lovely city wilderness escapes, is one of the premium spots for cherry-blossom viewing. Also known as a sporting park, it features soccer and baseball fields and cycling courses. The site would have played host to the 1940 Olympic Games, which were skipped when the Second Sino-Japanese War broke out in 1937. The Setagaya Art Museum (p. 362) can also be found here.

Inokashira Park

1-18-31 Gotenyama
Musashino 180-0005
Since its opening in May 1918, Inokashira has become one of Tokyo's premiere green spaces and a key destination in Tokyo's far west. On the edge of Kichijōji, Inokashira Park has its own train line and station. Most notably it is home to the Ghibli Museum (p. 362) and is also a popular location for cherry-blossom viewing. The park features a petting zoo, a small aquarium and the charming Inokashira Benzaiten shrine (p. 334). Red pines and cedars feature prominently in the park and there are several bee 'sanctuaries' set up among the trees. A stroll from Kichijōji to Inokashira Park makes for a wonderfully pleasant day.

Ueno Park

(p. 175)
Ueno Park covers a huge tract of land near JR Ueno Station and is home to lakes, a zoo, museums and shrines. Another favourite for cherry-blossom viewing, it boasts some 1000 cherry trees, and swan-boating on the lake through the lotus flowers is popular. Visitors to the park can find the Tokyo National Museum (p. 362), the National Museum of Western Art (p. 354), the Tokyo Metropolitan Art Museum, and the National Museum of Nature and Science (p. 362). The Shitamachi Museum (2-1 Uenokōen), built in 1980, is dedicated to the history of Tokyo's 'under city'. The land was once part of the Kan'ei-ji Buddhist temple (p. 334), though many buildings were destroyed by fire. The temple and an elegant five-tiered pagoda (hiding within Ueno Zoo) are striking reminders of the park's age, and relics can still be seen, including the face of a large statue of the Buddha. Many tree species, including *Ginkgo biloba*, and bird species, including the popular tufted duck, make Ueno Park their home. Edo-period shogun Ieyasu Tokugawa is enshrined at Ueno Tōshō-gū, a Shinto shrine that dates back as far as 1651.

Yoyogi Park

2-1 Kamizono-chō, Yoyogi
Shibuya 151-8557
Despite its festive atmosphere today, Yoyogi Park has had a varied history, acting as a military parade ground and US Army barracks from 1945. The land was returned to the Japanese government in the early 1960s in preparation for the 1964 Olympic Games, when it played host to the athletes and to many of the events, most notably the gymnastics, which were held in the stunning mid-century Yoyogi National Gymnasium (p. 351). It's best known now as the home of Sunday cosplayers, Elvis impersonators, martial-arts aficionados, buskers and more. A host of rowdy flea markets also take place on the grounds at various times. On the other end of the spectrum, one of Tokyo's biggest and most peaceful shrines, Meiji Jingu (Meiji Shrine, p. 334), can be found on the edge of the grounds. It's also a prime spot for cherry-blossom viewing and a stroll-worthy hub that connects the neighbourhoods of Shibuya (p. 234), Harajuku (p. 252) and Yoyogi (p. 291). NHK Studio Park (p. 365) is in the southern part of the grounds, at the tip of Kōen Dōri in Shibuya.

Shinjuku Gyoen

11 Naitomachi
Shinjuku 160-0014

One of Tokyo's biggest gardens, Shinjuku Gyoen was once the sole domain of the Imperial Family. Sadly, most of the garden was destroyed by bombing in 1945 and its original landscape has been lost forever. Although still known as an imperial garden, it was opened to the public in 1949 and has since become one of the prime spots for picnics during cherry-blossom season (p. 76), as it boasts an astounding 1500 cherry trees. It's also a prime spot for autumn-leaf viewing (p. 62). The regular 200 yen entry fee remains the same during *hanami* (flower viewing). Other standout features of the park include tulips, towering Himalayan cedars, and Japanese-, English- and French-style gardens. The Shinjuku skyline, including the Metropolitan Government Building, can be seen from the southwest side of the garden.

CLASSIC JAPANESE GARDENS

Kiyosumi Teien

3-3-9 Kiyosumi
Kōtō 135-0024
Kiyosumi Teien, near the MOT Museum of Contemporary Art (p. 360), is a Meiji-era garden and an interesting counterpoint to other gardens around Tokyo. Tucked away in a quiet part of the city, the area alone is worth a stroll, but beautiful Kiyosumi is the jewel in the crown. A tea house in the middle of the lake, with stepping-stone walkways that cross koi carp–filled waters, will transport you to a magical era. Perfectly manicured lawns and islands covered in twisted trees and brightly coloured flowers complete the picture.

Koishikawa-Kōrakuen

1-6-6 Kōraku
Bunkyō 112-0004
Established by feudal lord Mito Yorifusa in 1629, this garden's ambitions were so extensive that it would fall to his son to finish it many years later. Another Edo garden, and an excellent choice for viewing both cherry and plum blossoms, Koishikawa Kōrakuen features magical moss-covered bridges, ponds with surfacing rocks and more of that fiery autumn magic. One of the many standout features is the stone *engetsu kyō* ('moon bridge'), where the shape of the full moon is formed by the arch of the bridge and its reflection in the water.

Rikugi-en

6-16-3 Honkomagome
Bunkyō 113-0021
Featuring the lovely Fukiage Tea House (p. 146) and the site of Michelle's kimono day out (p. 64), Rikugi-en is a wonderful example of an Edo-period garden, having been established in the 1700s. For a mere 300 yen you can stroll about this piece of history. Designed around the six principles of Japanese poetry, this beautiful garden features charming stone bridges and lanterns and, in autumn, trees that glow with fiery red-and-gold foliage. Wander the grounds and spend some time in the tea house; you'll feel like you are living in Edo-period Tokyo.

WESTERN-STYLE GARDENS

Hibiya Kōen

1-6 Hibiyakōen
Chiyoda-ku, Tokyo, Tokyo
Host to the Hibiya Library Christmas Market and a place to see striking autumn colours, Hibiya Kōen is one of Tokyo's well-known Western-style parks, with plantings of European flowers and trees and installations of Western-style statues. With a history of riots and protest, some violent, Hibiya Kōen is still a site of rebellious activity today: musical gatherings and rallies are common. A restaurant, Matsumotoro (1-2 Hibiyakōen), sits in the shade of a towering 400-year-old ginkgo tree, an impressive interloper among the Western features of the park.

OTHER GREEN SPACES & PLACES

Gardens at Asakura Museum of Sculpture

(p. 363)

Gardens at Tokyo Tower

4-2-8 Shibakōen
Minato 105-0011

Hama Rikyū Gardens

1-1 Hamarikyūteien
Chūō 104-0046

Happō-en

1-1-1 Shirokanedai
Minato 108-0071

Institute for Nature Study National Reserve

5-21-5 Shirokanedai
Minato 108-0071

Jindai Botanical Garden

5-31-10 Jindaiji-Motomachi
Chōfu 182-0017

Lawns at Tokyo Midtown

9-7-1 Akasaka
Minato 107-0052

Meguro River Walk

2-6 Nakameguro
Meguro 152-0000

National Shōwa Memorial Museum

1-6-1 Kudan-Minami
Chiyoda 102-0074
www.showakan.go.jp

Nezu Museum

(p. 352)

Sumida Park

1-2-5 Mukojima
Sumida 131-0033

Hibiya Kōen (opposite bottom left); Rikugi-en (opposite, all other images)

ARCHITECTURE

—— One thing that we both love to do is travel for architecture, and Tokyo has never failed to deliver. Over the past twenty years, we have witnessed many new developments and constructions in the city. It has been exciting to see the evolution but, at the same time, it has been sad to see small communities disrupted to make way for big business, and classic buildings torn down to be replaced by looming high-tech towers.

We love mid-century architecture and anything with a sense of history, but we also love the simplicity and boldness of the Japanese aesthetic and how that can translate into stunning contemporary buildings. Our favourite structures range from capsule hotels and small eateries with dark-wood interiors and sliding paper doors, to bold, colourful reinventions of apartment blocks and space-age monoliths of glass and steel. Many of Tokyo's buildings, new and old, are truly memorable and notable from an architectural point of view.

Most of the entries in the following list are retail, residential and public buildings. Galleries and museums with wonderful architecture can be found in their own section (p. 356), as can the shrines and temples that embody traditional Japanese architecture (p. 330), and they all certainly form part of this dialogue as well.

A NOTE ON METABOLISM

In 2012, we attended an exhibition on Metabolism at the Mori Art Museum (p. 357). As lovers of architecture, we knew a lot about Western architectural movements, but the concept of Metabolism was completely new to us: a fascinating take on Futurism and Brutalism designed to cope with the booming Tokyo population and a foreseeable lack of future housing.

Space-age capsules to be built on stilts in the actual ocean were proposed, and people thought pods and capsules would redefine housing for a new age. Many of the ideas never made it from the planning stage, but some did, and stand as a testament to a bold vision that was probably a little frightening for those out of the Metabolist loop, as the ideas were perceived to lack organic warmth.

Just like its Western cousin, Brutalism, Metabolism is seen as an ugly duckling to some, but it had serious principles and was clever beyond its years. The darlings of the movement, Kisho Kurokawa and Kenzō Tange, are both loved and revered by architects and designers globally, but are sometimes misunderstood by their own public.

See page 354 for a list of Metabolist gems in Tokyo.

MODERNIST ARCHITECTURE

Hotel Okura Tokyo; Yoshiro Taniguchi, Hideo Kosaka, Shiko Munakata and Kenkichi Tomimoto; 1962
2-10-4 Toranomon
Minato 105-0001
hotelokura.co.jp/tokyo
Now mostly demolished, the simply gorgeous main lobby is set to reopen in 2019 (and is being designed by Yoshio Taniguchi, son of Yoshiro Taniguchi). In the lobby of the current building you can still glimpse a small remaining piece of the modernist masterpiece that has the charming echoes of days gone by.

International House of Japan; Maekawa Kunio, Sakakura Junzō and Yoshimura Junzō; 1955
5-11-16 Roppongi
Minato 106-0032
i-house.or.jp/eng
A beautiful example of mid-century Japanese architecture with a stunning garden.

Hara Museum of Contemporary Art, Jin Watanabe, 1938
(p. 360)

GINZA ARCHITECTURE

Ginza Place, Klein Dytham, 2016
5-8-1 Ginza
Chūō 104-0061
Compare and contrast: the arresting white woven look of the contemporary Ginza Place building sits opposite the stately, Art Deco–inspired Wako Building by Jin Watanabe (1932).

Louis Vuitton Ginza, Jun Aoki & Associates, 2000
3-6-1 Ginza
104-8130
An extraordinary building by day or night. Aoki & Associates took the ubiquitous LV monogram and used it as a building block to construct a flagship store as elegant and refined as the label itself. With few traditional windows to speak of, light comes through the signature Louis Vuitton pattern etched into the facade, and the building ends up looking almost holographic in appearance. At night the structure glows with an otherworldly presence.

Mikimoto 2, Toyo Ito, 2005
2-4-12 Ginza
Chūō 104-8145
mikimoto.com/en/stores
A tall white monolith with a stencil-cut facade, Mikimoto 2 fills you with an urgent need to slot blocks into the empty shapes that pockmark its surface. At night, lights shining through the misshapen portholes gives the impression of a futuristic lighthouse guiding explorers through Tokyo's neon jungle.

Yamaha Ginza, Nikken Sekkei, 2010
7-9-14 Ginza
Chūō 104-0061
www.yamahamusic.jp/shop/ginza.html
A retro-inspired, coloured jacquard/diamond-patterned stunner (with a café to match), the Yamaha building makes its own statement among the big names of Ginza.

Nakagin Capsule Tower, Kisho Kurokawa, 1972
(p. 209)
8-16-10 Ginza
Chūō 104-0061

Odaiba (opposite top); International House of Japan (opposite bottom)

Tod's Omotesandō; Tama Art University Library; St Mary's Cathedral; Tama Art University Library; Yoyogi National Gymnasium (clockwise from top left)

SUPERSTAR ARCHITECTS

KENZŌ TANGE, THE MODERNIST MASTER: Traditional Japan meets a retro vision of the future

Fuji TV Building, Odaiba, 1997
2-4-8 Daiba
Minato 135-0091

A building like no other, this pod-robot of a structure forces you to contemplate the future of buildings – and of the society that uses them. With its metal bubble and shining struts framing open space, this is a perfect embodiment of the Metabolist (p. 348) school of design. As an added bonus, the pod has a stunning view of the area.

St Mary's Cathedral, Sekiguchi, 1964
3-16-15 Sekiguchi
Bunkyō 112-0014
cathedral-sekiguchi.jp

A Roman Catholic church with a full Japanese makeover, St Mary's Cathedral is another building that modernists can't miss. Outside, towering, glinting metal reaches toward the heavens, while inside, light diffuses through organic, flowing shapes. A stunning building.

Yoyogi National Gymnasium, 1964
2-1-1 Jinnan
Shibuya 150-0041
jpnsport.go.jp/yoyogi

One of our favourite pieces of architecture in Tokyo; beautiful from every angle, flowing and pulsing with dynamic energy, the Yoyogi National Gymnasium still looks fresh more than fifty years after its construction.

Embassy of Kuwait, Mita, 1970
4-13-12 Mita
Minato 108-0073

TADAO ANDO, THE UNLIKELY INNOVATOR: A self-taught weaver of beauty

21_21 Design Sight, 2007
(p. 362)

Co-designed with fashion icon Issey Miyake, this understated building sits low to the ground in a clear space of manicured lawn and is juxtaposed with a wall of tall trees.

Tokyo Skytree, 2009
(p. 161)

TOYO ITO, THE MASTER OF HIGH-CONCEPT & INNOVATION

Mikimoto 2, Ginza, 2005
(p. 349)

Sometimes affectionately called the Ginza Jewel – or the Swiss Cheese Building – Mikimoto 2 showcases Ito's ability to bring light, shadow and depth to the traditional skyscraper.

Tama Art University Library (Hachiōji), Yarimizu, 2007
2-1723 Yarimizu
Hachiōji 192-0394
tamabi.ac.jp

A university library so inspiring that students enrol just so they learn inside it, exhilarated by its extraordinary design.

Tod's Omotesandō, Jingūmae, 2004
5-1-5 Jingūmae
Shibuya 150-0001
tods.com

Breathtaking at night, Tod's on Omotesandō Dōri (p. 260) is distinguishable by its 'paper cut-out' design that makes it a striking figure on a boulevard already populated with stand-out buildings.

OMOTESANDŌ & AOYAMA ARCHITECTURE

Chloé building, Sophie Hicks, 2006

5-3-2 Minami-Aoyama
Minato 107-0062

The Chloé building's playful yet precise angled panels of wooden slats cover a tower that dwarfs nearby Cartier's half-sunken glass box. Along with the Prada store, this little cluster of buildings certainly adds an air of glamour and prestige to an already impressive Aoyama Dōri. The eponymous retailer no longer resides in the building, but the exterior is still worth visiting.

Comme des Garçons, Takao Kawasaki, 1999

5-2-1 Minami-Aoyama
Minato 107-0062
comme-des-garcons.com

The building's wide, angled windows and in-store divisions are more about display than making a major statement, but the window-dressing is second to none and as challenging as the clothing: contemporary artwork and cutting-edge fashion colliding in a parallel universe.

Prada Epicenter, 2003, and Miu Miu, 2015, Herzog & de Meuron

5-2-6 Minami-Aoyama
Minato 107-0062
prada.com/en
5-5-8 Minami-Aoyama
Minato 107-0062
miumiu.com/en

The populist face of Aoyama architecture, Prada arrived in the noughties and brought hordes of architecture and photography buffs along with it. Prada's subsidiary brand Miu Miu had big shoes to fill, so it went in almost the opposite direction. Where Prada is all glass and open-plan, inviting voyeurism, Miu Miu makes itself nigh inaccessible. Its dramatic sloping roof with a just a peek of copper lining makes it look like it could close and become an impregnable bunker in the event of nuclear war.

SunnyHills, Kengo Kuma, 2013

3-10-20 Minami-Aoyama
Minato 107-0062
www.sunnyhills.com.tw/index/ja-jp

An upscale cake shop, home of the famous Taiwanese pineapple cake, SunnyHills looks like a god threw down some wooden pick-up sticks and they landed in a semi-organised pile of diamond latticework. Bold, amusing and unlike anything you've seen, the garden-trellis theme continues throughout. At night, the light diffuses through it in the most magical way.

TOBICHI 2, Hobonichi Techo, 2014

4-25-14 Minami-Aoyama
Minato 107-0062
1101.com/store/techo/en/

A shop and gallery devoted to Hobonichi, the wildly popular daily recorder of thoughts and events loved by stationery and paper nerds (think a super-cool Filofax), TOBICHI 2 stands in stark contrast to the neon gods looming over Omotesandō and Aoyama. This building, with its layered wooden edifice and whitewashed walls, is smaller and more traditional, and emits an enticing warmth.

Nezu Museum, Kengo Kuma, 2009

(p. 267)
6-5-1 Minami-Aoyama
Minato 107-0062
www.nezu-muse.or.jp/en

SHINJUKU ARCHITECTURE

Mode Gakuen Cocoon Tower, Tange Associates, 2008

1-7-3 Nishi-Shinjuku
Shinjuku 160-0032

When it comes to statement buildings, the Cocoon Tower is one of the finest. A tall, lattice-covered futurist steeple, it is powerful in its intent, striking in its aspect and one of the true marvels of the Shinjuku skyline. Home to a fashion-focused vocational school, the building needed to be something that said fashion, design and commerce in one hit, and Tange Associates delivered it with a religious intensity. See it (and snap pics of it) from the curved byways of Nishi-Shinjuku Junction.

Shinjuku Rurikō-in Byakurenge-dō, Amorphe Takeyama & Associates, 2014

2-4-3 Yoyogi
Shibuya 151-0053
byakurengedo.net

A modernist block balanced on an alarmingly thin 'handle' base, an 'eye to god' on the front and cut-out side windows that bleed heavenly light at night: statement buildings don't come much more statement than this. It's also a temple, where people actually come to worship. The interior walls of multicoloured, glass Buddhas are impressive for their sheer scale. The rooftop garden is certainly worth a visit.

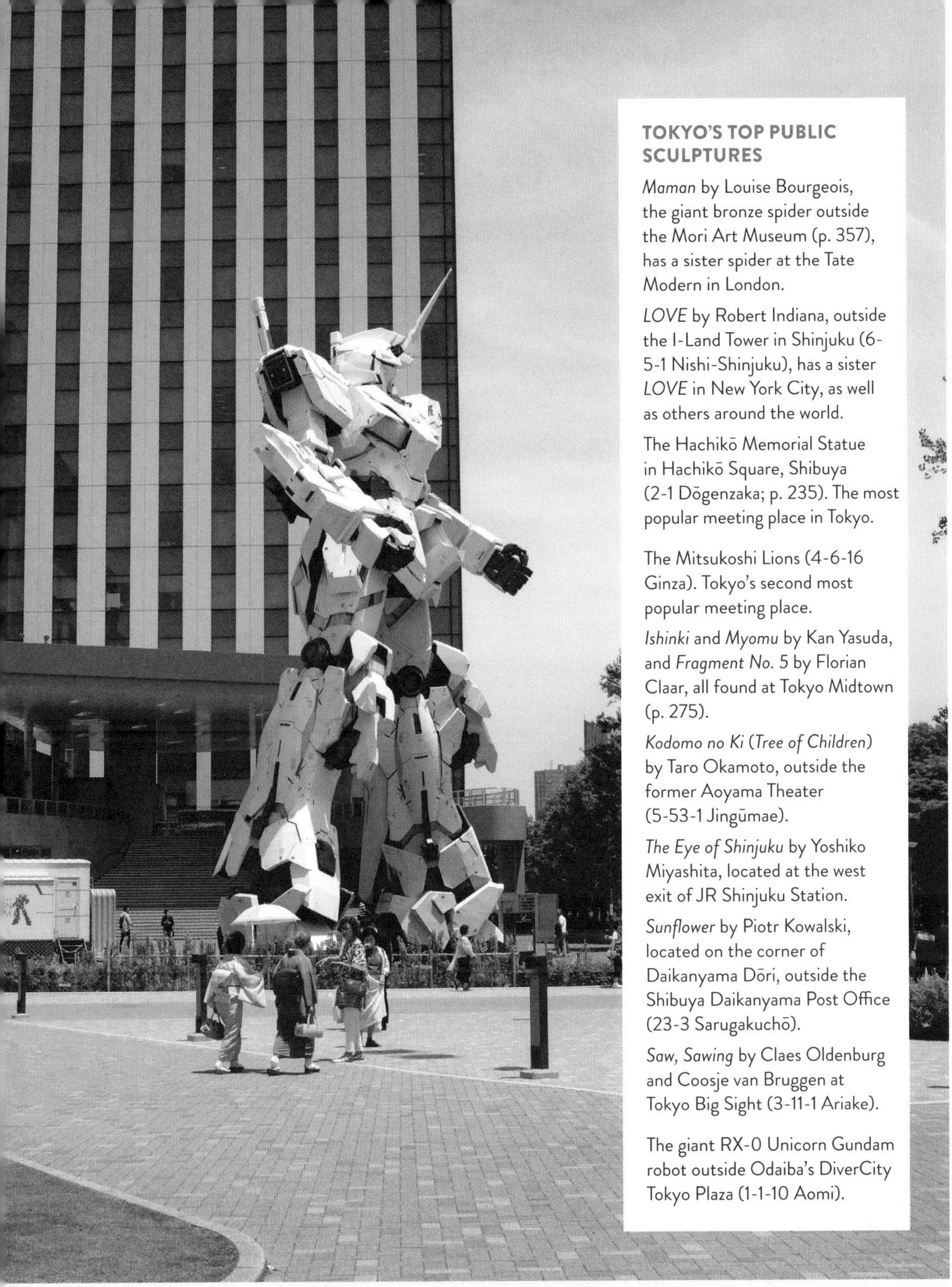

TOKYO'S TOP PUBLIC SCULPTURES

Maman by Louise Bourgeois, the giant bronze spider outside the Mori Art Museum (p. 357), has a sister spider at the Tate Modern in London.

LOVE by Robert Indiana, outside the I-Land Tower in Shinjuku (6-5-1 Nishi-Shinjuku), has a sister *LOVE* in New York City, as well as others around the world.

The Hachikō Memorial Statue in Hachikō Square, Shibuya (2-1 Dōgenzaka; p. 235). The most popular meeting place in Tokyo.

The Mitsukoshi Lions (4-6-16 Ginza). Tokyo's second most popular meeting place.

Ishinki and *Myomu* by Kan Yasuda, and *Fragment No. 5* by Florian Claar, all found at Tokyo Midtown (p. 275).

Kodomo no Ki (*Tree of Children*) by Taro Okamoto, outside the former Aoyama Theater (5-53-1 Jingūmae).

The Eye of Shinjuku by Yoshiko Miyashita, located at the west exit of JR Shinjuku Station.

Sunflower by Piotr Kowalski, located on the corner of Daikanyama Dōri, outside the Shibuya Daikanyama Post Office (23-3 Sarugakuchō).

Saw, Sawing by Claes Oldenburg and Coosje van Bruggen at Tokyo Big Sight (3-11-1 Ariake).

The giant RX-0 Unicorn Gundam robot outside Odaiba's DiverCity Tokyo Plaza (1-1-10 Aomi).

RX-0 Unicorn Gundam

METABOLIST GEMS

Fuji TV Building
(p. 351)

Hillside Terrace, Fumihiko Maki, 1969
18-8 Sarugakuchō
Shibuya 150-0033

Nakagin Capsule Tower
(p. 349)

Shizuoka Press and Broadcasting Center, Kenzō Tange, 1967
8-3-7 Ginza
Chūō 104-0061

Yamanashi Press and Broadcasting Center, Kenzō Tange, 1966
2-6-10 Kitaguchi, Kōfu
Yamanashi 400-0024

BRUTALIST ARCHITECTURE

Reiyukai Shakaden, Takenaka Corporation, 1975
1-7-8 Azabudai
Minato 106-8644
reiyukai.jp
A Brutalist-style temple that wears its 1970s badge proudly. With a multi-layered design that sits somewhere between a *kabuto* (samurai helmet) and Darth Vader's mask, Reiyukai Shakaden is imposing and proud.

National Museum of Modern Art, Yoshirō Taniguchi, 1969
3-1 Kitanomarukōen
Chiyoda 102-8322
www.momat.go.jp/english

Nippon Budōkan, Mamoru Yamada, 1964
2-3 Kitanomarukōen
Chiyoda 102-8321
nipponbudokan.or.jp

Science Museum, Kiyō Matsushita and Takashi Hirayama, 1964
2-1 Kitanomarukōen
Chiyoda 102-0091
www.jsf.or.jp/eng

OTHER NOTABLE ARCHITECTURE

National Museum of Western Art, Le Corbusier, 1959
7-7 Uenokōen
Taitō 110-0007
www.nmwa.go.jp/en
One of the very few examples of European mid-century modern architecture in Japan, Le Corbusier's concrete monument is the perfect thank-you note to the country, whose architecture had a major influence on the modernist movement. Despite its square lines and gloomy colour, the building radiates a surprising amount of warmth. One of Ueno Park's stand-out sights, and a must for anyone on a modernist pilgrimage.

Reversible Destiny Lofts, Shusaku Arakawa and Madeline Gins, 2005
2-2-8 Ōsawa
Mitaka 181-0015
Appropriate for the quirky suburb of Mitaka (where the Ghibli Museum resides), this brightly coloured playbox of ideas was built posthumously from the inventive plans of artists and architects Arakawa and Gins. With curves and undulations in the style of architect Friedensreich Hundertwasser's work, playful rooms with floors that rise and fall like waves carry you along to your destination or provide you with a place to relax. Subtitled 'In memory of Helen Keller', you can certainly see how something so tactile invites touch. Made up of globes, tubes and cubes, the end result is pure Tokyo and yet unlike anything else you might see, except perhaps in a child's toybox. If you fancy trying out one of the lofts, they can sometimes be available to rent on Airbnb.

UCCJ Harajuku Protestant Church, Ciel Rouge Création, 2006
3-42-1 Jingūmae
Shibuya 150-0001
harajuku-church.com
With organic waves and bold edifices punctuated by unusually shaped windows, the UCCJ Harajuku Protestant Church is part exultation of God and the gift of divine inspiration, and part celebration of the French design team's extraordinary skills. Both the exterior and the interior of the building are spectacular in their own right. Well worth the diversion into Aoyama Dōri's backstreets.

Nakagin Capsule Tower (opposite)

中銀

GALLERIES & MUSEUMS

——— To the Japanese, life is art and art informs life – and centuries of perfecting intricate handicrafts has given rise to a nation of makers where art is a part of the everyday. Tokyo, as a large and multi-faceted capital city, is a major centre for art in Japan. Countless galleries and museums ensure that art-lovers can exhibition-hop for the best illustration, contemporary art, graphic design and traditional art that the country has to offer. Many of our gallery recommendations could sit just as easily in the architecture section (p. 346), the buildings being works of art themselves. From large-scale exhibitions to small, one-room spaces, there is always something in Tokyo that will intrigue, astound, move, perplex and inspire.

THE ART TRIANGLE

Three of Tokyo's best art galleries are all within walking distance from each other. The Roppongi art triangle is credited with kickstarting a Roppongi revival of sorts, with the once rough-and-ready, expats-and-nightclubs, sleep-in-the-train-station town now family-friendly and crammed with destination spaces (spoiler alert: it's still vomit-on-the-streets nightclub-crazy as well, so you have the best of both worlds). Add 21_21 Design Sight (p. 362) and Fujifilm Square's amazing store-turned-photography-gallery (p. 365) to the mix and you have some heavyweight art destinations.

Mori Art Museum

Mori Tower 53F
6-10-1 Roppongi
Minato 106-6108
mori.art.museum

No matter when you visit or what is on, the Mori Art Museum always puts on an unforgettable show – and that's just the view. From the fifty-third and fifty-fourth floors you can see architect Richard Gluckman's vision of an urban utopia, an extraordinary city sprawl that reaches out to the very edges of Tokyo. Just riding the elevator up can give you vertigo. The museum itself has no permanent collection; it's constantly evolving, and as a result you'll find some truly unforgettable exhibitions of cutting-edge Japanese art. If you are there in February of the right year (2019, 2022, 2025, and so on), you'll be able to catch a taster of the best emerging Asian contemporary artists in a trienniale exhibition called Roppongi Crossing.

National Art Center

7-22-2 Roppongi
Minato 106-8558
www.nact.jp/english

Kisho Kurokawa's showstopping steel-and-glass waveform made its grand debut in 2006 and Roppongi has never looked back. As art havens go, the National Art Center has it all. With numerous exhibition spaces, there are plenty of shows to choose from – international and local, solo and joint. There are free exhibitions, as well as paid and combined-ticket shows. The centre often boasts some of the most visited exhibitions in the world. Add the upside-down conical pillar that props up the popular Brasserie Paul Bocuse, a great basement souvenir shop and endless photo opportunities (it's possible to go in and just marvel at the building itself), and you have one of Tokyo's premiere art experiences.

Suntory Museum of Art

9-7-4 Akasaka
Minato 107-8643
suntory.co.jp/sma/

Housed on the third floor of chic shopping centre Tokyo Midtown, the Suntory Musuem of Art is the corner of the art triangle that is dedicated to traditional Japanese and Asian art. Anyone with an interest in anything that tells a story of old Japan – *noren* curtains, screens, ancient artefacts – will find the permanent collection mesmerising. There are some serious pieces here, all housed in a display that gives new meaning to the phrase 'mood lighting'. Regular changing exhibitions showcase some amazing art, design and craft from years gone by.

Roppongi Hills (opposite top); Midtown Design Awards (opposite middle and bottom right); Steve at Espace Louis Vuitton (opposite bottom left)

MODERN & CONTEMPORARY ART

Hara Museum of Contemporary Art
4-7-25 Kita-Shinagawa
Shinagawa 140-0001
haramuseum.or.jp
Built by Jin Watanabe for the Hara family, this stunning house is now a contemporary-art museum showcasing the Hara dynasty's modern-art purchases. The building and gardens are an essential part of the experience. The mid-century modern–style gallery is one of the finest examples of the era in the world. Similar to Peggy Gugghenheim's wonderful museum in Venice, this is a small, precise gallery with exhibits to match. Even within the bustling transport hub of Shinagawa, the Hara Museum remains a small island of calm.

MOT Museum of Contemporary Art
4-1-1 Miyoshi
Kōtō 135-0022
mot-art-museum.jp
We've seen some of our favourite exhibitions at this modernist gallery. Starting at Kiyosumi-Shirakawa Station, follow the signs down charming 'Heart Street' and soak up the gentle feel of the area before reaching the main road where MOT's stunning angled contemporary/modernist exterior comes into view. The exhibitions here are always enthralling and challenging, and showcase some of the very best of Japanese contemporary art. Towering ceilings, wide spaces and a superb bookshop add extra heft to an already spectacular destination gallery. Extensive renovations since 2016 should see some interesting changes. The gallery reopens in March 2019.

Bunkamura
2-24-1 Dōgenzaka
Shibuya 150-8507
www.bunkamura.co.jp

National Museum of Modern Art – Crafts Gallery
3-1 Kitanomarukōen
Chiyoda 102-0091
www.momat.go.jp/english/cg/visit

National Museum of Western Art
(p. 354)

Tokyo Station Gallery
1-9-1 Marunouchi
Chiyoda 100-0005
www.ejrcf.or.jp/gallery

Watarium Museum of Contemporary Art
3-7-6 Jingūmae
Shibuya 150-0001
watarium.co.jp

TRADITIONAL & HISTORIC

If you are interested in the history of Edo and its evolution through art, science and architecture, there are plenty of amazing museums and galleries, many of which are located around Ueno Park (p. 342) and in older parts of town, like Sumida. The Edo-Tokyo Museum will give you a detailed account of the history of Tokyo, complete with artefacts from and recreations of the thirty-five eras of the Edo period (1603–1868; p. 26). The Edo-Tokyo Open Air Architectural Museum features life-size Edo environments (and some from later eras) so you can imagine what it was like to live in those times. Many other notable exhibition spaces dot Ueno Park, including the National Museum of Western Art, National Museum of Nature and Science. Beautiful Nezu Museum at the end of upscale Aoyama Dōri (p. 352) is notable for its wonderfully curated exhibitions and its tranquil garden, and anyone wanting to learn more about Japan's traditional handicrafts (including weapons, clothing and textiles) should head to Mingeikan, the Japan Folk Crafts Museum, a stunning building in its own right.

Edo-Tokyo Museum
1-4-1 Yokoami
Sumida 130-0015
edo-tokyo-museum.or.jp/en

Edo-Tokyo Open Air Architectural Museum
Koganei Park
3-7-1 Sakurachō
Koganei 184-0005
tatemonoen.jp/english

Hatakeyama Memorial Museum of Fine Art
2-20-12 Shirokanedai
Minato 108-0071
www.ebara.co.jp/csr/hatakeyama/english.html

Japan Folk Crafts Museum
4-3-33 Komaba
Meguro 153-0041
www.mingeikan.or.jp

Japan Folk Crafts Museum (above); Doraemon exhibition at the Mori Art Museum, 2018 (pp. 358–9)

National Museum of Nature and Science
7-20 Uenokōen
Taitō 110-8718
ww.kahaku.go.jp/english

National Museum of Western Art
(p. 354)

National Shōwa Memorial Museum
(p. 345)

Nezu Museum
(p. 352)

Ōta Memorial Museum of Art
1-10-10 Jingūmae
Shibuya 150-0001
ukiyoe-ota-muse.jp/eng

Samurai Museum
2-25-6 Kabukichō
Shinjuku 160-0021
samuraimuseum.jp/en

Setagaya Art Museum
1-2 Kinutakoen
Setagaya 157-0075
www.setagayaartmuseum.or.jp/en

Tokyo National Museum
13-9 Ueno Park
Taitō 110-8712
www.tnm.jp

DESIGN-FOCUSED

21_21 Design Sight
9-7-6 Akasaka
Minato 107-6290
2121designsight.jp
Honorary member of the Roppongi art triangle, Tadao Ando's building rises from Tokyo Midtown's pleasant lawns like a beautiful metal butterfly waiting to take flight. Designers and the design-obsessed will be in heaven, not only for the building's iconic exterior or its stark grey concrete interior (a minimalist dream), but also for the design-focused exhibitions, which showcase product, creation and experimentation in perfectly curated shows.

Ginza Graphic Gallery
DNP Ginza Building 1F
7-7-2 Ginza
Chūō 104-0061
www.dnp.co.jp/gallery/ggg_e
A small side-street gallery devoted entirely to graphic design – a field in which Japan is a world leader. We would go so far as to say that Japan invented graphic design, with its rich history of calligraphy, kimono patterns and *ukiyo-e* woodblock prints. It follows, then, that Japanese (and international) graphic design, both new and historical, is a fertile source of inspiration and material for stunning and informative exhibitions. Hard to believe entry is free.

Creation Gallery G8
Recruit Ginza 8 Building 1F
8-4-17 Ginza
Chūō 104-8001
rcc.recruit.co.jp/g8/en

Muji Yūrakuchō store and gallery
3-8-3 Marunouchi
Chiyoda 100-0005
muji.com
TIP: *Stop by minimalist grocery store D'Marge on the ground floor. It's almost a gallery in itself, except that fruit and vegetables are the art …*

Tokyo Midtown Design Hub
5F Midtown Tower
9-7-1 Akasaka
Minato 107-6205
designhub.jp
TIP: *Some design,* zakka *(handicraft, p. 372) or craft stores have small gallery spaces. Hobonichi Techo (p. 352) and Tegamisha (1-17-5 Kikunodai 2F) are two examples.*

SINGLE ARTIST

Ghibli Museum
1-1-83 Shimorenjaku
Mitaka 181-0013
ghibli-museum.jp
Sitting on the lip of beautiful Inokashira Park, the Ghibli Museum is something of a pilgrimage for many people. The famous animation company Studio Ghibli, founded by Hayao Miyazaki, Isao Takahata and Toshio Suzuki, has been responsible for some of the most loved and lauded animations in Japanese history, including *Sen to Chihiro no Kamikakushi* (*Spirited Away*; 2001), *Hotaru no Haka* (*Grave of the Fireflies*; 1988), *Hauru no Ugoku Shiro* (*Howl's Moving Castle*; 2004) and *Mononoke-hime* (*Princess Mononoke*; 1997). The museum is the epitome of Tokyo's quirky and *kawaii* ('cute') side, an organic blob sprouting grass and ivy, with famous Ghibli characters poking their heads around every corner – kids will love it. It's all presided over by the robot soldier from *Laputa: Castle in the Sky*. Naturally, you can get the *Nekobasu* (the cat bus of *My Neighbor Totoro* fame) from Mitaka Station.

A brief word on ticketing: you have to buy tickets for a specific time slot in advance. Tickets can be purchased from Lawson convenience stores, Lawson Online (l-tike.com/st1/ghibli-en) or JTB Online (jtbgmt.com/eng/ghibli/TicketSystem.html). Pick the slot you want, be on time and enjoy the magical Ghibli experience!

Yayoi Kusama Museum
107 Bentenchō
Shinjuku 162-0851
yayoikusamamuseum.jp

Part of the avant-garde scene of sixties New York, Matsumoto-born Kusama is now acknowledged as one of Japan's most important artists. The pop artist, whom Yoko Ono cites as an influence, is instantly recognisable for her pumpkins and spots – giant, joyous visuals. The museum, designed by Kume Sekkei, is a blue beacon that simultaneously sits in and breaks up the grey Shibuya landscape. Glass cutaways are used to light the gallery up at night, a celebration of the light and love in Kusama's work.

Asakura Museum of Sculpture
7-18-10 Yanaka
Taitō 110-0001
taitocity.net/zaidan/asakura

Sumida Hokusai Museum
(p. 168)

2-7-2 Kamezawa
Sumida 130-0014
hokusai-museum.jp

SINGLE THEME

Tokyo is great at doing mid-sized galleries that specialise in a single theme, whether it's a particular art form, medium or subject. The cherry blossom and its history is celebrated in Nakameguro's Sakura Museum, while advertising from the fifties onwards at the Ad Museum gives you the Japanese take on Don Draper. The Tokyo Metropolitan Museum of Photography is a must-do. In its recently renovated spaces you'll get the best of the best in pictorial excellence from Japan and around the world.

Ad Museum
Caretta Shiodome
1-8-2 Higashi-Shimbashi
Minato 105-0021
admt.jp/en

Sakura Museum
1-7-13 Kamimeguro
Meguro 153-0051
satosakura.jp/english

Tokyo Photographic Art Museum (TOP)
Yebisu Garden Place
1-13-3 Mita
Meguro 153-0062
topmuseum.jp/e/contents/index.html

QUIRKY

Anyone looking for an oddball experience is spoiled for choice when it comes to gallery-hopping. Take, for instance, the frightening (and surprisingly interesting) parasite museum in Meguro, where you can witness, of all things, a giant nine-metre tapeworm rescued from the stomach of an unfortunate soul. Worms and all manner of things that attach to a human host can be found in jars and cases. It's a research facility as well, so you get the added bonus of it being free. Just don't blame us if something escapes and goes on a rampage!

If you're a little squeamish, there's always the Toto Tokyo Center Showroom, dedicated to the art of the toilet – something the Japanese have truly perfected. Anyone wanting a history of the toilet in Japan will be flushed with excitement.

The Cup Noodles Museum, an hour's train ride away in Yokohama, is a riot of colourful packaging from past and present, and a great place to take the kids. Sit in on some classes and learn the way of the noodle. Or head to the Museum of Yebisu Beer if you need some adult time. This is the tip of the wonky iceberg of quirk in Tokyo, so seek out your own favourites.

Cup Noodles Museum (Yokohama)
2-3-4 Shinko
Naka, Yokohama 231-0001
cupnoodles-museum.jp/en/yokohama

Meguro Parasitological Museum
4-1-1 Shimomeguro
Meguro 153-0064
kiseichu.org

Museum of Yebisu Beer
Yebisu Garden Place
4-20-1 Ebisu
Shibuya 150-8522
sapporobeer.jp/yebisu/museum

Tobacco and Salt Museum
(p. 168)

1-16-3 Yokokawa
Sumida 130-0003
jti.co.jp/Culture/museum

Toto Tokyo Center Showroom
JR Minami-Shinjuku Building
7–8F
2-1-5 Yoyogi
Shibuya 151-0053
showroom.toto.jp/showroom.aspx?sr=028

SMALL, INTERESTING COLLECTIONS

Fujifilm Square
9-7-3 Akasaka
Minato 107-0052
fujifilmsquare.jp

Okuno Building
1-9-8 Ginza
Chūō 104-0061

Scai the Bathhouse
6-1-23 Yanaka
Taitō 110-0001
scaithebathhouse.com/en

Tomio Koyama Gallery
Complex 665 2F
6-5-24 Roppongi
Minato 106-0032
tomiokoyamagallery.com/en

GALLERIES IN DESIGNER STORES

Espace Louis Vuitton
Louis Vuitton Omotesandō Building 7F
5-7-5 Jingūmae
Shibuya 150-0001
espacelouisvuittontokyo.com

Seibu Shibuya Art Gallery
Seibu Shibuya B Building 8F
21-1 Udagawachō
Shibuya 150-0042
sogo-seibu.jp/shibuya

Shiseido Gallery
Tokyo Ginza Shiseido Building BF
8-8-3 Ginza
Chūō 104-0061
shiseidogroup.com/gallery

MUSEUMS FOR KIDS BIG & SMALL

Dagashiya Game Museum
17-8 Miyamotochō
Itabashi 174-0054
dgm.hmc6.net

NHK Studio Park
2-2-1 Jinnan
Shibuya 150-8001
www.nhk.or.jp/studiopark

Nurie Colouring Book Art Museum
4-11-8 Machiya
Arakawa 116-0001
www.nurie.jp/foreign/index_eng.html

OTHER GALLERIES

Art in Gallery
4-25-3 Jingūmae
Shibuya 150-0001
art-in-gallery.la.coocan.jp

Case Gallery
55-6 Motoyoyogichō
Shibuya 151-0062

Doinel
3-2-9 Kita-Aoyama
Minato 107-0061
doinel.net

Galerie Doux Dimanche
3-5-6 Jingūmae
Shibuya 150-0001
2dimanche.com

Gallery 360°
360.co.jp/en
1-17-14 Oyamadai
Setagaya 158-0086

Gallery Éf
2-19-18 Kaminarimon
Taitō 111-0034
www.gallery-ef.com/e.htm

Gallery Ma
Toto Nogizaka Building 3F
1-24-3 Minami-Aoyama
Minato 107-0062
www.toto.co.jp/gallerma

OCO Gallery
1-8-2 Tomigaya
Shibuya 151-0063
ocogallery.jp

Ōta Fine Arts
Piramide Building 3F
6-6-9 Roppongi
Minato 106-0032
otafinearts.com/en

Prismic Gallery
4-1-9 Minami-Aoyama
Minato 107-0062

Rathole Gallery
5-5-3 Minami-Aoyama BF1
Minato 107-0062
ratholegallery.com

Vanilla Gallery
Tosui Building B2F
8-10-7 Ginza

Michelle photographing the Minä Perhonen exhibition at Spiral Gallery, Aoyama (opposite)

KABUKI, NOH & BUNRAKU THEATRE

—— Kabuki is an extremely high-end Japanese soap opera on stage, often centred around historical themes. Originally performed by women, it is now performed mostly by men due to the Tokugawa shogunate's ban on female performers in the 1600s; many male kabuki performers specialise in playing women, a role known as *onnagata*. Kabuki captures the heart and mind with stories of intrigue, family feuds and romantic trysts. Actors are extremely expressive and wear elaborate costumes and detailed make-up. The sets are complex, often involving moving parts, trapdoors, shifting scenes, revolving stages and the *hanamachi*, a footbridge that runs through the audience, which gives the actors the perfect platform for theatrical entrances. Quite often a kabuki show is only part of a larger story – the meatiest part – so prior knowledge is helpful. Despite this, shows can go for many hours, although they can be taken in short doses. You can choose to see only one act, which usually takes around two hours.

Kabuki-za (above); Akane Imai and her *Noh* theatre troupe and Kabuki-za details (opposite)

だんご

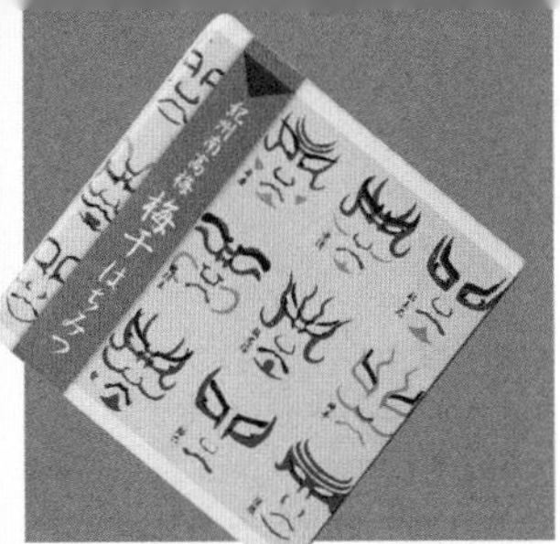

大関株式会社
大関
長部
天下無双

for KID's
KABUKI
FACE
PACK

Noh is more enigmatic than kabuki, uses masks instead of make-up, and is thought by some to have been developed by the samurai class as a way to impress the wealthy elite. Plays are usually based on historical themes. Performers – once again, mostly male – move slowly, precisely and rhythmically, with elements of dance integrated into their performance. The costumes are highly designed, rich and elaborate, but the sets are less complex than those of kabuki: a roof, four pillars and a backdrop depicting a pine forest, emulating the outdoor space where *Noh* theatre was once performed. *Noh*, with its shadowy spectres saying ethereal things while floating through a spirit world, influenced the work of German playwright and director Bertolt Brecht. You can still catch *Noh* performances outside (in Kamakura, for example) and it is an atmospheric way to enjoy the show.

The third popular form of traditional Japanese theatre is *bunraku*, where beautiful, detailed puppets play out high dramas onstage. You can catch *bunraku* performances at the National Theatre. There is also a small *bunraku* puppet museum on the eighth floor of the Hikarie complex in Shibuya (2-21-1 Shibuya, www.hikarie.jp/en).

WHERE TO SEE KABUKI THEATRE

Kabuki-za

4-12-15 Ginza
Chūō 104-0061
kabuki-za.co.jp

Anyone wanting to catch a Kabuki show in Ginza is in for a treat. Kabuki-za was built in 1889, then rebuilt in 1911 … and 1924 … and 1950, a victim of fires and bombings over the years. The most recent rebuild in 2013 was controversial, with the design by architect Kengo Kuma aimed at fortifying the building against earthquakes and making it more accessible. It's a striking facade: sake barrels and brightly colored lanterns are stacked under a towering gabled roof; bright purple *noren* curtains welcome visitors at the entrance; and rows of photographs of famed kabuki actors past and present gaze out over the space. Inside, apart from the theatre itself, you'll find a museum, a tea shop and a beautiful rooftop garden. In the basement there is a fun, rough-and-tumble market full of kabuki-themed gifts and merchandise. You can get kimono, lanterns, postcards – all sorts of things related to kabuki (and beyond). It's a bustling affair; people will often go there just to shop, even if they haven't taken in a show.

WHERE TO SEE NOH THEATRE

Cerulean Tower Noh Theatre

26-1 Sakuragaokachō B2F
Shibuya 150-8512
www.ceruleantower-noh.com/language/english

Kanze Noh Theatre

Ginza Six B3F
6-10-1 Ginza
Chūō 104-0061
ginza6.tokyo

This theatre is home to the famous Kanze *Noh* troupe, which performed in Shibuya as far back as 1900.

National Noh Theatre

4-18-1 Sendagaya
Shibuya 151-0051
www.ntj.jac.go.jp/english.html

WHERE TO SEE BUNRAKU THEATRE

National Theatre Tokyo

4-1 Hayabusachō
Chiyoda 102-8656
www.ntj.jac.go.jp/english.html

A GUIDE TO NOH THEATRE

AKANE IMAI, NOH THEATRE STUDENT & PERFORMER

What is the allure of *Noh* theatre for you?
The magnificence of the costumes, and being able to learn so much about history.

How often do you perform?
Once a month, when my *sensei* comes from Kyoto and I practise notation, dance and mimetic movement (which is called *shimai*). I practise for about an hour each day at home. The school of *Noh* I am learning, Kongō-ryu, comes from Kyoto.

How often do you attend a professional *Noh* theatre performance?
I go and see my *sensei* (teacher) perform two to three times a year, and also go another two to three times a year to see other *Nohgakushi*, or *Noh* performers.

Do you wear kimono? What percentage of the audience wear traditional dress?
Unless the weather is really poor, I would always wear kimono. I would say that twenty to thirty per cent of the audience wear kimono, too.

What kinds of people attend?
It's usually older people and students of *Noh* theatre, as well as young people who are interested in *Noh*, and members of the five *Noh* schools.

Is there anything else a visitor should know before attending a performance?
When visitors see a *Noh* theatre performance, I think it would be good for them to try to imagine and understand what the story is trying to tell them, and to read what it is implying.

A KABUKI STORY

COCO TASHIMA, KABUKI FAN & SENIOR EDITOR AT PAUMES BOOKS

When I see kabuki, it's like I am in another world, far from reality. The stage looks like a moving picture scroll, and seeing it for the first time is a beautiful and magical moment. Each kabuki theatre has its own atmosphere, and I like Kabuki-za's atmosphere best of all.

WWW.PAUMES.COM

How often do you attend a performance?

It depends – in 2017, I went seven times. Every month at Kabuki-za there's a new program with matinee and evening shows. I wish I could see all of the performances, but I would end up going bankrupt!

What do you wear? Do many guests wear kimono?

I try to wear respectable, beautiful clothing that's appropriate for this brilliant theatre. But I don't think you need to go too far – comfortable clothes are also important, because the performances are quite long. Actually, one of the pleasures of going to Kabuki-za is watching women in kimono. There are a lot of snappy dressers, especially the wives of the kabuki actors! Last year I attended one play that was based on the ancient Indian epic the *Mahabharata*, and there were women wearing sari, which was wonderful. I would like to go to see kabuki in kimono someday.

Do you arrive early to look around the basement level?

Yes, I like to look around the basement level. If I don't have enough time to browse before the play starts, I'll just drop by the *bentō* shop, Yagura, for something to eat. They sell selected *bentō*, including a special *bentō* based on the performance of the month, as well as sushi. I also love the beef cutlet sandwich from Grill Bon.

If you're not seeing a kabuki performance, you can still enjoy shopping in the basement complex. You can find beautiful Japanese sweets and kabuki-themed hand towels, postcards and washi tape, as well as kimono accessories and more. There's also a Yamada-Ya stall there, which sells *manjū* (sweet steamed buns). I love their tiny *manjū*!

The souvenir shop, Kao-Mise, is the only place you can get Agemaki Soft Cream – vanilla soft-serve ice cream, topped with deep-fried rice cakes.

What is the price of a performance, and how do you book?

Tickets cost between 4000 yen and 20,000 yen, and I book my tickets online. It's possible to see kabuki for less by purchasing a single-act ticket, or *hito-maku-mi-seki*. You'll have to arrive early and stand in the box-office line, but it's worth a try. One-act tickets start at around 800 yen.

Do you eat and drink in the interval? If so, what?

There are two or three intervals during kabuki. The short intervals are around ten to fifteen minute. I usually get a program and learn the story, or check the souvenir shop. The long interval is roughly thirty minutes, which is better if you want a meal. There are some restaurants in the Kabuki-za theatre (it's best to make a reservation in advance), but in my case, since I prefer sweets, I usually just eat a quick snack like sushi or a sandwich in my seat or the second-floor lounge. Sometimes I buy a glass of sparkling wine …

Speaking of Kabuki-za's sweets, I especially love the Mede-Taiyaki stall on the third floor. They sell a fish-shaped waffle filled with sweet red-bean paste and tiny red-and-white rice cakes. They're very popular, so there's always a long line, and sometimes they sell out quickly!

What kinds of things should a non-Japanese visitor look out for in a performance?

That's a difficult question! I'd also like to know the answer!

Traditional stories might be appealing to visitors, as they have been performed many times over the centuries and would be a good way to get to know the basics of kabuki.

My first kabuki was *Kyo Kanoko Musume Dojoji*. The main *onnagata* was so gorgeous, and I enjoyed the beautiful costumes and stage design, which featured *sakura* (cherry blossoms). It was also more dance-focused – there are quite a few kabuki plays that are mainly dance. This style of kabuki would be enjoyable for visitors, even if they can't understand the story.

Alternatively, there have recently been a few new kabuki plays based on manga. In 2015, I saw one based on the *One Piece* manga – it became very popular, and was performed again and again. This autumn, *Naruto* is coming to kabuki. If you like manga or anime, it would be a nice introduction to the kabuki experience.

TRADITIONAL CRAFTS

Traditional Japanese handicrafts are among the world's most refined and beautiful. Whether it's delicate woven textiles and hand-turned ceramics, or tea, beer and homewares, the Japanese have a deep affinity for creating things without the use of complex machinery – something that may seem at odds with the country's position at the forefront of technology. But the past sits comfortably beside the present (and the future) in Japan, and traditional crafts like ikebana (flower-arranging), *shibori* (indigo-dyeing) and *shodō* (calligraphy) are still practised and perfected today.

For an immersive introduction to Japan's traditional crafts, try visiting one of Tokyo's old-school tea houses. Artful ikebana displays may adorn the space where you take the tea ceremony, and you might be seated on a chair covered in *shibori* textile. Tea made from hand-ground *matcha* (green tea) powder will be mixed in front of you and delicately served up in a vintage ceramic cup by your host, whose kimono is likely handmade and hand-dyed.

You can find unique markets around town with great examples of handmade wooden items and vintage textiles for sale (we saw some amazing examples of *boro*, p. 373, at the Oedo Antique Market, p. 309). The Edo-Tokyo Museum (p. 360) and the Nezu Museum (p. 352) will take you on a craft journey and inspire you to try a few of the crafts for yourself. Areas such as Kuramae (p. 154) have lots of maker stores, as do Nishi-Ogikubo (p. 311), Kichijōji (p. 303) and Aoyama (p. 252). So put on your walking shoes, turn your phone off and wander through the streets as if you were living in a less cluttered, less digital time, finding your own treasures and experiences.

CRAFT MUSEUMS & CENTRES

Japan Calligraphy Museum
2-10-4 Negishi
Taitō 110-0003
taitocity.net/zaidan/english/shodou

Japan Folk Crafts Museum
(p. 360)

Japan Traditional Craft Centre
Akasaka Oji Building 1F
8-1-22 Akasaka
Minato 107-0052
kougeihin.jp

National Museum of Modern Art – Crafts Gallery
3-1 Kitanomarukōen
Chiyoda 102-0091
www.momat.go.jp/english/cg/visit

Ōta Memorial Museum of Art
1-10-10 Jingūmae
Shibuya 150-0001
ukiyoe-ota-muse.jp/eng

WHERE TO BUY FABRIC

Fabric Street, Nippori Textile Town
6-7-2 Higashi-Nippori
Arakawa 116-0014
nippori-senigai.com
Fabric Street is full of fabric stores, including the iconic Tomato Fabrics (6-44-6 Higashi-Nippori). The wider area is home to more than seventy stores related to fabric and fashion. There is a map at Nippori Station to help you navigate, or you can download one from the Nippori Textile Town website above so you don't miss anything!

Maito Kuramae Work & Shop
4-14-12 Kuramae
Taitō 111-0051
maitokomuro.com

Minä Perhonen Materiaali
Hillside Terrace G–1F
29-10 Sarugakuchō
Shibuya 150-0033
mina-perhonen.jp/en/shop/tokyo/materiaali/

Nuno
Axis Building B1F
5-17-1 Roppongi
Minato 106-0032
nuno.com

ZAKKA 雑貨

Zakka is a design movement based around making your life more meaningful by taking the time to arrange, make and display everyday objects. *Zakka* stores see the extraordinary in everyday items, celebrating handmade, repurposed, whimsical and forgotten utilitarian pieces. This includes everything from journalling with washi tape and stickers to arranging and pressing flowers, knitting, stitching and repairing clothing, and shopping for cute versions of everyday items such as tea and coffee cups, pots and pans, chopsticks, socks, buttons, vases, plants and planters, and more.

BORO & SHIBORI

——— *Boro* means 'rag', and in the context of Japanese handicrafts is the technique of stitching small pieces of (often mismatched) fabric together to form one large piece – an unpolished yet striking take on patchwork that arose from the poverty of the Edo-period working class. Cold winters and the scarcity and expense of cloth meant that every garment was precious. Hemp and *shibori* (indigo-dyed) fabrics that were once part of household furnishings or clothing were masterfully stitched together, updated, re-dyed and re-shaped throughout a working-class person's lifetime.

Boro makes an art of creating new from old, and many fine examples are highly detailed, with great care taken with the placement of patches and decorative flourishes added with *sashiko* stitching, which also serves to reinforce the piece. A recent resurgence in both *shibori* and *boro* has meant fashion labels, especially ones that use denim, have started incorporating yesterday's lessons into the clothes of today. Kapital in Ebisu (2-20-2 Ebisu-Minami 1F) is a perfect example of this.

Although *boro* tends to be associated with a dreamy, romantic feeling these days, with vintage *boro* only affordable and appealing to some, the roots of this craft are purely working class. *Boro* is an object lesson in preservation, building on tradition, reducing waste, and the willingness to change and update something already owned. In fact, we've been inspired to use *boro* techniques to mend and re-use linen tea towels and sheets at home. Perhaps the next time you find a hole in your favourite sweater or a moth eats through your best shirt, you too might consider repairing it rather than throwing it away – making it so that the patch shows, and telling your own special *boro* story.

——— When we think of *shibori*, we imagine working-class people of the Edo period dyeing and hanging large sheets of patterned indigo fabric in and around classic Japanese buildings, with hinoki cypress and cherry trees swaying in the breeze, the smell of miso and incense in the air. We are transported back to a society where everyday people wore outfits made of one-off, artisan-crafted cloth; an age of creativity and invention, of making the most of what you had and elevating everyday chores to fine arts and crafts.

Shibori is a textile art that involves binding, twisting or folding cloth before dyeing it with indigo, giving each piece of fabric its own unique design. It was first practised in the Nara period (710–794), and became popular in the Edo period, when the technique was used by the working class to dye inexpensive hemp, as silk and cotton were unaffordable. Natural dyes from readily available sources like madder root and beetroot were used to obtain the rich purple-blue colour. When clothes wore out, they were mended (see *boro*, left) and re-dyed to appear new again. In essence, *shibori* was a method of reusing and recycling, only with added artisan qualities: born out of necessity, but made to be beautiful as well as practical. Delve deep into the history of *shibori* and you'll find microcosms where unique styles and trends have developed, keeping this ancient art alive through the ages.

There are six major techniques in *shibori*: *arashi*, where fabric is wrapped around, bound to and scrunched on a pole; *itajime*, where cloth is sandwiched between wooden shapes to prevent the dye from penetrating; *kanoko*, which we know in the West as tie-dye; *kumo*, which involves pleating and binding fabric before dyeing; *miura*, where thread is wrapped around small sections of cloth; and *nui*, which is made from fabric that has been gathered using a running stitch. Fabric choice determines which technique is used, and each one results in different patterns and shapes. By selecting one technique over another, indigo-dyers can create complex beauty or timeless simplicity.

To find vintage *shibori*, visit flea markets (p. 308) or Fabric Street in Nippori Textile Town (p. 372). UGUiSU, the Little Shoppe (p. 282) sells artisan-made indigo-dyed earrings, as well as a host of handmade items using traditional techniques. The Edo-Tokyo Museum (p. 360) is a wealth of inspiration.

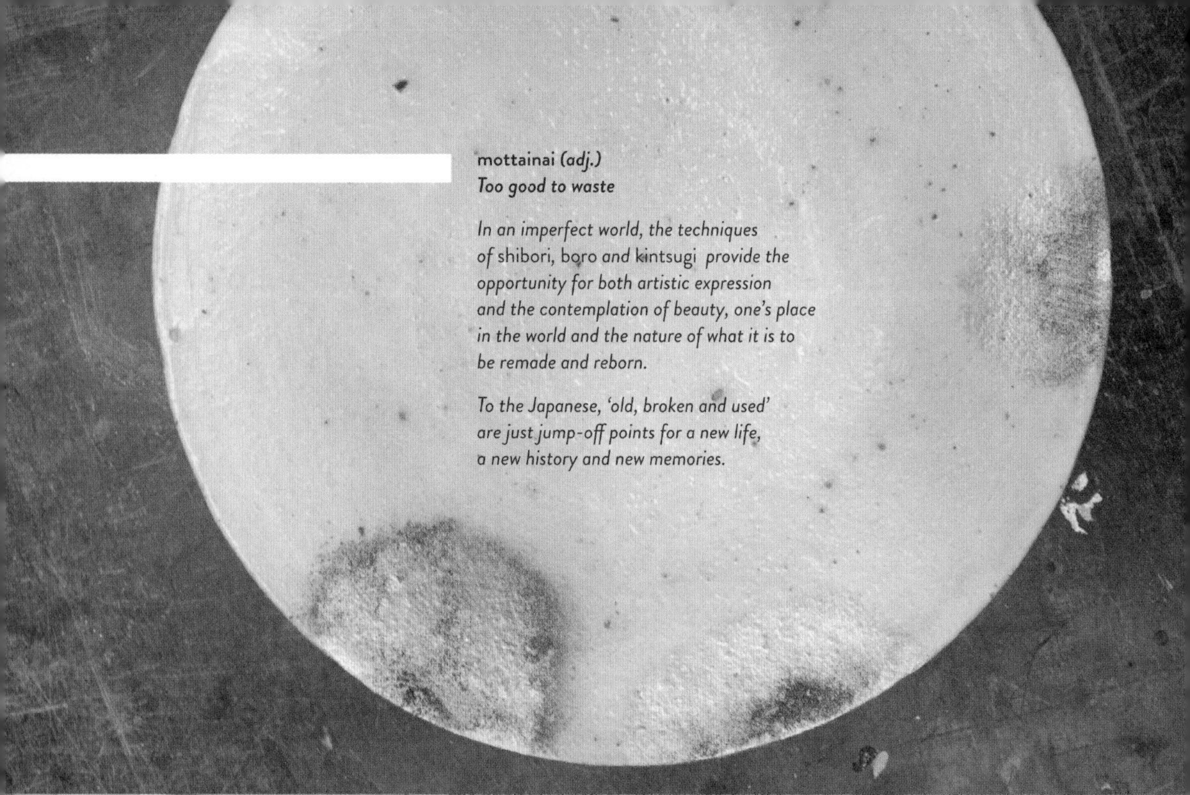

mottainai (*adj.*)
Too good to waste

In an imperfect world, the techniques of shibori, boro and kintsugi provide the opportunity for both artistic expression and the contemplation of beauty, one's place in the world and the nature of what it is to be remade and reborn.

To the Japanese, 'old, broken and used' are just jump-off points for a new life, a new history and new memories.

—— *Kintsugi* ('golden joinery') or *kintsukuroi* ('golden repair') is the repairing of glass, porcelain, earthenware and other forms of pottery with *urushi* lacquer mixed or dusted with gold or other precious metals. Its origin is thought to go back as far as the fifteenth century: a famous story tells of the eighth shogun of the Ashikaga shogunate, Yoshimasa, who sent his favourite tea bowl to be repaired by Japanese craftsmen. As the bowl could not be properly put back together (at the time ugly metal staples were used, a technique that has since become one of the arts of *kintsugi*), they decided instead to transform the bowl using gold powder and lacquer. Yoshimasa loved it, and the art of *kintsugi* was born.

With *kintsugi*, if a plate or cup breaks into large pieces, it can be put back together in a way that allows it to wear its breaks with pride, showing its history and emerging more beautiful and unique than it once was. If the piece suffers a chip, the hole can be filled, sanded and painted, transformed into something better than new – something that has a story to tell.

Kintsugi's value as a metaphor for overcoming the hardships in our lives is hard to ignore. The band Death Cab for Cutie released an album called *Kintsugi*, which dealt with the issues of being broken and remade, of being more beautiful because of our fractures and cracks. Like healing ourselves in real life, *kintsugi* can take a long time. Days or even weeks are needed for planning, filling, drying and curing. A piece can take up to a month to be transformed into something wonderful and unique. But the beauty in the end is worth the wait, like witnessing a caterpillar emerge as a butterfly.

MICHELLE SAYS:

I distinctly remember the first time I saw a kintsugi tea cup. It was in a small ryokan (inn) in the countryside. On a cold, wintery day, we were given tea as we checked in. I'd never seen anything quite like it. Fine gold lines like tiny veins threaded through the blue-and-white porcelain of the cup. I thought it was one of the most beautiful things I'd ever seen and asked the owner about the technique. She explained that the cup had been in her family for generations as part of a set. It was the last remaining piece left and had broken during an earthquake decades earlier; it had been repaired using kintsugi. The story not only told me about the history of the cup but spoke of the owner's family history, of earthquakes and the sentimental value of that last remaining piece of a tea set. Years later, our friend Hiki organised a class for us to learn the technique together.

Another friend, Kylie Johnson, is an incredibly talented Australian potter who owns the Paper Boat Press ceramic studio in Brisbane. She has just spent three months in Japan with the assistance of the Churchill Fellowship to complete a course in kintsugi. Pictures of her work are on the opposite page, bottom left and right.

IKEBANA

MICHELLE SAYS: *I must admit to being a collector of ikebana scissors before I realised that they were especially made to cut flowers. When I first saw them in Japan, I just thought they were so beautiful. I used them to cut herbs from my garden, so I guess I wasn't too far from the mark.*

Ikebana literally means 'living flowers', but Michelle has always preferred its other name, 'kadō', which means 'way of flowers'. This form of flower-arranging brings nature indoors, giving it a place of importance in the home and allowing it to lighten the heart and spirit of those who cross the threshold. In ikebana, flowers and foliage twist and bend as nature intended; they favour one way or another, depending on the season and their position in relation to the sun.

Unlike Western flower-arranging, ikebana is often minimal and sparse, and makes use of twigs, bracken, seed pods and fronds. Seasonal foliage, stem height, vessel choice, balance and harmony are all taken into consideration. White flowers are popular; red flowers less so, as they are used for funerary arrangements. Ikebana can be used for celebrations, ceremonies and condolences. You will often see white orchids arranged beautifully outside a shop; this signifies that the shop has just opened.

The beauty and mystique in ikebana is grounded in the Japanese love of the seasons. The way seasons affect the appearance of flora also affects the appearance of ikebana. For instance, in March, when it is windy, arrangements are often curved or bent as if in a strong wind. On p. 54 we go into more detail about seasons in Japan and the importance of nature in day-to-day life as a source of transient beauty and as a marker of time.

Of course, there is a practical use for ikebana as well. The preparation, methods and style of the arrangements often prolong the life of the cut flowers.

Ikebana is an ancient art, with origins dating back to the late eighth century, but it was not until the eighteenth century that it reached peak popularity. There are different philosophies and more than 1000 schools of ikebana; however, its roots lie in Buddhist theory, and in fact flower-arranging was first brought to Japan from China at the same time as Buddhism.

Interestingly, many military leaders (including Hideyoshi Toyotomi and Yoshimasa Ashikaga) were versed in the art of ikebana. It is said that it helped calm the mind when strategising in wartime, something that seems quite at odds with the beauty of the pursuit.

RESOURCES:

Ohara School of Ikebana
Ikebana lessons in English
(you can participate or observe)
ohararyu.or.jp/english/lesson.html

Sogetsu Ikebana
Ikebana lessons and
demonstrations in English
sogetsu.or.jp/e/study/hq/tokyo/
international.html

SHODŌ

Shodō – 'the way of writing' – is Japanese calligraphy, a practice that turns pictorial characters into art. Using handmade brushes, dark inks and porous paper, practitioners of *shodō* channel deep concentration into graceful, subtle lines. Each character written in *shodō* requires precise application and an exact order of strokes, which makes calligraphy a very focused discipline. Hand angle, brush size, speed, paper choice, and the poetry of what is being written all factor into the quality of a piece of *shodō*. It can take years to learn, let alone master.

The Japanese language is made up of three scripts: *kanji* (Chinese characters), *hiragana* (a syllabic script used to write native Japanese words) and *katakana* (a syllabic script mostly used to write foreign words). The complex beauty of *kanji* takes precedence in the practice of *shodō*, but since the end of the eighth century *hiragana* and *katakana* have also been used.

Tracing back to China, with roots thought to be around the twenty-eighth century BC, calligraphy was introduced into Japan in the seventh century. Like ikebana and the Japanese tea ceremony, *shodō* is deeply connected to Buddhism, and is still practised by Buddhist monks. To master *shodō*, and in particular Zen calligraphy, practitioners must 'clear the mind' and let the letters flow out themselves, without trying too hard.

In Japan, children are taught *shodō* in primary school, as it is thought to bring a quiet harmony to the spirit. In high school it is an art elective, and some prestigious universities around the country, including Tokyo Gakugei University, even have dedicated *shodō* departments.

In the West, the art of calligraphy is having a resurgence. Hand-type and lettering has made its way into contemporary graphic design and onto cherished book covers, and a new generation of calligraphers are discovering that it can help with everyday tasks like writing memos, thank-you notes and sending postcards. *Shodō* can be harder for left-handed people (Michelle, being left-handed, knows this well!). You'll need to hold your brush and apply pressure a little differently.

Tokyu Hands and Sekaido (both p. 212) have great brushes and paper, and serious calligraphy enthusiasts can buy sets that include brushes, ink, ink stone, desk pad, brush rest, water dropper, paperweight and washi paper. Hanging scrolls, or *kakejiku*, are the visual face of calligraphy and are often seen in Buddhist temples, tea houses and other cultural spaces. You can sometimes buy them at vintage markets (p. 308).

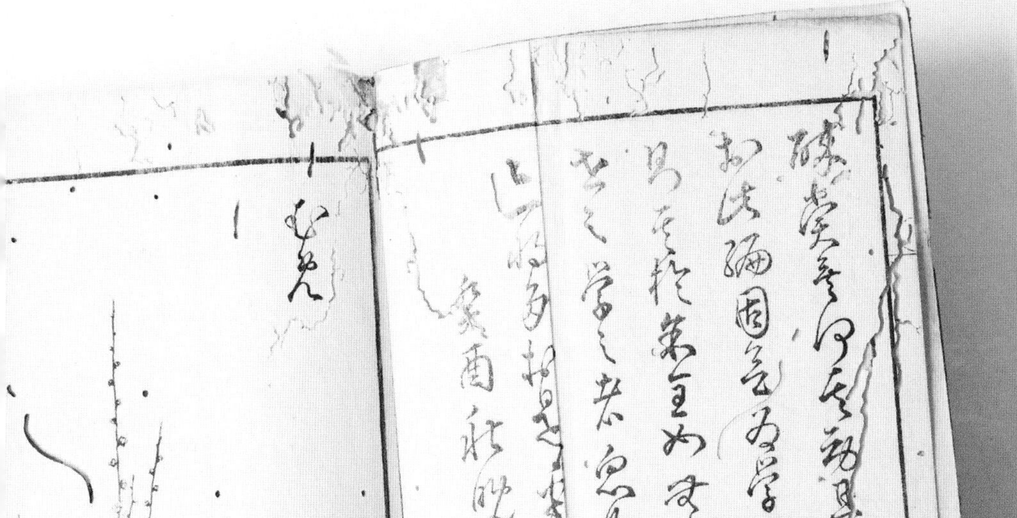

PAPER-MAKING WORKSHOPS:

Ozu Washi
OzuHonkan Building, 3-6-2 Nihombashihoncho, Chuo-ku, 103-0027
ozuwashi.net/en/

Paper Museum
1-1-3 Ōji
Kita 114-0002

ARIGATŌ GOZAIMASU

Thank you to our visionary publisher, Mary Small, for the amazing opportunity to make a book we are so proud of. For hatching an idea and giving it form and substance. Your insight, thoughtful guidance and publishing acumen made this book a pure pleasure from start to finish. Thank you for your friendship and support over so many years.

Thank you to Clare Marshall. We could not have made this book without you. Your creativity and sensitivity blur the boundaries of editor, writer and conductor. Your ability to turn ramblings and ideas into a structure shaped this project. Thanks for listening to everything and making sure we were happy at every step. Your patience, kindness and thoughtfulness, not to mention all the late nights and so much hard work, made this project an unforgettable experience.

To our Japanophile editors, RR and LW:

Rihana Ries. Thank you for sifting through the mountain of a manuscript, organising and sorting a book with bilingual leanings into a concise and comprehensive read, for making sure both our voices have their own tone, and for understanding us and the way we wanted to articulate our passion for Tokyo. Thank you for always going above and beyond.

Lauren Whybrow. Thank you for scouring the text, ironing out the wrinkles, winkling out imperfections, dotting the I's, crossing the T's and minding the P's and Q's. And for being our London correspondent.

To Clare Keighery, for PR-ing things and helping to send a book born in a small house out to the big wide world.

To Jane and Ashley at Plum for all the behind-the-scenes support and love.

Thanks to our up-late typesetter, Pauline Haas, for all your hard work.

To Chris Middleton. Thank you for taking beautiful and natural photos of two people who don't like getting their photo taken, and for all your ephemera shots that are scattered throughout the book. Always a pleasure to work with you.

Dear Hiki Komura. Thank you for always taking great care of us. For the very special kimono day out and *hanami* picnic. For your friendship, support, advice and translating. To both Hiki and Ryo, thank you for taking time out to spend with us for Oshōgatsu, for all the fun nights out and days spent together. For making us laugh and try new things and for helping us to love and understand Japan from your perspective.

Coco Tashima, thank you for your friendship, garden dates, kabuki and family pictures.

Thanks for spending time with us (mostly eating sweets and laughing way too much). Thank you for being part of our book and sharing your knowledge of the old arts.

Shoko Seko, thanks for letting us into your world of intricate beauty and extra-*kawaii* toys. For your friendship and kindness. For being part of our book and sharing your story.

Akane Imai, thank you for dressing Michelle in a kimono, and for sharing your wonderful *Noh* theatre story and knowledge of traditional Japanese arts.

Kenta Sato, thanks for taking one for the team and hitting the late-night bars, clubs and watering holes.

Flora Waycott and family, thanks for being part of our Shōwa-era section and for drinking way too much tea with us.

Nina Larkins, thanks for your endless cuteness and curiosity. And for being an even bigger fan of Totoro than Michelle.

Thanks to Kylie Johnson for sharing your *kintsugi* images and to Tiffany Johnson for your amazing printing – and to you both for being two people we look forward to seeing, knowing we can ramble on about Japan for hours with you.

To all the booksellers who promote local, ethical and interesting publishing. To our favourite small businesses, Alasdair, Eddie and Ruby at The Boroughs, and Chris at Happy Valley, who are always passionate in supporting our books.

To our families and friends who have had to listen to so many Tokyo stories: a heartfelt thank-you to the Mackintosh extended family; Marlene, Andrew, Carolyn and families, the Wide extended family; Margaret, Chris, Heather, Tracy and families, and to our absent fathers who will be forever missed. Thanks to Olive and Leo for starring in the book with Totoro. Thanks to our incredibly supportive friends: Olivia and Joel; May and Sylvie; Dawn and Steve; Ingrid and Adrian; Jane and Chris; Will and Phu; Tina and Andy; Gregory and Chris; Pacquita, Mark and Will; Melinda, Hugo and Audrey; Graham; Dave and Gerry; Kate and James; Shainne; Beci and Raph; Alice; Mary, Max and girls; Clare, Pete and Nina; Lucy; Paul; Heather; Rihana; Hannah; Trisha and Simon; FHA girls; Flora; Pip; Stephen, Christine and Karl; Makiko; Chizuru; Shoko. Most of all, to that person we forgot: we left you out on purpose because you are so special.

Thank you to Hisashi Tokuyoshi, Hiroki Osaki from Hoshino Resorts, Hiroaki Matsumoto from Hotel Okura Tokyo, Motomi Mizuishi from Temarino-Ouchi, Cheese Hedgehog, Tama Art University Library and Pete Spark for your kind help and support.

INDEX

• S

• T

A PLUM BOOK

First published in 2018 by
Pan Macmillan Australia Pty Limited
Level 25, 1 Market Street,
Sydney, NSW 2000, Australia

Level 3, 112 Wellington Parade,
East Melbourne, VIC 3002, Australia

Design by Michelle Mackintosh
Edited by Rihana Ries
Index by Helena Holmgren
Photography by Michelle Mackintosh, with additional photography as listed

Typeset by Pauline Haas
Colour reproduction by Splitting Image Colour Studio
Printed and bound in China by 1010 Printing International Limited

A CIP catalogue record for this book is available from the National Library of Australia.

10 9 8 7 6 5 4 3 2 1

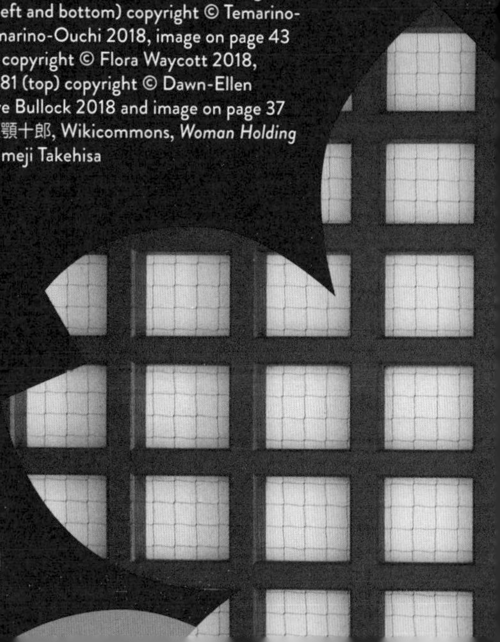